To Jeff
With Friendship and Gratitude

Michael

TRADE LIBERALIZATION

— AND —

TRADE PREFERENCES

(Revised Edition)

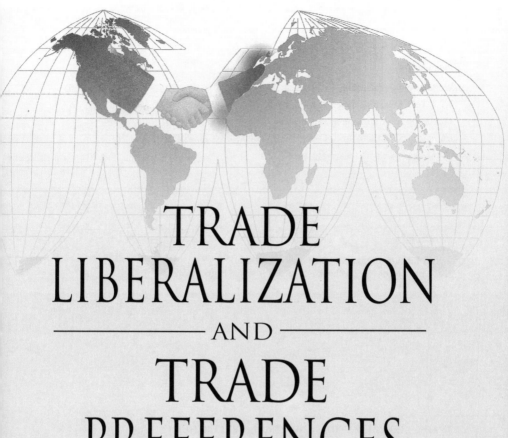

TRADE
LIBERALIZATION
— AND —
TRADE
PREFERENCES

(Revised Edition)

Michael Michaely

Hebrew University of Jerusalem, Israel

World Scientific

NEW JERSEY · LONDON · SINGAPORE · BEIJING · SHANGHAI · HONG KONG · TAIPEI · CHENNAI

Published by

World Scientific Publishing Co. Pte. Ltd.

5 Toh Tuck Link, Singapore 596224

USA office: 27 Warren Street, Suite 401-402, Hackensack, NJ 07601

UK office: 57 Shelton Street, Covent Garden, London WC2H 9HE

British Library Cataloguing-in-Publication Data
A catalogue record for this book is available from the British Library.

ISBN-13 978-981-283-229-0
ISBN-10 981-283-229-7

Typeset by Stallion Press
Email: enquiries@stallionpress.com

Printed in Singapore by B & JO Enterprise

Preface to First Edition [2004]

This book is a collection of papers written over the last decade on the topics of trade liberalization and trade preferences. Four of these have been published previously. "Goods vs Factors: When Borders Open, Who Moves?" *The World Economy*, Vol. 26, April 2003, pp. 533–554 is reproduced as Chapter 2 in this book; "The Pattern of Removal of Trade Barriers" (Michael Michaely, Demetris Papageorgiou, and Armeane M. Choksi, Liberalizing Foreign Trade: Lessons of Experience in the Developing World, Basil Blackwell, 1991, Appendix A1) appears here as Chapter 3; "Partners to a Preferential Agreement: Implications of Varying Size" (*Journal of International Economics*, Vol. 46, October 1998, pp. 73–85) forms Chapter 5; and "Assessing the Promise of a Preferential Trade Agreement" (Trade, Development and Political Economy, Palgrave, 2001, pp. 121–140) appears as Chapter 9. These papers are reprinted here under almost identical titles, and with very minor changes required for stylistic uniformity in the book. Permission by the four respective publishers for reproduction is gratefully acknowledged.

The rest of the chapters are new. Their substance largely derives from work, which has circulated in a variety of mimeographed forms; but they have gone here through considerable transformations. Chapters 6 and 10 rely to a large extent on studies I have carried out for the World Bank, mostly presented in "Small Economies: Trade Liberalization, Trade Preferences and Growth" (January 1996, written jointly with Demetris Papageorgiou) and "Trade Preferential Agreements in Latin America: An *Ex-Ante* Assessment" (March 1996). Chapters 4, 7 (new Chapter 12) and 8 (new Chapter 7) are based on work performed during my stay in the fall of 2000 as Visiting Professor at the Center for Research on Economic Development and Policy Reform at Stanford University, which appeared as a Working

Paper of the Center titled "Trade Liberalization and Preferential Trade Agreements: Some Unexplored or Unresolved Issues" (February 2001).

My prime debt is to Demetris Papageorgiou, my colleague at the World Bank at the time, whose involvement was instrumental in implementing much of the work presented here, and whose advice contributed substantially to its design and formulation. I also wish to express my gratitude to the Center at Stanford, and to its then Director Anne O. Krueger, whose hospitality enabled me to pursue the research there. Suggestions by Max Corden, Nadav Halevi, Ronald Jones, Ephraim Kleiman, and the late Richard Snape led to many improvements. Helpful comments were also provided by participants at seminars given on various occasions at the World Bank and at Stanford. My indebtedness for all these contributions is sincerely acknowledged.

Preface to Revised Edition [2008]

Aside from a variety of editorial changes, the revision of this volume consists of the addition of three chapters representing research conducted over the last two years: Chapter 8, "The Impact of Liberalization on Trade Structure"; Chapter 13, "Proximity: The Role of Distance"; and Chapter 14, "Trade Relationships within Regional Groupings."

Alexander Elbert has expertly carried out the computation work in this added research and has also made substantive comments on the studies; his contribution has been invaluable. I am also greatly indebted to Jeffrey Bergstrand for comments and advice on much of this material.

Contents

List of Figures

List of Tables

Chapter 1

Introduction

This book is a collection of individual essays. Yet they all have a common theme: trade liberalization and preferential trade agreements (PTAs). Trade liberalization is arguably the major issue of the conduct of commercial policy. And, as a component of it, the relationship between universal, multilateral trade liberalization and the conclusion of PTAs — that is, a process of liberalization that discriminates between trading partners — has been a focus of analysis and debate in recent years. This book is thus designed as a contribution to the understanding of several salient elements of these issues. It is a search for answers to significant questions, which have not been raised and explored before; an attempt to clarify and elaborate upon others which, although they have been discussed (sometimes extensively) in the literature, have not been settled; and an analysis trying to provide bridges for moving from generalities to the comprehension of concrete instances and developments.

A few themes keep recurring in the analyses of the separate essays. One revolves around issues of stages in the process of liberalization. Another is the *impact* of both trade liberalization and preferences. Still another is the role of *size* of economies in liberalization and in the conclusion of preferential agreements. Similarly, the role of *proximity* of economies in the conduct of trade policy. And, probably most prominent, the possibility of *assessing* the desirability and outcome of policies.

Chapter 2 raises a fundamental question for the outcome of opening up economies to movements of both goods and factors between them: which of the two will actually move? It analyzes the *ex-ante* expectation, given the circumstances of the economies, discusses the issue of how, in fact, to assess the outcome of opening up, and suggests an illustration through the analysis of a concrete recent case.

Chapter 3 addresses four issues, which are commonly faced when trade liberalization is introduced in stages, rather than at one stroke. One is the significance, and meaning, of the existence of "tariff redundancy." Another is the preferred method of gradually collapsing an existing system of tariffs. A third one is the treatment of tariffs on intermediate inputs in the process. Finally, the chapter provides an analysis of the implications of the industrial structure of an activity (that is, the degree of competitiveness in it) for the order of the activity in the implementation of liberalization.

Chapter 4 examines the desirability of a PTA, not in the "second-best" framework — as is the practice in the customs-union theory, when preferences are compared with no liberalization at all — but as a "first-best" question, namely, how should a PTA be compared with *free* trade? The former is obviously inferior (given a conventional set of assumptions); but what is the impact of various economic attributes on the extent of such inferiority?

Chapter 5 turns to the significance of the size of an economy for the desirability of a partner for a preferential agreement. The conventional wisdom has been that "large is beautiful": the larger an economy the more promising it should look, *ceteris paribus*, as a potential partner. This premise has been disputed in recent years, and the chapter's analysis suggests the circumstances under which one presumption or another should be adopted.

Chapter 6 again focuses on the size of economies, addressing a much wider range of issues. It first specifies the attributes that distinguish small from large economies, and examines whether these attributes should lead to faster or slower growth of small economies, and whether indeed observed growth rates differ in small economies as compared with large ones. Then, coming to the major themes of this book, the analysis turns to the issue of trade liberalization, asking whether small economies benefit more or less than others from freer trade, and whether the introduction of liberalization should be easier or, on the contrary, more difficult in a small economy. Similarly, it inquires whether the desirability of preferential agreements between small countries is different at one or both ends of the partnership, given the attributes of such economies, than it is for agreements concluded between large countries.

Chapter 7 addresses an issue of PTA analysis which has been brought up recently, and to which little analysis has been applied, namely, in considering the promise of a PTA, does it matter whether the home country's current trade with the potential partner is due to any significant extent to "history" rather than (or in addition to) present circumstances by which trade flows would otherwise be determined? The analysis of the chapter provides a positive answer to this question. Moreover, it shows that the possibility that the past participates in forming the present ascribes significance to the *order* in which the two trade policies considered here — universal trade liberalization vs a PTA — are introduced.

Chapter 8 is devoted to an issue whose importance may have been realized, but which has been subjected to only little investigations, namely, beyond (generally recognized and often studied) the impact of trade liberalization on the *size* of trade — leading to its expansion — does the policy have also a substantial impact on the *structure* of trade? Using a variety of elements to define the nature of a structural change and employing several indices to measure these elements, the weight of the evidence suggests that liberalization does indeed affect the structure of trade — both exports and, probably to a lesser extent, imports — in a given pattern. This conclusion carries implications about issues such as the impact of liberalization on dependence on the outside world, on the country's terms of trade, on the structure of employment, or on the derived level of welfare.

Chapter 9, as well as the two chapters that follow it, turns to issues of *assessment* of a PTA. How should the promise of a contemplated, concrete PTA be judged? Much of the analyses of the earlier chapters, such as the examination of the role played by size of the economies, or by their past trade relationships, is obviously meant to contribute to the ability to make such *ex-ante* assessments. However, in this chapter, a general review of the relevant criteria is provided. And — based on it, and probably of more importance — a set of tools of measurement is suggested for this task.

Chapter 10, then, following in the footsteps of its predecessor, proceeds to illustrate the usefulness of such tools by applying them to a concrete case: the promise of PTAs concluded within Latin America — a region that has contributed a major share of the world's experiments with PTAs in recent decades, and in which further PTAs are continuously being contemplated.

Chapter 11, on the other hand, addresses the issue of an *ex-post* assessment of the conclusion of a PTA. It tries to determine whether, and to what extent, the PTA changes the geographic pattern of the home country's trade; specifically, the extent of the bias in the expansion of the country's trade toward its PTA partners. The chapter develops, again, a set of indices whose use is likely to contribute to such assessment. And, as in the earlier *ex-ante* analysis, it then provides an application to a concrete, recent case — the PTA among five countries in Latin America that is known as the Andean Pact.

The last three chapters of the volume are all related to the likelihood of a country being a "natural trade partner", and, specifically, to the role played by geographical proximity of countries. Chapter 12 addresses two issues. First, whether proximity of economies should be expected to make a preferential agreement between them more promising — an issue which in recent years has been hotly debated. Second — an issue to which less attention has been paid — whether a general nondiscriminatory liberalization should be expected to expand trade between neighbors more (or less) than between distant partners. This analysis is important, among other things, for distinguishing between the impact of preferential agreements and that of overall trade liberalization.

Chapter 13 looks more closely and specifically at the impact of distance on trade. It points out that estimates of the relationship between the two, normally derived from "gravity model" equations, consistently indicate a very strong influence of distance on the size of trade flows: an increase in the former contracts the latter by the same proportion, or even more (that is, the elasticity of trade on distance is unity or above). However, the size of international transportation costs is normally very low, as a proportion of the price of the good, and the increase in these costs with distance, involving only a minor change in the price of the good, could not possibly explain a large reduction in the trade flow. Hence, "distance" must involve, and represent, attributes other than transportation costs, which are not directly observed and which presumably have a stronger impact than that of a change of transportation costs.

Finally, Chapter 14 addresses the issue of "natural" trade partnership through the investigation of intra-regional trade relationships within each of nine regional groupings in the world — including, altogether, most of the countries which might be classified into such groupings. The findings indicate that in each and every region, intra-regional trade is indeed much more intensive than trade of the region's members with outsiders, and, similarly, that complete absence of trade with any member of a region is practically nonexistent; whereas it may be common in relationships with potential partners outside the region. Trade is particularly intensive between contiguous countries. In most regional groupings, an overwhelming weight is found for a "center" country — a weight far exceeding its general role as a heavy trader. Trade of each member of the region with this "center" is the essence of intra-regional trading; whereas trade flows among the "periphery" countries are minor. This hub and spokes pattern is mostly explained by the center's attributes as a more developed economy than its periphery partners, offering a particularly broad range of goods to satisfy the demands of its partners.

The methodology of the essays in this book is eclectic. Parts of the analysis are pure theory — often conducted through diagrammatic representation. Beyond this, an important analytic goal is the development of tools for measurement and assessment. Empirical studies constitute another major component of the analysis. While there are different analytic elements, a common thread is shared by these essays: all consist of steps designed to lead from theory to policy. This process requires the transformation of theory to assessment through the development of appropriate tools, and a demonstration of the validity and usefulness of the latter by illustration through empirical studies. The fundamental character of this collection of essays is thus the use of theory to enhance the ability to carry out assessment and, in this manner, to contribute to the improvement of trade policy.

Chapter 2

Goods vs Factors:
When Borders Open, Who Moves?

The Issue

Take the case of two countries that, having been completely insulated from each other, open their mutual border to a free movement of both goods and factors of production. "Pure" situations like this, of a one-step change from complete isolation to a perfect freedom, are naturally hard to find; however, several close approximations may be observed in recent experience. One is the unification, in the late 1980s, of West and East Germany. Another is the change in the relationship between Israel, the territory of the West Bank of Jordan and the territory of Gaza, formerly ruled by Egypt, following their occupation by Israel in the 1967 war — a case that will serve later for illustration. And, if current winds continue to blow, a similar development may yet take place in the foreseeable future should the two parts of Cyprus, or South and North Korea, unite (or at least reach full economic integration). The issue indicated here will be relevant also for less extreme changes; that is, movements from less than full insulation to less than full openness.

One of the best known propositions in the theory of international and inter-regional trade is that movements of goods and of factors of production substitute for each other. Given certain conditions, either one of them can equalize the prices of both goods and factors among the economies participating in the exchanges. And being substitutes, the larger one of these movements, the smaller the need (or the room) for the other, to reach equilibrium, and the smaller this other movement will become.

In the situation at hand, when the borders open, which movement will it be — of goods or of factors? Or, less extremely — as we might reasonably expect the case to be — if both movements take place, what would be the extent of one vs the other? Beyond its economic context, this issue involves the political and cultural implications of the international exchange, which are different when factors, particularly, labor, move, from when goods are transacted — a set of issues which clearly lies beyond the scope of the economic analysis.

The present chapter will address this issue. In the following section, *a priori* considerations will be suggested. In the next one, problems involved in an attempt to contrast *ex post* the extent of movement in the two markets will be raised. Finally, the last section will provide an illustration through a reference to the experience of partial integration of the economies of Israel and of the West Bank and Gaza.

Theoretical Considerations[1]

While an extensive literature exists addressing the welfare implications of inter-relationships of movements of goods and factors, analyses of the specific issue at hand are rather scarce. Perhaps the most important contribution to the topic is still Bertil Ohlin's celebrated *Inter-regional and International Trade*.[2] Ohlin's treatise is devoted to factor markets and factor movements just as much as to the exchanges of goods — a practice that was not adopted in the mainstream of international-trade theory in the following two generations. The following may best summarize Ohlin's analysis:

> "... The movement of goods to some extent takes the place of factor movements.... Nevertheless the exchange of goods cannot bring about a complete equalization of factor prices, inter-regional differences remain and call forth factor movements.... Factor prices are in this way brought closer together in the different regions; the need for inter-regional trade and consequently its volume are reduced. Factor movements act as a substitute for the movements of commodities. Inter-regional price equalization seems to be furthered either by both movements or by the one that meets with less resistance."

And

> "... Everything depends upon the intensity of the reaction of factor prices and therefore factor movements when trade varies, and upon the intensity of the reaction of commodity prices and

therefore trade when factor movements vary.... For all practical purposes, however, one may assume that either commodities alone or both commodities and factors move between the various regions (p. 116)."

Ohlin appears to be of two minds. In part, he seems to assign predominance to the exchange of goods, and it is only because this exchange does not fully equalize factor prices[3] that factor movements are called forth. However in other statements, Ohlin appears to give *a priori* equal chances to movements of goods and of factors: the predominance of one or the other will be established by the level of obstacles to mobility in each market, and by the cross elasticities between the volume of movement in one market and the change of prices in the other. Note, however, that these elasticities participate in determining the volume of exchanges in *both* markets, but not their relative importance: the lower *either* of these elasticities, the larger the volumes of movements of *both* goods and factors in the international exchange. These elasticities thus do *not* indicate the primacy of movements in one market or the other. More generally, the volumes of movements of goods and of factors do not necessarily indicate the importance of each in equilibrating the prices of goods and of factors.

James Meade's (1955) contribution, another classic, analyzes the relationships between the international movements of goods and of factors quite extensively; however, it refers to the issue at hand only in an indirect manner. Meade's approach is *normative*, and it takes the movement of goods as the basic phenomenon. It then proceeds with the question: given this movement, under what conditions will it not be sufficient to maximize world welfare, so that the movement of factors will be called upon to achieve this goal.[4] By inference, the stronger the fulfillment of such conditions (for instance, the higher the transportation costs of goods), the stronger the movement of factors will be. Perhaps the most important specific circumstance which Meade introduced is the effect of "atmosphere" — a factor by which the whole production function in one economy differs from that of the other.[5] The larger this scalar, it is implied, the stronger the movement of factors will be in relation to the movement of goods.

Yet another seminal contribution to the topic — again, not quite contemporary — is that of Robert Mundell of some forty-five years ago.[6] We recall that Mundell demonstrated that given complete freedom of movement of factors, any restriction on the movement of goods will become *prohibitive*: no exchange of goods will take place at all, and equalization of both good and factor prices will be achieved fully and exclusively by factor movements. Conversely, if even partial impediments exist to the movement of factors and none to the movement of goods, factor movement will not exist, and the full equalization of both sets of prices will be carried out just by the movement of goods (this situation, roughly, has been assumed in the conventional analysis of international trade). However, what would be the outcome if *both* types of movements were completely free? Or, a situation which is more probable, if both are subject to one (partial) constraint or another? Here, a rigorous answer of "either-or" appears to be impossible, and we are reduced to probabilistic propositions and to a discussion of the circumstances that would make any outcome more or less probable.

Before proceeding, an element of dissimilarity of the two markets should be noted. A movement of goods means, by and large, an *exchange* of goods: one country exports good X in exchange for the other's good Y (whether as a barter trade, as is normally assumed — implicitly — in "real" analyses, or through the intermediation of money). A movement of factors, on the other hand, implies no such exchange: labor does *not* move from country A to country B "in exchange" for capital moving in the opposite direction. The transformation, in this case, is of the movement of a factor one way in exchange for the reward for the factor's *services* moving, by way of goods, the other way — not necessarily simultaneously, but at some (often unspecified) point of time in the future.[7] Thus, aside from the question of movement of goods vs movement of factors, we shall have to ponder the issue of the movement of one factor vs the other — with each, again, conceptually able to perform the whole equilibrating process (in *both* markets) by itself.

As a matter of curiosity, it should be noted that — unlike most issues in economics — there is no symmetry of directions in the general issue raised here. That is, one cannot sensibly pose the question of what and who moves, or does *not* move, when borders *close* — aside from the obvious observation, which owes nothing to economic responses that what stops are precisely the pre-closing movements. As a counter example to a case like the unification of Germany, take a case like that of the recent (hostile) disintegration of Yugoslavia into separate republics. Presumably, when borders are completely shut, *nothing* moves. The only issue which can be raised, and which may sometimes be of value, is: what past, pre-disintegration movements of goods and of factors have been eliminated by the imposition of closed borders in the area?

To the basic questions posed — of who moves first and most — there are no universal *a priori* answers. I shall try, however, to classify here the elements involved in making one outcome or another more likely.

To start with, when all goods and factors enjoy perfect, cost-free mobility, the outcome will be indeterminate; *anything* can happen, and the equilibrating process will be determined by pure chance. Although in the narrow technical sense the equilibrium achieved will be stable, the outcome will indeed be completely fluid and highly unstable: any minute change in one of the system's variables could conceptually lead to a complete upheaval. This extreme situation may be a useful analytical construct; however, it does not provide an answer to the issue with which we are concerned.

In the concrete world, impediments to movement do, of course, always exist. As is suggested by Mundell's analysis, the degree of imperfection of the mobility of goods and of factors is of crucial importance. In the simplified world of two goods and two factors (and two countries), it is enough for *one* of the factors to move freely to equilibrate prices in the two markets (and equalize them for the two partners). If none of the factors enjoys perfect mobility, nor at least one of the goods, this will not happen. Here, the degree of imperfection can intuitively be expected (as it was by Ohlin) to determine the extent to which goods vs factors, and one factor vs the other, will move between the two geographic markets.

Imperfection of mobility is the product of two categories of impediments. One consists of the "natural," inherent costs: transport costs in the narrow sense, the need to overcome unfamiliarity with foreign markets, the reluctance of labor to migrate to foreign countries, and the like. The other consists of man-made barriers — primarily, most often, barriers imposed by governments, but also by nongovernmental organizations (labor unions, trade associations, or other organs of monopolistic collusion).

One aspect of mobility, however, which may be of major importance for the present issue, is somewhat less obvious (or at least less familiar). Movement of goods between trade partners depends on (and is implied by) the specialization of each partner in some goods; that is, the expansion of some activities and the contraction of others. For that — this again follows by definition — factors would have to move from one activity to another. In most analyses, we (notionally) move smoothly from one point on a transformation curve to another; but in fact, such movement of resources must also be subject to a variety of constraints and barriers (including, for instance, the need to gain information) and is a time-consuming process. The issue of movement of goods vs movement of factors between countries may thus be (partly) translated into another issue, in which we compare not two geographical movements but one which is *inter-regional* and another which is *inter-sectoral.* That is, we ask whether the movement of factors between *countries* is subject to a lower or higher degree of imperfection than the movement of factors among *activities* (in either of the trading countries).

To be more concrete — and inevitably more speculative — it may be presumed, on this score, that the opening of borders between two less-developed countries, in which production tends to be more concentrated in a few activities and to depend more heavily on natural resources, will not lead to much specialization in goods. Equilibrating the markets may then depend more on factor movements (although presumably not much of this will take place, since no radical differences in factor prices — other than in prices of natural resources, which are immobile — can be expected under autarky among the countries involved). Opening the borders between two highly developed countries, on the other hand, can be expected to lead to a rapid and substantial specialization in production activities, leaving less room for movement of factors.

The impact of *size* of the economy, and particularly of the *difference* in sizes of partners, is worth noting. Suppose that one of the two partners that open up to each other is substantially larger than the other. In all likelihood, though this is obviously not an inevitability, the larger economy is also the richer one — its very richness making it "large," in terms of its GDP, and is hence the capital-rich partner.[8] In such a case, labor will be the factor that moves from the small to the large partner. As is well known, the exchange of goods *may*, under such circumstances, be insufficient to equilibrate factor prices: in the small economy, full specialization in some goods may take place (without fully eliminating the production of these goods in the large, importing country), and equality of factor prices will not be achieved. The movement of factors (that is, of labor from the small to the large country, or of capital in the opposite direction) will thus be an inevitable component in the process of reaching a new equilibrium. An element of asymmetry is thus present in this case: no such limitation exists with regard to the achievement of equilibrium through the movement of factors. When factors move, full equalization of factor (and goods) prices must be achieved *before* any given factor fully moves from the small to the large economy.

In determining the identity of the factor that will move most (between the trading partners), imperfection of mobility will definitely be a prime consideration. However — again, a less obvious component — the answer will also depend on the *pace* at which the movement of one factor leads toward equilibrium. Does one factor's movement generate a more or less intensive change in relative factor prices than a movement of the other factor?[9] In the concrete case of labor vs capital, it is normally assumed that capital movements, when free, lead very rapidly to equalization of interest rates (in the sense of interest-rate parities). This then leaves relatively little space for a movement of labor, where the market prices — the wage rates — move slowly in comparison. However, the interest rate on highly liquid assets is not the relevant price of capital for the purpose at hand, although the two are related: it is, rather, the rate of return on capital invested in production activities (in the long run, the marginal productivity of capital), and this, presumably, moves at a much slower pace than the interest rate on liquid assets. In this concrete case, thus, this consideration does not *a priori* provide a clear answer.

The analysis thus far has assumed, explicitly or implicitly, a world of *two* countries: the two had been closed to each other — hence, by definition of the case, completely autarkic — and have now opened up (to "the world"), completely or partially. When the two are just a pair in a multi-country world, the channels of change obviously become more complex. We shall attempt here not much more than a taxonomy.

Prior to the mutual opening up, each of the two partners might have been (i) completely open to the rest of the world (ROW); (ii) completely autarkic (no movement of goods and of factors taking place at all); (iii) partially open to the ROW. In addition, starting from the initial situations indicated in either (i) or (iii), the post-opening situation might involve: (iv) one or both partners becoming closed to the ROW. It is hard to find concrete examples in recent history of situations (i) or (iv). The (potential) unification of Korea would involve something approximating situation (ii), as far as North Korea is concerned. The unification of Germany, on the other hand, approximates situation (iii).[10]

The analysis for situations (ii) and (iv) should resemble the one applied to the two-country world — at least for one of the two partners.[11] Situation (iii) offers many varieties of analysis. In situation (i) — if it were to be found — the opening of borders between the two partners would be irrelevant, both of them having previously made equilibrating changes through their contacts with the ROW, that is, goods and factor prices would be equal between the two partners even when they were isolated from each other.[12] Strictly speaking, though, this would be true in the absence of transportation costs. When such costs do exist — and they can normally be expected to vary in transactions with different countries — the introduction of a new trade partner will lead to price changes.

Continuing along similar lines, the following inferences can be noted. Designate the two countries involved as "A" (home country) and "B" (partner). If the mobility of both goods and factors between partner B and the ROW is perfect, while country A has been closed to it and remains so, the outcome will look as if country A too is open (that is, as if A has opened its borders not just with B but with everyone else). This follows from the fact that in these circumstances, the partner's prices of goods and of factors will be equal to what they are in the ROW. If B is a large country in relation to the ROW, but a small country in relation to A (implying that A is a large country in relation to the world as a whole), this new opening up will change the world prices of goods and services; however, it remains true that the same outcome will be reached by A's opening up toward B as by its opening up to the world as a whole. This becomes less true the stronger the impediments to mobility of goods and factors between B and the ROW. Similarly — this is more intuitively obvious — if A is not completely but only partially closed to the ROW, the higher the barriers between these two, the stronger the (equilibrating) movements of goods and factors will be between A and B when the two open up to each other.

One final note. Although the present discussion addresses the topic of "when borders open — who moves?" and is so titled, it may be relevant for other issues. In fact, it can be applied to any instance in which disequilibrium appears due to any set of circumstances, in the relationship of two economies to each other. Suppose — to take a widely discussed case — an initial equilibrium is disturbed by an exogenous development, which leads to the emergence of production of an important new tradable good; the discovery of oil, or (more importantly in the past) gold, is an obvious instance of this nature. An equilibrating mechanism will now come into operation. In the "conventional" trade theory, this will involve a real appreciation, leading to the creation of an import surplus in the aggregate of all items other than the "new" tradable. However, the changes in relative prices of goods will lead to consequent changes in the prices of factors. Hence, once factor movements are allowed into the analysis, it follows that such movements will take place, contributing to the process of establishment of a new equilibrium. The question of the relative importance of movements of goods vs factors, between the economy at hand and the ROW, thus presents itself in this case as well.

The Assessment of Movements in the Two Markets

In assessing *ex post* performance, is there a concrete way of actually gauging the contribution of each of the two markets to the equilibrating process? As will be indicated here, the answer, unfortunately, must be negative; hopefully, some approximations may be offered.

In principle, the extent of movements in the two markets — for goods and for factors — in relationship to each other, will probably best be assessed through their impacts on relative prices: to what extent has either of these movements contributed to the degree of convergence of relative prices — again, of both goods and factors — in the partner economies?

Even on the level of "principle," complications abound. One is that *full* convergence may be expected never to materialize. And, when it is not full, a tendency toward convergence should be evident in both markets; but its *degree* (namely, the ratio of actual convergence to what it would be were it full) will not (except by sheer chance) be the same in the two markets. Thus, the extent of convergence, to which the movements at hand are supposed to have contributed, is not a well-defined term.

Beyond that — again, short of full convergence — the degree of convergence cannot be well defined (or, amounting to the same thing, can be defined in a variety of ways) in a multi-good, multi-factor world: neither the differences in the pre-opening situation nor those found in any post-movement position can be summarized by a meaningful quantitative index.

However, suppose these formidable considerations could be ignored, and a "degree of convergence" could actually be defined. It would still not be possible to estimate the "contribution" of movements in each of the two markets to this convergence. Specifically, the degree of price convergence in each market could *not* be identified with the contribution of this market to the "aggregate" convergence. The reason is simple: price convergence in each of the markets — for goods and for factors — originates in principle from movements (of goods, or of factors) in *both* markets, and convergence in one market is thus a function of convergence in the other. Thus, price changes in each of the markets cannot be an indication of the extent of this market's contribution to aggregate price convergence. Perhaps, though, not the extent but the *order* of convergence in the two markets may be meaningful: it is conceivable that a specification of some dynamic model, and its estimation, might reveal causal relationships, identifying one or the other of the two markets as the origin of price convergence.

One price that may merit observation is the relative price between tradables and nontradables. If, to take one extreme outcome, no factor movements at all take place, there is no *a priori* reason for a change of this price: the price of exportables should increase, and that of importables should fall, but as a rule, no trend of change of the aggregate price between tradables and nontradables should be expected. If, on the other hand, factor movements do occur, and they do *not* take the form of a permanent migration, they should give rise to the transfer of factor remittances, and these, in turn, should lead to a relative fall of the price of tradables in the economy in which the factors originate, and an opposite trend in the factor-receiving economy.[13] This would be a complementary measure to the observation of *quantities*, to which we now turn. As we shall see, such observation too is not devoid of serious complications.

In comparing movements of goods and of factors, the only possible common denominator is the quantity of *factors* involved: in the movement of factors, it is observed directly, and in the movement of goods, it will be the factor content of these goods. The size of this movement — the volume of factors — must then be reduced to a *single* common denominator, and the only way of performing this is through the use of money values, based on market prices of the various factors.

The first is a relatively easy issue. In assessing the factor content of a given movement of goods, it is the *value added* (in the economy), rather than the gross value of the goods, which should be estimated: by definition, this is the (home economy's) factor content of the good.

A point that may seem obvious, but should nevertheless be mentioned, is that the "movement (or exchange) of factors" stands not for the value of the "factor" (which sometimes, as in the movement of labor, may be defined and estimated only with great difficulty), but to the value of factor *services* involved in the transaction.

A major issue, which clearly does not have a single, definite answer, is whether the movement of factors (directly, or through the exchange of goods) should be estimated by its *gross* or *net* size. If factors are regarded as uniform and homogenous, the net concept would seem to be appropriate; thus, the values of factors contained in the (value added) imports of the economy from its partner will be subtracted from the value involved in the home economy's exports of goods, to yield the (net) size of factors moving between the two economies through the exchange of goods.

Should, on the other hand, the factors be defined in minute detail, those involved in the imports of goods will be found to be different from those represented in the exports of goods, and the *gross* value, combining *both* the export and the import trade, will then provide the appropriate estimate. These considerations will be similar when direct movements of factors are observed. Unfortunately, no clear-cut answer, or even clear-cut criteria for judgment, may be offered on this (rather important) issue.

Estimating the net size of factor movements implied in the exchange of goods also raises a substantial practical difficulty. For the gross value, just an estimate of the value added component in the total value is required, and this, at least in rough approximations, is available with a reasonable amount of work. Estimating net factor content, on the other hand, will inevitably require Leontief-type data of individual factor inputs in the production of the goods involved — a much more demanding task.

An entirely separate issue concerns an aspect of the asymmetry between movements of goods and of factors referred to earlier. This may best be illustrated by reference to the two extreme outcomes. Suppose, at one end, that the whole equilibrating process is performed through the exchange of *goods*. This would be the beginning and the end of the process, and the actual estimates would show just this movement. Suppose instead — taking the other extreme — that the new equilibrium is reached exclusively through the movement of *factors*. Here, several alternative forms of movement should be distinguished. Take, first, the case where the movement of factors is generated through a change in the location of *ownership* of *labor*, which migrates *permanently* from one economy to the other. Here, no return of rewards for factor services will be involved, and no further changes; however, the estimates will show just a one-time migration, and no exchanges of factor services from then onward. Assume, on the other hand, that the location of ownership remains unchanged. Payments for factor services will thus be remitted from the factor-receiving economy to the factor-sending one, and data of such remittances will indeed, in this case, provide the required estimates of "factor movements." However, at some time, such remittances will be offset (via an equilibrating mechanism involving the real exchange rate) by an import surplus of *goods* (and nonfactor services) of one economy, forming an export surplus of the other.[14]

Thus, assessing the process will inevitably reveal (beyond some brief adjustment period) an exchange of goods, so that it will appear as if such an exchange did participate in the equilibrating mechanism — contrary to what we have assumed the case to be. This also applies to the situation in which *capital* movements are involved, leading at some time to the transfer back of interest and dividend yields. However, in the case of capital, a further element is involved. Whether with or without change of ownership, the movement of capital leads, while it lasts, to an export surplus of the capital-exporting economy. This does not necessarily mean an increase of aggregate trade in goods — an opposite outcome is also possible; however, in all probability, it will involve an increase in the exchange in factors implied in trade in goods.[15]

The analysis of changes of *structures* of economic activity may complement the evidence gathered directly from observation of flows of goods and of factors. One element of change ties in with the inference noted earlier about the relative price of tradables to nontradables. The larger the (nonmigrating) factor flow, the larger the transfer back of factor remittances; the larger, hence, the deficit of trade (in goods and nonfactor services) will become; and the more the share of nontradables will increase in the factor-exporting economy. Another element of contrasting structural changes is concerned with the share of exportable vs importable goods in the economy's product. Compare, again, the two extremes. With only an exchange of goods — the "conventional" case — trade and specialization imply an increase in the production of exportables and a decline in the share of importables. On the other hand, with only a movement of factors, the production of exportables (in the factor-exporting country) should *fall*; and that of importables rise. This is demonstrated more rigorously in the Annex, which concludes this chapter.

An Illustration: Israel, the West Bank, and Gaza[16]

In the war of June 1967, Israel occupied two territories of pre-1948 Palestine: the West Bank of the Kingdom of Jordan and the Gaza Strip held prior to the war by Egypt. Before the 1967 war — with Israel, on the one side, and Jordan and Egypt, on the other side, being technically "enemies" — the borders between Israel and each of the two territories (which do *not* share a border with each other) were completely sealed. The West Bank, as a part of Jordan, naturally had a completely open (imaginary) border with the East Bank (for movements of both goods and factors), and, as a part of Jordan, enjoyed open borders (for goods) with most of the ROW (subject, of course, to general restrictions on Jordan's trade with the outside world). The Gaza Strip, on the other hand, not being formally part of Egypt, had only a limited access to Egypt — in either movement of goods or of labor, or, through Egypt, to the ROW.

In terms of freedom of movements of goods, the situation was almost completely reversed following the war. Both the West Bank and Gaza came to have largely open borders with Israel — with a degree of imperfection due to administrative regulation, which was to a large extent nontransparent. The West Bank continued to enjoy partial trade relations with Jordan (with the latter admitting limited quantities of goods originating in plants existing prior to the 1967 war). Gaza, on the other hand, had such access neither to Egypt nor to any other Arab country — prior, of course, to the Egypt–Israel peace treaty of 1980 (except, in a very limited form, via Jordan), and its trade was directed almost exclusively to Israel (with one important exception, namely, exports of citrus fruit).

Differences in factor intensities between Israel and the two territories are too obvious to require much empirical verification. In comparison, Israel is rich in capital and in skilled labor; whereas the territories are rich in unskilled labor.[17] Movement of labor from the two territories to Israel became virtually free, but full migration was not allowed; the large majority of workers commuted daily, without establishing permanent residence. Labor movement in the opposite direction, from Israel to the two territories, was in fact not of much relevance. Capital was also roughly free to move across the former borders; however, probably due to political uncertainties, there was only very little capital movement (from Israel to the West Bank and Gaza). The two economies (regarding, for such statements, the two territories as a single entity) differed dramatically in size. By end 1968, the territories' labor force numbered 128,000 (83,000 in the West Bank, and 45,000 in Gaza); Israel's labor force, at 915,000, was seven times as large. Owing to substantial differences in the level of development, the gap in aggregate incomes was even more striking: the combined GDP of the West Bank and Gaza was, in 1968, less than 3.5 per cent of Israel's GDP. In terms of the size of external trade (considering, for such purpose, the pre-1967 trade of the West Bank with the East Bank of Jordan as "external") the gap between the two economies was probably even larger.[18]

An obvious implication of this difference in magnitudes of the economies is that economic relationships of the two — and changes in them — would be expected to be of much significance to the two territories, and of only very limited relevance to Israel. For this reason, the present analysis refers almost exclusively to the impact of the events under consideration on the economies of the two territories, with only scant references to their significance for Israel.

The data used in this study refer to the years 1968–1982. This 14-year period should be long enough to reveal features of a permanent nature, in which the transition from one situation to another will have been completed, rather than just short-term developments or attributes of transitory stages. The period could conceivably be lengthened — but only by a few years: political developments since the mid-1980s, and in particular the first popular uprising ("the Intifada") in the two territories, reversed many of the changes introduced by the opening up in 1967. Actual openness, particularly to movements of labor, declined materially. Thus, the predominant part of the period in which a high degree of openness between the economies involved was actually maintained is studied here.

Table 2.1 presents, separately for the West Bank and for Gaza, their exports to Israel of goods and nonfactor services, on the one hand, and of factor services, on the other hand. The latter are overwhelmingly

Table 2.1: Exports to Israel of goods and of factor services (in percentage of GDP, at current prices).

	WEST BANK		GAZA	
	Exports of goods (1)	Exports of factor services (2)	Exports of goods (3)	Exports of factor services (4)
	13.2	5.1	7.5	1.5
1969	10.9	12.6	6.4	6.0
1970	13.4	21.1	8.9	16.3
1971	13.6	29.7	14.2	18.4
1972	12.2	33.5	19.2	38.6
1973	16.8	32.8	22.6	43.6
1974	15.0	27.5	24.3	41.5
1975	17.6	35.2	31.2	44.6
1976	16.6	33.8	33.1	40.5
1977	15.7	31.7	35.9	37.5
1978	14.9	29.1	40.0	48.7
1979	15.1	35.1	31.1	54.5
1980	14.8	29.0	39.3	55.0
1981	19.0	37.9	52.3	61.9
1982	14.8	38.1	49.6	69.3

Source: The sources for this table and for the two following tables are a variety of publications of Israel's Central Bureau of Statistics, as well as special processing of data made by the Bureau for the aforementioned study, from which these tables are drawn. This note will not be repeated in the rest of the tables.

remittances of West Bank and Gaza workers in Israel and are thus the best representation of the volume of factor transfers from the two territories to Israel. The data are far from perfect and, in the present context, suffer from a bias: movements of goods are to some extent under-recorded; whereas labor remittances are somewhat over-stated.

In comparing the two types of transfers, we recall that it is the *value added* (rather than the gross value) in the exports of goods (and nonfactor services), which should be the object of comparison. From evidence not shown here, we know that the value added component is particularly low in the case at hand. About half of the exports from the West Bank to Israel, and the almost exclusive component in the case of Gaza, consisted of garments. In the West Bank production, the value added was low. In Gaza, considerations go even beyond this. Here, the production of garments was mostly of the "maquilladora" type — only the finishing stage of a mostly Israeli product being carried out in the territories. No transaction in goods actually took place — just a contract of the Israeli manufacturer with providers of the territory's labor (predominantly female labor who, being unable due to inhibitions of tradition to move to the Israeli location of production, had the work assigned to them in their own homes). Thus, this was in fact not a trade in goods but in factors, which should be added to the value of labor movement estimated through remittances. In view of this, it may be concluded that in Israel's exchanges with the West Bank, and even more so with Gaza, the transfer of factors (that is, labor) played an overwhelming role in the equilibrating mechanism.

It may also be observed that a new steady-state (presumably equilibrium) position was reached in the case of the West Bank within roughly five years: no trend changes seem to have taken place beyond 1973. In Gaza, on the other hand, this required some dozen years. This difference might be a function of the fact that the *size* of transfers — whether of factors directly or through goods — was much more substantial in Gaza (as a proportion of GDP) than it was in the West Bank.

Tables 2.2 and 2.3 provide another insight concerning the issue at hand. Both record the shares of major sectors in economic activity — in the GDP, in Table 2.2, or in occupation of the labor force, in Table 2.3. The most important observation, common to both, is a substantial decline in the share of agriculture, in both the West Bank and Gaza. Had the opening of borders led exclusively to the movement of goods between the partners, the share of agriculture in economic activity in the two territories would have been increased, probably substantially: in trade relationships with Israel

Table 2.2:   Shares of major sectors in the national product (percentage of total).

Year	Agri. (1)	Manu. (2)	Constr. (3)	Public services (4)	Other services (5)	Total (6)
(A) *West Bank*						
1968	38.4	8.5	4.3	16.8	31.8	99.8
1969	37.6	9.1	5.7	16.3	31.2	99.9
1970	35.7	9.5	6.5	15.8	32.5	100.0
1971	36.4	8.8	7.6	13.9	33.2	99.9
1972	35.4	8.2	9.3	13.5	33.5	99.9
1973	39.0	8.2	10.7	13.1	28.3	99.3
1974	n.a.	n.a.	n.a.	n.a.	n.a.	n.a.
1975	31.5	7.3	14.5	11.7	34.8	99.8
1976	31.5	6.7	14.7	11.5	35.5	99.9
1977	31.9	6.8	14.6	11.8	34.7	99.8
1978	32.6	6.7	15.1	11.6	33.8	99.8
1979	34.1	6.5	15.1	11.2	32.8	99.7
1980	35.2	6.2	14.4	12.0	32.0	99.8
1981	31.2	6.2	16.0	13.3	33.2	99.9
1982	28.4	6.3	16.7	14.3	34.2	99.9
(B) *Gaza*						
1968	28.1	3.1	3.1	20.3	45.3	99.9
1969	26.4	4.1	6.1	20.3	43.2	100.0
1970	28.0	6.0	6.6	20.3	39.0	99.9
1971	29.3	6.0	6.4	19.7	38.6	100.0
1972	31.9	6.9	10.2	19.9	31.0	99.9
1973	27.9	6.9	13.8	19.6	31.9	100.1
1974	24.8	8.2	15.0	21.0	31.0	100.0
1975	28.4	10.1	17.2	21.0	23.3	100.0
1976	31.6	11.3	19.1	18.6	19.4	100.0
1977	30.7	11.5	17.1	17.6	23.1	100.0
1978	28.9	12.5	21.3	19.0	18.2	99.9
1979	23.2	12.1	24.8	16.3	23.7	100.1
1980	18.8	9.9	21.4	19.5	30.4	100.0
1981	20.9	8.3	23.9	22.0	25.0	100.1
1982	16.3	8.8	23.4	23.0	28.4	99.9

it seems, from all the evidence, that the two territories should specialize in agriculture (at least where production is not irrigation-intensive), and Israel in manufacturing. If, on the other hand, it is the factors market in which the action takes place, an opposite trend might be expected: the labor which moves from the two territories to Israel is overwhelmingly low skilled (at least at the time the movement starts) and is drawn primarily from agricultural activities in its place of origin. The fact that the share

Table 2.3:   Allocation of domestically employed labor force by major sectors.

	In thousand workers					In percentage of total				
Year	Agri. (1)	Manu. (2)	Constr. (3)	Serv. (4)	Total (5)	Agri. (6)	Manu. (7)	Constr. (8)	Serv. (9)	Total (10)
(A) *West Bank*										
1969	46.3	15.6	8.9	29.7	100.5	46.1	15.5	8.9	29.6	100.1
1970	42.4	14.6	8.4	34.4	99.8	42.5	14.5	8.4	34.5	100.0
1971	36.6	13.4	5.6	35.6	91.2	40.1	14.7	6.1	39.0	99.9
1972	34.3	13.2	6.5	36.4	90.3	38.0	14.6	7.2	40.3	100.1
1973	30.0	14.4	6.7	36.6	87.7	34.2	16.5	7.6	41.7	100.0
1974	36.1	14.1	6.8	37.8	94.8	38.1	14.9	7.2	39.9	100.1
1975	31.8	14.5	7.7	38.0	91.9	34.6	15.8	8.4	41.4	100.2
1976	31.4	13.8	9.3	38.3	92.6	33.9	14.9	10.0	41.4	100.2
1977	30.7	13.9	9.6	27.6	91.9	33.4	15.1	10.5	40.9	99.9
1978	32.3	14.3	10.2	37.2	94.0	34.4	15.2	10.9	39.6	100.1
1979	29.1	14.7	10.9	37.8	92.5	31.5	15.9	11.8	40.9	100.1
1980	31.3	14.3	10.1	38.6	94.3	33.2	15.2	10.7	40.9	100.0
1981	28.5	14.7	11.1	39.2	93.5	30.5	15.7	11.9	41.9	100.0
1982	31.3	15.5	10.3	40.4	97.5	32.1	15.9	10.6	41.4	100.0
(B) *Gaza*										
1969	17.4	7.4	4.8	23.2	52.8	33.0	14.0	9.1	43.9	100.0
1970	16.8	6.4	4.5	25.2	52.9	31.8	12.1	8.5	47.6	100.0
1971	16.0	6.3	2.4	26.8	51.5	31.1	12.2	4.7	52.0	100.0
1972	11.4	5.8	1.9	26.9	46.0	24.8	12.6	4.1	58.5	100.0
1973	11.7	5.8	1.7	26.5	45.7	25.6	12.7	3.7	58.0	100.0
1974	11.6	5.7	1.9	27.5	46.8	24.8	12.7	3.7	58.0	100.0
1975	12.3	5.6	2.4	26.5	46.7	25.3	12.0	5.1	56.8	100.0
1976	12.8	6.5	2.2	26.7	48.3	26.5	13.5	4.6	55.3	99.8
1977	12.4	6.2	3.3	27.6	49.5	25.1	12.5	6.7	55.8	100.1
1978	10.3	7.5	3.42	27.5	48.7	21.2	15.4	7.0	56.6	100.1
1979	9.5	8.4	3.1	24.5	45.5	20.9	18.5	6.8	53.9	100.1
1980	8.7	8.6	3.4	25.6	46.3	18.8	18.6	7.3	55.3	100.0
1981	8.4	7.7	3.9	26.6	46.6	18.0	16.5	8.4	52.1	100.0
1982	8.3	6.8	3.9	27.1	46.1	18.0	14.8	8.5	58.8	100.1

of agriculture did indeed fall, in such a significant measure, thus provides support to the supposition that factor movements did indeed dominate the exchange of goods.[19] The construction sector is of particular interest. Its share in GDP appears to have increased substantially in both the West Bank and Gaza; but the share of the sector in employment seems to have been rather stable. Since the construction sector in Israel was a major recipient of labor from the two territories, its wage level increased in particular, with a parallel increase in its source (that is, in the territories).

Hence, a large increase in the relative price of construction. This, again, is a demonstration of the major impact of labor movements on the economic structure.

This leads to a more general observation about relative prices. Without showing the data, we may indicate that, save for a trend reversal for imports in the West Bank in the early 1980s, a significant fall of the relative price of tradables to nontradables took place over the period. This trend (like other changes indicated earlier) is more pronounced in Gaza than in the West Bank — a finding consistent with the larger share (relative to GDP) of income of the territory's labor in Israel. It is the remitted income, evidently, which gives rise to the relative decline of the price of tradables.[20] While this observation, by itself, does not yield a direct inference about the importance of labor movements vs the exchange of goods, it does again provide a representation of the importance of the former. It is interesting to observe that here, too, the adjustment to the new openness seems to have taken place within some five or six years: by about 1973–1974, a new steady state appears to have been approached.

The main finding of the analysis of this case is thus that following the opening of borders, adjustment took place predominantly through the movement of factors, almost exclusively labor, and only to a very limited extent through the exchange of goods. The analysis also indicates that most of the adjustment was achieved within a period of some five to seven years, with something approaching a new steady state being achieved by that time.

Much caution, though, is required in interpreting this finding. Beyond the "normal" problems of quality and reliability of data, it should be noted — as has been remarked earlier — that "openness" was much less than perfect. Various constraints, both formal and, to a large extent, uncodified and nontransparent, were imposed (by the Israeli authorities) for political or economic reasons. These were evidently much more severe when applied to the movement of goods rather than of labor. Similarly, other constraints on economic activity in the territories (such as on potential investment) were practiced on occasion. Owing to the informal nature of such constraints, no general data (but much anecdotal evidence) exist to verify their extent or precise application. It can thus only be assumed, or guessed — as the present author does — that the unrecorded constraints were less important (during the period under consideration) than the operation of the fundamental economic forces.

With this proviso, we may try to suggest potential generalizations. One is concerned not with the substance of the findings, but with their very existence. It appears that despite all the prior reservations about the ability of empirically verifying the issue under consideration, the use of several complementary measures, or the observation of phenomena from various angles, does provide an answer — at least a tentative one — when these measures tend to support each other.

A unique feature of the experience at hand is the geographical proximity of the markets involved: the movement between the centers of economic activity in Israel, on the one hand, and in the West Bank and Gaza, on the other hand, is at the extremes a matter of a few hours travel. This should lead to particularly large volumes of movement of both goods and factors, when borders open. It is possible, however — this is a guess, rather than an inference — that the existence of short (or, at least, *very* short) distances has a greater effect on the ease of movement of factors (labor) than that of goods. If this is the case, the lesson from the experience at hand may not be of general application.

This leads to the most important *unique* feature of the present case. The closeness of the markets to each other enables the existence of daily labor movement from the territories to Israel. This phenomenon will not be as prevalent in most other instances where, even when countries share a common border, the distance between major sources of labor and major centers of demand for it in the recipient country is large. Given the prohibition on shifting of residence of labor, virtually all labor movement from the territories to Israel took this form. Thus, in the steady state, a constant amount of labor movement is recorded; whereas when labor shifts its residence, labor movement should disappear altogether in the steady state. These circumstances thus led to a labor movement between the economies involved, which is both particularly *large* and of a *sustained* nature. It is thus likely that in other instances of opened borders between economies formerly closed to each other, factor (specifically labor) movements should be smaller (and, hence, the role left to the exchange of goods in the equilibrating mechanism larger) than in the present case. Moreover, in other instances — as was noted earlier — estimates of the role of factor movement would have (partly, at least) to aim at the integral of movements during the adjustment period, rather than (or in addition to) the observation of steady-state values.

Annex: Production of Exportables and Importables under the Two Types of Exchange

The analysis is presented by means of Fig. 2.1. PQ in this figure is the initial, closed-economy transformation curve between the two goods X (potential

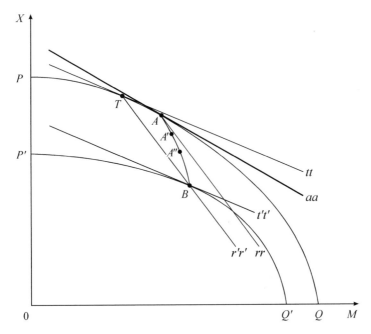

Figure 2.1:   Production of exportables and importables.

exportable) and M (potential importable). A is the autarky production (and consumption) locus. The familiar conditions required for trade to achieve full equalizations of good prices and factor prices at home and abroad are assumed to be fulfilled.

With the economy opening up fully to its partner (taken, in this analysis, to be the "world"), we shall examine two alternative extreme positions. Suppose, first, that only an exchange of goods takes place between the two economies, and no movement of factors. The production locus will move to T, where line tt, whose slope represents the partner's (constant) price ratio between the two goods, is tangent to PQ. Consumption will be on tt at some point southeast of T. Note the obvious: in comparison with autarky, production of the exportable good (X) increases; whereas that of the importable good (M) diminishes. This is, of course, the essence of trade and specialization.

Suppose now, instead, that *no* trade in goods takes place; a new equilibrium, following the opening of borders, is achieved exclusively through the movement of factors. Assume that just one factor moves: the relatively cheap factor at home (say, labor), in which good X is intensive, leaves home for the partner country. Had the relative price of goods remained unchanged, the new production locus would have been somewhere on line rr: this is Mundell's "Rybczynski line," which indicates the path along which, following the exit of a factor, the production of the good intensive in that factor contracts, whereas production of the other good expands not just in relative but in absolute terms.[21] However, prices of goods at home are *not* constant: with a fall of the production (= consumption) of X, and an increase of M, the relative price of X will rise. Consequently, the contraction of production of X, and the expansion of M, will be *smaller* than at constant prices. For exposition, let us follow in steps the path along which the production locus moves. First, it changes from A to A'. The line connecting A with A' will be steeper, representing a smaller substitution of X by M, than the Rybczynski line rr. In the next step, the shift will proceed to a point like A''. With the relative price of X rising still further, a line A'A'' will be still steeper than AA'. The curve AB, which connects all the points like A' or A'', may be termed the "production–contraction curve." By the reasoning just presented, it should be concave (from the origin), and steeper throughout than the Rybczynski line rr (which is a "production–contraction curve" at constant goods prices).

When the (step-by-step) movement reaches B, it will stop. This is the position at which the home price of X rises enough to make it equal to the partner's price, with a concomitant equalization of factor prices. No further factor movement will then take place. The new transformation curve will become P'Q'; with t't', tangent to the transformation curve at B, representing both the "world" and the home relative price between the two goods. Note, now, an important observation for our purpose. In comparison with autarky, the new equilibrium production locus represents a *smaller* production of the exportable good (X) and a larger production of the importable good (M). This is, obviously, the exact opposite of the outcome we have observed when the exchange taking place was that of goods rather than factors. The source of this difference is the fact that the "home economy" is not the same economy with or without its cheap factor leaving it.

To establish the precise location at which point B will actually be found, consider the shift from A to B as taking place, notionally, in two separate stages. First suppose that a minute barrier is imposed on the movement of factors, so that only goods are exchanged. Production then moves from A to T. At this stage, a minute barrier is imposed on the movement of goods, whereas it is removed from the movement of factors. A factor (labor) will then move out, to the partner. With goods prices remaining constant throughout, at the partner's level, the production locus will move southeast along r'r', an "unadulterated" Rybczynski line (that is, a line along which the price of goods is constant, at the "world" level). At point B, line r'r' is intersected by the "production–contraction" curve AB (and its notional extension). This is, hence, the new equilibrium position, at which home prices of goods and of factors are equal to the external prices.

Notes

1. The analysis suggested here runs within the framework of the factor-proportions model of the origin of trade and of the process of reaching equilibrium in the markets for goods and for factors. With alternative models and alternative origins, exchanges of goods and of factors may appear to be not substitutes but *complements* — with the trade in goods giving rise to a movement of factors from which, in turn, further trade in goods originates (see Markusen, 1983). However, much of the observations made here about the likelihood of one exchange or the other will remain valid beyond the context of a factor-proportions model.

2. See Ohlin (1935, 1967). Citations are to the 1967 edition, which is probably more widely accessible. Except for very minor linguistic changes, the two editions are identical for the present purpose.

3. An assumption of Ohlin noted, of course, in the Stolper–Samuelson analysis (1941).

4. "We wish to inquire how probable it is that (under free-trade) circumstances situations may still arise in which... the full maximization of world production would require the free movement of factors of production not only domestically within each country but also internationally between the trading countries" (p. 331).

5. This is similar to the scalar multiplier defining a "Hicks neutral" growth process, except that it is assumed in a comparison over space rather than over time.

6. See Mundell (1957).

7. Hence, when constraints on movement of factors are concerned, costs of repatriation of *factor rewards* constitute such impediment.

8. In all the four concrete cases cited earlier — the two Germanys, Israel and the two territories, the two Koreas, and the two parts of Cyprus — one partner is much larger than the other. Typically, one

has a population 5 times larger than its partner (the range is from two to seven), and a GDP 15 times (ranging from some 10 to 20 times that of the other), implying that it is much richer in terms of per capita income.

9. This question is posed here in a vague manner. To be more precise, it should be coined through the use of some elasticity concept, though both the numerator and the denominator of such elasticity could be formulated in more than one way.

10. One might put in category (iv) the situation of Central and Eastern European countries subjected to Soviet hegemony a short time after World War II; however, economic annexation into a centrally planned world largely defies analyses based on the operation of the market. This comment partly applies also to the case of the German unification, East Germany having been a centrally planned economy prior to the change.

11. This is a *positive* statement. Welfare implications are obviously quite different between cases (ii) and (iv).

12. As an illustration: The West Bank and Gaza, discussed later, do not exchange much directly; however, real wages and (perhaps less so) prices of goods in the two territories have tended to converge through exchanges with Israel.

13. If, on the other hand, the factor movement (specifically, that of capital) does involve a change of location of ownership, the change of the relative price of tradables should be in the opposite direction *during a transition period*. More on this later.

14. In a multi-country world, and multilateral trade, this is true for the aggregate trade of each of these two partners; but not necessarily for the balance of trade between the two.

15. As could naturally be expected from a major (future) contributor to the "transfer problem" debate, Ohlin paid much attention to this point. He noted (pp. 124–125) that "... Capital holds a unique position in one respect: it can move from one region to another only in the form of goods and services. Export of capital assumes an excess of commodity exports over imports." However, "the effects of capital movements and interest payments in opposite directions are obviously neutralized so far as the mechanism of trade is concerned; the net sum alone moves in a given direction in the form of goods or services." It is not clear whether Ohlin has in mind a "steady-state" situation, in which *only* the repatriation of the yield of capital takes place. On the one hand, he puts this analysis in the context of a transition period: "... factor

movements require time . . . [and they] have special effects while they are actually in progress." However, he also implies that over time, ". . . the influx of capital proceeds at an even rate."

16. This section draws heavily on an ongoing research conducted by Ephraim Kleiman and the present author, on "The Process of Economic Integration: A Case Study of Israel, the West Bank, and Gaza." The study has been supported by the Ford Foundation and the Earhart Foundation.

17. So far as land, water, or other natural resources are concerned, one would have to go into more specific attributes. For the issue at hand, relative differences in these factors — which do not move directly — are of secondary importance.

18. This is a guess: naturally, no data about goods crossing the imaginary "borders" *within* Jordan are to be found.

19. A comparison of Tables 2.2 and 2.3 will show a larger fall in the share of agriculture in employment than in production. That is, in relation to other sectors, labor productivity in agriculture increased materially. *Aggregate* production of the agriculture sector increased substantially, in both the West Bank and Gaza.

20. A regression analysis clearly confirms the association between these two variables.

21. In Mundell's analysis, just as in that of Rybczynski's original development (1955), a factor moves *into* the home country, rather than leaving it as in the present case.

References

Markusen, J R (1983). Factor movements and commodity trade as complements. *Journal of International Economics*, 14, 341–356.

Meade, J E (1955). *Trade and Welfare, The theory of international economic policy*, Vol. 2. Oxford: Oxford University Press.

Mundell, R A (1957). International trade and factor mobility. *American Economic Review*, 47, 321–335.

Ohlin, B (1935). *Inter-regional and International Trade*. Cambridge, Mass.: Harvard University Press (Revised Edition, 1967).

Rybczynski, T M (1955). Factor endowment and relative commodity prices. *Economica*, 22, 336–341.

Stolper, W F and Samuelson, P A (1941). Protection and real wages. *Review of Economic Studies*, 9, 58–73.

Chapter 3

The Pattern of Removal of Trade Barriers

The Issues

When a trade liberalization is undertaken, it is normally introduced in steps (though in many recent experiences the whole liberalization process has been so fast as to make the nature of steps, and their order, of less relevance). Four issues involved in the pattern of implementation of liberalization are the subject matter of this chapter. One is the possibility of the existence, prior to liberalization, of "tariff redundancy" — with the implication of this for the concreteness of a process in which such tariffs are lowered. Another is the preferred method of gradually collapsing the existing tariff system. A third one is the advisability of starting the liberalization (as has often been the case) with the removal (or lowering) of tariffs on inputs. The fourth issue, finally, concerns the relationship of the preferred order of removal of trade barriers to the industrial structures of the various economic activities. These issues will be addressed, respectively, in the following four sections of the chapter.

"Redundancy" of Tariffs

It is often observed, or expected, that in earlier stages of tariff reductions these are (or would be) apparent rather than real, in that they merely remove redundancy in the system — "water in the tariff." Some redundancy is to be expected from time to time — a government may err on the high side when intending to impose a prohibitive tariff or, if circumstances change, a tariff that originally constituted a real restraint may become redundant. Neither eventuality, however, can account for the massive tariff redundancies inferred in many studies of concrete experiences. Two possible explanations will be explored (a) that the redundancy, not the tariff reduction, is more apparent than real and (b) that a genuine redundancy exists, whose source may have some important implications.

The argument that the redundancy is illusory originates from the observation that goods with a common designation are not generally homogeneous and identical. This characteristic can lead to a misperception in two totally different ways. First, the statement that a tariff is "redundant" is often derived from a price comparison: the home price of the good is compared with the foreign price, and the proportional excess of the former over the latter is found to be smaller than the posted tariff rate. However, quite often, the same good is not being compared in the two markets: the designation is the same, and some essential features are similar, but vast differences exist between the foreign "good" and the home-produced one. Generally, the latter has less inherent value (as seen by the user) than the former. The price comparison may well therefore involve a misleading bias toward finding an apparent tariff redundancy. A lowering of the "redundant" tariff would then indeed have an economic consequence and would (most often) be an act of trade liberalization.

The second argument is more complicated. The tariff code may distinguish thousands, perhaps tens of thousands, of different "goods." However, even with such detailed distinction, few "goods" will be genuinely uniform. Normally, a "good" will consist of several, probably many, homogeneous subunits, each with its own cost structure. The implication of this pattern is analyzed with the aid of Fig. 3.1. Assume, for simplicity, constant marginal (and average) costs of production of each subunit ("branch"); this assumption is immaterial for the outcome. The unit of a product of each branch is defined so that its foreign price is one (say, one dollar). The branches 1 to n are represented in an ascending order of domestic costs (for simplicity, again, assume equal quantities — hence values in foreign currency — of production of all branches). The tariff level is meant to prohibit any imports of the good, that is, of all its branches. It is therefore set at level t, which will prohibit imports of n, the product of the highest-cost branch in this activity. For branches 1 to $n - 1$, then, there will inevitably be a positive level, higher or lower, of tariff "redundancy." Any actual estimation, whether it takes an average of all branches or happens to hit upon one of them as a sample, will be likely to record a tariff redundancy in this activity. However, lowering the tariff level would *not* be meaningless: branch n at least — and others, depending on the extent of tariff reduction — would become exposed to foreign competition. We may think of a curve SS as the supply curve of the "good," where changes in the

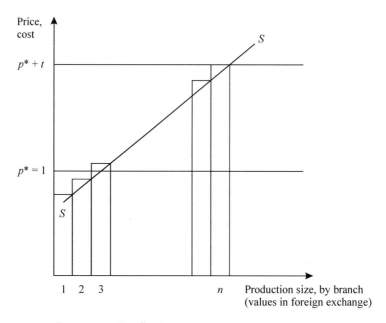

Figure 3.1:   Tariff redundancy and production structure.

quantities supplied originate not from changes in the level of production of a homogeneous unit but from the addition, or subtraction, of "branches." What we see, then, is a normal supply response: a price reduction will lower the size of production — a certain level of production was profitable before the tariff reduction, and less of it remains so after the tariff change. If, for any activity, the costs of sub-marginal units are calculated, the tariff will be found to be "redundant" for them. Only in this sense is tariff "redundancy" present. The more important consideration is that here, too, a tariff reduction would change an economic constraint and *would* be of economic consequence.

The argument may be extended further. Normally, no thousands or tens of thousands of tariff levels in the tariff code match the number of "goods" in the tariff classification: many goods (assuming, now, each "good" to be homogeneous) must differ in their cost levels. Hence, for all "sub-marginal" goods, a tariff "redundancy" will be found. Once more, the important consideration is that a tariff reduction *would* be a relevant economic change.

One source of genuine redundancy is common — the "change of circumstances" involved in a radical change of the real exchange rate.[1] Many tariff levels are contemplated and formulated as "prohibitive" under a given exchange rate will become redundant under a substantially higher exchange rate, and this redundancy will indeed be real. However, reduction of such "redundant" tariffs would still not necessarily be irrelevant. Presumably, in economies with histories of widely fluctuating real exchange rates, many decisions are based on some average past levels of the rate, as predictors of relative prices in the medium and long-term future, rather than on current exchange rates. If and when this is the *modus operandi*, a reduction of apparently "redundant" tariffs when the real exchange rate is high would still be relevant for expectations about future relative prices in the importable activities concerned and would again be of economic consequence.

Methods of Tariff Reduction[2]

Suppose that tariff levels are to be lowered in stages and through some *uniform* scheme.[3] The scheme can have a variety of formulations, but three methods in particular recur in deliberations on alternative routes of tariff reduction.

One is the across-the-board reduction of all tariffs by equal amounts, that is, by an equal percentage of the foreign price of each good, until a final target level (whether zero or otherwise) is reached.[4]

A variant of the across-the-board method reduces tariffs by *proportional* rather than equal amounts: at each stage, tariffs are cut by equal proportions of themselves rather than of the (foreign) prices of the goods.

The third scheme, finally, is the "concertina" method (Corden, 1974) in which the highest tariffs are lowered to a given level, with no change in tariffs below that level; this is then repeated at each stage so that the top level becomes progressively lower. By the last stage all tariffs have been lowered to the target level.

As a method that will most reduce *dispersion* in the tariff system, the concertina method seems intuitively to be the preferred scheme, since it is the dispersion that distorts the economic system and lowers welfare. Figure 3.2 demonstrates this proposition more formally. Assume two activities A and B, identical except for their tariff level. Specifically, supply (or cost) curves are identical for the two, as are demand curves. Thus, S_H is the home supply curve and D_H is the home demand curve for either A or B. (For simplicity, the figure represents these curves as straight lines.) P^* is the foreign price for the two activities. Initially, a tariff at the level of t_a is imposed on imports of A, and a lower tariff t_b applies to

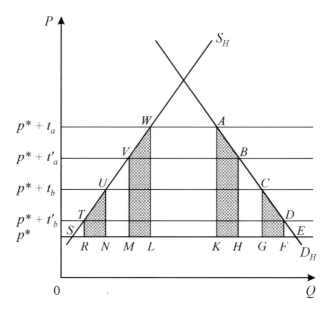

Figure 3.2:   Analysis of the "concertina" scheme for tariff reduction.

imports of B. The two domestic prices are thus $P^* + t_a$ for A and $P^* + t_b$ for B. Assume, now, an equal reduction of both tariffs, so that the domestic prices become, respectively, $P^* + t'_a$ and $P^* + t'_b$. Domestic production of A will decline by LM, and production of B will decline by NR, which is equal to LM. Similarly, domestic consumption levels will increase by the same amount in both goods — KH in A and GF in B. In as much as transitory short-term *costs* may arise, they will originate from the production side, that is, from the lower level of domestic activity. Since the reduction of levels of production will be equal in the two activities (given the assumption of similarity of activities, which amounts to the absence of any specific knowledge of differences between the two), the short-term losses should be identical.

Not so, however, the (permanent) gains from the tariff reduction. In activity A, the production loss from trade restriction will decline from WLS to VMS; the gain from the tariff reduction will hence be the shaded area WLMV. Similarly, the gain from the tariff reduction of B will be the shaded area UNRT. The production gain is thus clearly *smaller* in activity B than it is in A. Similarly, the *consumption* gain from the tariff reduction in A (shaded area ABHK) is necessarily larger than the consumption gain in B (shaded area CDFG). Both the production and the consumption gains, from an equal size of tariff reduction, are thus necessarily larger in the activity in which the initial tariff level is higher.

Observe, now, an alternative in which the tariff for B is kept at its original level (t_b remains its tariff and $P^* + t_b$ its domestic price). Instead, an equal amount is added to the tariff reduction in A, that is, this tariff will now be reduced not by the difference between t_a and t'_a but by twice that much. The aggregate changes in consumption and in production, and the aggregate (presumed) short-term transitory costs, will be the same as before. However, the (permanent) gains from tariff reductions will *not* be the same. The new areas of gains and losses will not be shown in the diagram, to avoid overcrowding. However, it should be easy to see that, in this alternative, both production and consumption gains from the tariff reduction will be *higher* than under the former alternative.

The first method illustrated in Fig. 3.2 represents our first-mentioned scheme, equal reductions of all tariffs; the second represents the concertina method. It is thus clearly established that the concertina method is superior.

Suppose, now, that the *proportional* scheme of across-the-board tariff reductions is adopted. Assuming the same "average" reduction of tariffs, this means that the tariff in A will be reduced to a lower level than t'_a. Again, this is clearly preferable to the equal-size tariff reductions, since any "transfer" of tariff reduction from B to A will be beneficial. The proportional scheme is inferior, though, to the concertina method, where the *whole* tariff reduction is "transferred," in a manner of speaking, from B to A.

The order of preference for the alternative schemes is thus, first, the concertina method, next, the proportional method, and last, equally large reductions of all tariffs.

It is further evident from the analysis that an *increase* in the lowest tariffs — as, once more, "transfer" of a tariff to the items that carry low tariffs — would be beneficial. This "extended concertina" should constrain tariff increases by the target uniform tariff level: when the latter is zero, no tariff should be raised. Since the planned uniform tariff is normally *not* zero (no actual case has in fact been observed); the zero tariffs at least should be increased. This relates to the issue discussed next.

The Imposition of Tariffs on Inputs

This section is concerned with the imposition of tariff duties on previously duty-free imports of inputs. (Inputs here refer to both intermediate and capital goods.)

To isolate the effects of various measures on the *protection* system, it will be assumed — as is usually done — that the *exchange rate* is in equilibrium, both before and after any change is introduced. In other words, an exchange rate adjustment is always carried out following a change in the protection system. However, it is the *effective* exchange rate that is in equilibrium; in other words, had the (positive or negative) protective devices been removed, the existing formal exchange rate would *not* be at its equilibrium level.

Designate by R_{vj} the *effective* exchange rate (the rate that includes trade taxes and subsidies, in addition to the formal exchange rate) for value added in the production of a good j; or the effective exchange rate for gross value in consumption. $\overline{R}$, which is some weighted average of all R_{vj} in the system, will stand for the equilibrium exchange rate. The *protective rate* in each activity j, designated g_j, would then be[5] $g_j = R_{vj}/R - 1$.

Had all R_{vj} been equal (that is, in a system with uniform rates of import tariffs and export subsidies), this level of the R_{vj} would also be the equilibrium level of the exchange rate $\overline{R}$; hence, all protective rates in the economy would be zero. In the normal case, the R_{vj} will, of course, be different in different activities. Hence, some protective rates will be positive; others negative. Specifically, when some imports are subject to tariffs and no export taxes are found, any activity with a zero tariff level must be subject to a *negative protection*: in comparison with a free-trade (or a "neutral") system, this activity is discouraged.

In a system in which export subsidies exist as well as import duties on final goods, and imported inputs are free of duties, the imposition of (low) tariffs on inputs would unambiguously be beneficial. The activities of production of inputs in this case are clearly subject to the highest (algebraically) negative protection, and reducing that discouragement must be an advantage. Moreover, imposition of input duties will also lower the effective protection rates in the (positively protected) production of final goods, and lower the dispersion of effective protective rates in the system.[6]

The outcome is not unequivocal when some other part of the economy is subject to negative protection. Specifically, suppose subsidies to exports are very low in comparison with the protection of import substitutes; for simplicity, we shall assume that export subsidies are zero, a situation not too far from the norm.[7] Here, exports clearly suffer from the infliction of negative protection and our inferences will have to be qualified.

First, assume that input duties do not apply for the production of exportables — a principle that operates in most developing countries, although the application of drawback schemes may often be far from perfect. In this instance, some distortion is introduced. The aforementioned benefits of the imposition of input tariffs will still be found; but, whereas without these tariffs the production of inputs and of exportables is equally (negatively) protected, their introduction leads to the discouragement of exportable activities vs the domestic production of inputs. The question of which impact is more important depends on the elasticities of substitution among the sectors involved. It may be presumed that the welfare-enhancing substitutions will dominate; however, this is an empirical judgment, or guess, rather than a logical necessity.

Let us now assume the opposite: no drawback at all of input tariffs is provided to exporters — whatever duties on inputs exist, they have to be fully paid by exporters as well as others. In this case, the imposition of input tariffs would *lower* the effective protection of exportable activities and would raise the level of dispersion (from initially zero, under our assumptions) of effective protection rates (all of which are negative) in the exports sector. These changes would tend to lower welfare and to offset, to one degree or another, the welfare-enhancing outcome of the inputs tariffs.

To understand the effect on *resource* movement in the economy, the resulting changes in the *formal* exchange rate must also be investigated. We classify all activities into four sectors: final consumption goods (C), intermediate inputs (I), exports (X), nontradeables (N). Distinguishing, again, between the two extreme situations concerning the availability of drawbacks on input duties in exports, we observe the following.

With a perfect scheme: The impact of the imposition of duties will be to reduce domestic production and increase imports of final consumption goods. Imports of inputs will decline too. Any fall of exports arising from the movement of resources into the inputs sector will be matched by falling imports in the latter. Whether an import or an export surplus is created will depend on whether the rise of imports of final goods is larger or smaller than the fall in imports of inputs. Thus, the change in the formal rate of exchange is uncertain. Since the average effective exchange rate for all tradeables must stay unchanged (to remain in equilibrium), we know that in the end this rate will fall in the final goods sector and rise in the inputs sector; however, the result is uncertain for exports.

With no drawback: Here, initially exports must fall, because of the decline of effective protection in this sector. Thus a contribution is made toward creating an import surplus, and a depreciation of the formal exchange rate. However, this result is still not logically inevitable. Once more we know that, in the end, since the protection of inputs increases in relation to that of final consumptions goods and exports, the effective exchange rate of either one of these two sectors or both must fall. In at least one of these two, resources will move from the sector to the nontradeable activities. In this instance, we do not know whether resources will move from the exports sector to the sector of final consumption goods or the other way around, since protection rates fall in both sectors.

The directions of resource flows, and their welfare implications, are summarized in Table 3.1. Note that no impact on welfare is assigned to movements of resources between nontradeables and either of the three tradeable sectors; these combined movements must be "neutral," since the effective exchange rate in the economy is assumed to be always in equilibrium.

We thus see, in sum, that in either case the welfare effect of the imposition of duties on inputs is uncertain. The presumption of a welfare increase is stronger with the existence of a drawback scheme for exports than without it (without a drawback scheme, in addition to the ambiguity about movements between final consumption goods and exports, the welfare-reducing movement of resources from exports to inputs production is stronger). However, even here, a welfare improvement is not inevitable. In either case, judgment on which flows of resources among sectors is likely to be important would have to be based on information about specific activities.

Table 3.1:   Movements of resources following the imposition of input tariffs.

Perfect drawback			No drawback		
Direction of resource flow		Welfare change	Direction of resource flow		Welfare change
C	→ I	+	C	→ I	+
C	→ X	+	C	? X	?
I	← X	−	I	← X	−
C	→ N		X	→ N	
I	← N		I	? N	
X	? N		X	? N	

←→, direction of movement; ?, ambiguity; +, enhancement; −, diminution; C, final consumption goods; I, intermediate inputs; X, exports; and N, nontradeables.

Industrial Structure and the Order of Removal of Barriers

In the reduction of trade barriers, should the industrial structure of a branch of production influence the placing of that branch in the schedule of reductions? Specifically, when a liberalization is carried out in stages, should a distinction be made between a competitive and a monopolistic activity?

In addressing this issue, our analysis will assume, for simplicity, extreme situations: a competitive industry is one with perfect competition; and a monopolized industry consists of a single firm. The compared activities will be assumed to be identical (in cost and demand conditions) except for the difference in industrial structure.

D_T, compensated demand curve for the good; D_H, demand for domestic production; MR, marginal revenue; MC, marginal cost (= domestic supply, under competition); P^*, international price.

Perfect competition: P^C, is consumer price; $P^*D(=P^C B)$, consumption; $P^*F(=P^C L)$, domestic production.

With the removal of quota: gain of consumer surplus $= P^*CBP^C$; loss of producer surplus $= P^*HLP^C$; loss of importer rent $= FDBL$. Therefore, net gain $= BDC$ ("consumption gain") $+ LFH$ ("production gain").

Monopoly: $P^*G(=P^m M)$, domestic production; P^m, consumer price; $P^*E(=P^m A)$, consumption.

With the removal of quota: gain of consumer surplus $= P^*CAP^m$, loss of producer surplus $= P^*HKMP^m$; loss of importer rent $= GEAM$. Therefore, net gain $= AEC$ ("consumption gain") $+ KGH$ ("production gain").

Comparison: With monopoly, consumption gain is larger by $AEDB$; production gain is smaller by $KGFL$. But: $GF–ED$ (the difference in consumption between the two cases is equal to the difference in production, since imports are given). Hence, necessarily, $KGFL < AEDB$. Therefore, the net gain from removal of the quota restriction will be larger under monopoly than under perfect competition. This holds for any import quota, including zero, that is, including the case of complete prohibition.

Removal of Quantitative Restrictions

It is sometimes argued that *ceteris paribus*, removing QRs in a monopolistic industry brings more benefits than when the industry is competitive. If so, QRs should be removed first from monopolized activities. The argument seems to be intuitively persuasive. A monopoly leads to distortion and waste, and removal of the monopoly power, through the introduction (or increase) of trade, should enhance welfare by eliminating that waste.

The precise meaning of the *ceteris paribus* assumption is crucial in the analysis. Three possible alternatives will be examined: (a) *import quotas* are the same in the competitive and the monopolized industries: (b) *prices* (before liberalization) are the same in both; and (c) *costs* are equal in both. The analysis under these three alternatives is carried out through Figures 3.3–3.5.

It is found that the answer to the basic question of whether more is gained from removing QRs from activities with one industrial structure than another is inconclusive. The following propositions emerge from the analysis.

(i) Starting from complete prohibition of imports (zero quotas), and abstracting from other considerations (or in the absence of other relevant information about activities), monopolized activities should be liberalized first, as bringing the greatest welfare gain. But an important observation should be made here. The monopolized industries, *ceteris paribus*, manifest the highest prices, and hence also the highest *differentials* (between the domestic and the international price). A policy rule that requires industries with the highest price differentials

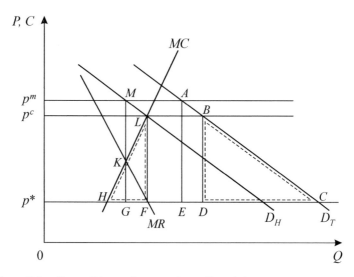

Figure 3.3:   Competition and monopoly — Case 1: import quotas are equal.

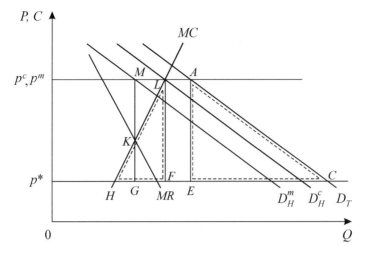

Figure 3.4: Competition and monopoly — Case 2: consumer prices are equal.

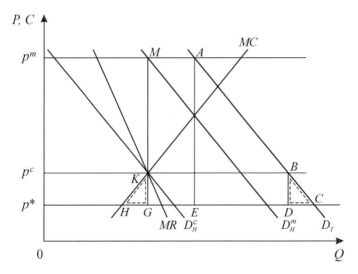

Figure 3.5: Competition and monopoly — Case 3: costs are equal.

to be liberalized first would thus take care of the discrepancy in welfare gains associated with the trade structure. Moreover, such a rule will not have to be concerned with whether the price differentials originate from differences in industrial structure (in otherwise identical activities) or in other attributes of non-identical activities — such as demand and cost functions or the size of the import quota.[8] There is *no separate* need to specify the industrial structure.

(ii) When price differentials are equal in otherwise identical activities, the welfare gain will be higher if import restrictions are lifted first from the *competitive* industry. In other words, there is a trade off: the welfare gain may be as high in a monopolized industry with a higher price differential as in a competitive industry with a lower differential. If anything, then, *competitive* industries should be prior candidates for liberalization when the price differential criterion is followed.[9]

(iii) A cost differential criterion would call for the opposite discrimination; but this inference has little practical use. To make any sense, the application of cost differentials as indicators of the expected gains from liberalization would require estimates of *marginal* costs, an effort which is obviously not feasible — even it were desirable — on the required scale.

Perfect competition: $D_H^C D_T (= LA)$, import quota; P^C, p^m, consumer price; $P^* F (= P^C L)$, domestic production; $P^* E (= P^C A)$, domestic consumption.

With the removal of quota: net gain $= AEC$ ("consumption gain") $+ LFH$ ("production gain").

Monopoly: $D_H^C D_T (= MA)$, import quota; PC, P^m, consumer price; $P^m M (= P^* M (P^* G)$, domestic production; $P^m A (+ P^* E)$, domestic consumption.

With the removal of quota: net gain $= AEC$ ("consumption gain") $+ KGH$ ("production gain").

Comparison: The consumption gain is identical under competition and monopoly. The production gain will be smaller under monopoly. Hence the total gain from the removal of restriction is smaller under monopoly.

The rationale is simple. An identical (consumer) price under competition and monopoly may be established only through a *larger* import quota under monopoly. Consumption is the same, but production is smaller (and imports larger) under monopoly. Hence, the gain from removal of the quota restriction is smaller under monopoly.

Perfect competition: $D_H^C D_T (= KB)$, import quota; P_c, consumer price; $P^* G (= P^c K)$, domestic production; $P^* D$, $(= P^c B)$, domestic consumption.

With the removal of quota: net gain $= BDC$ ("consumption gain") $+ KGH$ ("production gain").

Monopoly: $D_H^m D_T (= MA)$ = import quota; P^m, consumer price; $P^*G(=P^m M)$, domestic production; $P^*E(= P^m A)$, domestic consumption.

With the removal of quota: net gain = AEC ("Consumption gain") + KGH ("production gain").

Comparison: The production gain is identical under competition and under monopoly. The consumption gain will be larger under monopoly. Hence the total gain from the removal of restriction is larger under monopoly.

This is the reverse of case 2. Identical costs under competition and monopoly imply a higher consumer price under monopoly. This may be established only by a *smaller* import quota, and hence also smaller consumption. Thus, while production and production loss are equal, consumption (and imports) are smaller under monopoly. Hence the gain from removal of the quota restriction is larger under monopoly.

Reduction of Tariffs

Whenever imports do exist with a given tariff — that is, whenever the tariff is not prohibitive — the industrial structure of the activity is completely irrelevant in the present context: a domestic monopoly has no monopolistic power as long as imports provide any part of the domestic consumption, so that the otherwise monopolistic firm faces a domestic demand that is infinitely elastics (in a "small country", which is assumed here all along). Industrial structure becomes of consequence only when the tariff is prohibitive.

In Figure 3.6, t_c is the prohibitive tariff in its strict definition: whatever the industrial structure, it is just at this tariff level that all imports will disappear. An increase of the tariff beyond that level in the competitive industry will merely create some tariff redundancy. For the monopolistic industry, however, increasing the tariff level will affect the domestic price, the quantity produced, and the quantity consumed (the last two being necessarily equal to each other).[10] Thus, raising the tariff from t_c to t_m would raise the domestic price from $P^* + t_c$ to $P^* + t_m$ and lower the quantity produced and consumed from P^*E to $P^* + t_m A$. Only beyond the level t would a further raising of the tariff become irrelevant under monopoly. We shall refer to the tariff level t_m as the "actually prohibitive" tariff, whereas t_c will be addressed as the "competitively prohibitive" tariff level.[11] It may readily be seen that the economic loss of the actually prohibitive tariff t_m is *higher* than the loss from a competitively prohibitive

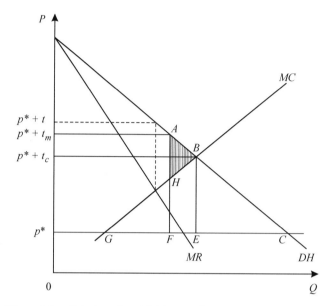

Figure 3.6:   Relation of prohibitive tariffs and domestic monopoly.

tariff t_c. The loss from the latter is the combination of the production loss BEG and the consumption loss BCE (that is, the area BCG). The loss of the former, on the other hand, is yielded by the (smaller than competitive) production loss HFG; and the (larger than competitive) consumption loss ACF. It thus *exceeds* the competitive tariff loss by the shaded area ABH. Hence, the *complete* removal of an actually prohibitive tariff, under monopoly, will yield a higher welfare gain than the removal of a prohibitive tariff under competition. The former may always be viewed as being undertaken in two stages: first, a reduction in the actually prohibitive tariff to the level at which it is competitively prohibitive, which will eliminate the excess loss ABH; and then a removal of the remaining part of the tariff, which will have the same effect under monopoly as under competition.

It is thus established — not surprisingly — that if an order of complete removal of tariffs has to be introduced, the prohibitive tariffs should first be eliminated in monopolistic industries. However, the same end would be achieved if the elimination of the *higher* tariffs first were to serve as a guiding policy rule. Moreover, it does *not* follow, from this analysis, that partial reduction, rather than complete elimination, of a tariff should be preferred when a monopolistic industry is in question. This will be the preferred course only if, given the *same* level of tariffs in the two industries, some tariff redundancy exists in the competitive industry, whereas in the monopolistic industry the tariff is only what we have termed "actually prohibitive" (and does not exceed the level t in Fig. 3.6). The opposite, of course, is not possible. In this case, the partial reduction in the tariff would be welfare enhancing in the monopolistic industry but irrelevant in the competitive industry (as long as the tariff is not reduced below its competitively prohibitive level).

When, on the other hand, no competitive redundancy is involved, the outcome is ambiguous (Fig. 3.7). Once more, the initial tariff levels are the competitively prohibitive tariff t_c in the competitive industry and the actually prohibitive tariff t_m in the monopolistic industry. Assume, now, an equal reduction of the tariff levels in both industries: from t_c to t'_c in the competitive activity, and from t_m to t'_m in the monopolistic industry. In the competitive industry, consumption will now increase to P^*M; and domestic production will fall to P^*N. The consumption and production welfare losses (in comparison with free trade) will now be LCM and TNG, respectively. That is, in comparison with the *initial* tariff, the aggregate welfare gain will be the shaded area BLMNT. In the monopolistic industry, consumption will increase from P^*F to P^*R (imports will still be actually prohibited).

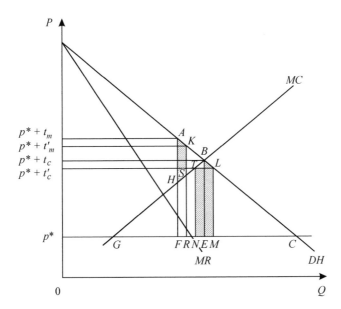

Figure 3.7:   Relation between prohibitive tariffs and domestic production.

The new consumption loss (in comparison with free trade) will become KCR, and the new production loss will be SRG — a higher production loss than before due to the expansion of production. In comparison with the initial tariff, the aggregate welfare gain will be the shaded area AKSH. Now, in general it is impossible to describe whether the latter is bigger or smaller than the aggregate gain under competition (BLMNT): the larger consumption gain under monopoly may be either more or less sufficient to compensate for the fact that the production loss increases, under monopoly, while under competition it must fall. Thus, no general *a priori* presumption is established as to whether, under a scheme of equal reductions of tariffs, a larger or smaller gain will be realized in a competitive or a monopolistic activity.[12]

Notes

1. Fluctuations of the real exchange rate may indeed be dramatic. Take, for instance, Argentina and Chile in the 1970s and the 1980s. In the former, the real exchange rate stood at 132 in the third quarter of 1976 (1970 = 100), 42 in the last quarter of 1980, and again 135 by the end of 1982. In Chile, similarly, the real exchange rate in early 1981 was less than one third its level in early 1974; by 1984, it regained most of this loss. See Cavallo and Cottani (1991), and de la Cuadra and Hachette (1991).

2. See also Bruno (1972), Corden (1974), and Harberger (1991).

3. A "uniform" scheme of tariff changes is defined here as one in which no activities are referred to by name or by any attribute other than the initial levels of their tariffs.

4. Needless to say, once the tariff level of a good reaches that (zero or positive) floor, no further tariff reduction in this activity will be undertaken. However, in our discussion we assume, for simplicity, that this stage has not yet been reached.

5. For a fuller elaboration of this formulation, see Michaely (1977).

6. Since protection is defined here in a way in which it is *zero* on average in the economy, only the measure of its *dispersion* will indicate the degree of economic loss brought by the protection system.

7. This is *not* an "extreme" case, since export *taxes* (or export quotas) are quite common.

8. In non-identical industries, differences in size are obviously relevant for the total gain. Properly formulated, the rule should state that

the highest gain *per unit of change of imports* (or of production, or consumption) will be realized where the price differential is highest.

9. But this is *not* recommended here as a policy rule. For a variety of other reasons, the gain in adhering to the principle of *uniformity* in the application of a rule (such as that of following price differentials) will far exceed any potential gain from discrimination.

10. We assume, again for simplicity, that no part of the domestic production turns, under monopoly, into *exports*. In view of the existence of transportation costs, and various other costs involved in turning from import substitution to exports, this is in any case not a highly restrictive assumption. As Fig. 3.6 is drawn, no exports would be forthcoming in the absence of this assumption; however, it could be drawn otherwise.

11. Referring to the issue discussed in an earlier section, another source of a *measured* tariff "redundancy" may be seen here: if the (actually prohibitive) tariff level is compared with the excess of domestic *costs* over the international price, the part AH of the tariff will be found to be "redundant."

12. Referring to our discussion earlier, it will be clear that, in a *proportional* scheme of tariff reductions, a higher likelihood is established that the welfare from the tariff reductions will be higher in the monopolistic industry. However, that will be due simply to the fact that this industry is subject to a higher level of an initial tariff than is the competitive industry; and hence, also, to a larger (absolute) tariff cut.

References

Bruno, M (1972). Market distortions and gradual reforms. *Review of Economic Studies*, 39, 373–383.

Cavallo, D and Joaquin C (1991). *Argentina*. In *Liberalizing Foreign Trade*, Papageorgiou, D, Michaely, M and Choksi, A M (eds.), Oxford: Basil Blackwell. Vol. 1, pp. 1–167.

Corden, W M (1974). *Trade Policy and Economic Welfare*. Oxford: Clarendon Press.

De la Cuadra, S and Dominique (1991). Chile. In *Liberalizing Foreign Trade*, Papageorgiou, D, Michaely, M and Choksi, A M (eds.), Vol. 1, pp. 169–319.

Harberger, A C (1991). *Trade Policy and the Real Exchange Rate*. Washington, DC: World Bank Economic Development Institute.

Michaely, M (1977). *Theory of Commercial Policy: Trade and Protection*. Oxford: Philip Allan, Chicago: University of Chicago Press.

Chapter 4

Preferential Trade Agreements vs Free Trade

The Issue

The desirability of a preferential trade agreement (PTA) has traditionally been analyzed within the Vinerian, second-best context[1]: the starting position is that of trade restrictions, and the introduction of trade preferences — that is, a geographically discriminating relaxation of restrictions — is compared with a situation in which no restrictions at all are removed. Surprisingly, little attention has been paid to the comparison of the conclusion of a PTA with the introduction of an overall, nondiscriminating liberalization (that is, at the extreme, with a free-trade situation).[2] This tilt of the analysis may perhaps be explained by the particular attraction of *sign*, rather than size. In the comparison of a PTA with general restrictions, the sign of the welfare change is ambiguous. When a PTA is compared with a general liberalization, on the other hand, the outcome (given the fulfillment of some well-known conditions) is in no doubt: a PTA is inferior to general liberalization. But how important is this inferiority? Or, put in a slightly different way, what are the circumstances, or attributes, which would assign more or less significance to the distortion introduced, in this comparison, by a PTA? The analysis of this issue, which has been mostly neglected in the main body of the customs-union theory, will be addressed in the present chapter.

An Analytical Framework: The Sources of Loss

For analytical purposes, it may be simplest to consider the conclusion of a PTA (starting from general, nondiscriminatory import restrictions) as consisting notionally of two steps. First, a general, overall liberalization is introduced, leading to the establishment of free trade. Next, a tariff (at the pre-liberalization level) is imposed only on the nonpartner countries (the "rest of the world" ROW), leaving free trade to be conducted only in trade with the partner. A comparison of a PTA with general liberalization would thus consist of the analysis of the impact of this second step.

To start with, we may define — in similarity with the Vinerian analysis — the components of welfare change; in this case, unlike the Vinerian, they are all elements of *loss*. First comes the impact of contracting the home production of exportable, shifting resources to the production of importables. This may be termed "trade destruction" (in similarity with the Vinerian "trade creation" — but, of course, with a welfare effect of the opposite sign). Next comes "trade dislocation" — the loss from shifting the source of imports from the cheaper nonpartners to the more expensive partner (this is entirely equivalent, in nature and in sign, to the Vinerian "trade diversion").[3] Finally comes the "consumption diversion" — similar in nature to the second-best analysis "consumption gain," but consisting here of a definite loss rather than a definite gain.

These three elements of loss are given quantitative representation in Fig. 4.1. PQ is the home country's transformation curve between X, the exportable good, and M, the importable good. All quantities will be measured by X, the exportable good (nothing would have changed were

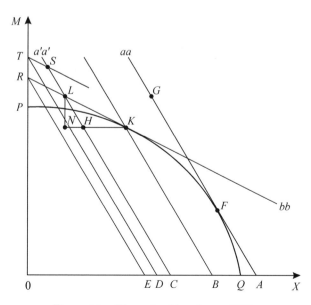

Figure 4.1:   Elements of loss from a PTA.

they to be measured by M, the importable good). The slope of *aa* represents the relative price between X and M in the nonpartner country (ROW); whereas the slope of *bb* represents, similarly, the price in trade with the partner (indicating a higher price of M than in ROW). The home country is "small," facing a fixed price in trade with either the partner or ROW. With free trade, the production locus will be at F; whereas consumption, given some demand conditions (not shown), will be at G, with FG representing the trade vector. The value of the country's national product, in terms of X, will be OA.

When the tariff on imports from ROW is imposed, two alternative changes are possible. One is that imports will continue to originate (exclusively, under the specified circumstances) from ROW, but production and consumption loci, and trade, will change.[4] This will be the outcome as long as the imposed tariff is lower than the price differential of imports originating in the partner country and in ROW. This outcome is not shown in the diagram, but will be discussed later. The alternative outcome will occur when the tariff is equal to (or, rather, higher than, by an infinitesimally small amount) this price differential (further tariff increases would be immaterial). In this instance, all trade will be shifted toward the partner, which will become the sole source of imports.[5] This alternative is shown in Fig. 4.1. The production locus will now become K, and consumption will shift to L, KL being the vector of trade (this time, with the partner).

The value, in terms of X, of the basket of goods represented by K, were trade still to be conducted with ROW, is the amount OB. This is evidently smaller than OA, the value of the country's production basket prior to the tariff. The difference, AB, thus represents the loss from trade destruction. Next, we observe the loss from buying the imports, as they are at their new level, from the more expensive source. The trade vector KL indicates the purchase of the size LN of imports, paying for it NK of exports. But had these imports been bought from ROW, only NH of exports would have to be paid. KH is thus the loss from trade dislocation, and it is represented on the X-axis by BC. The aggregate of these two components of loss — trade destruction and trade dislocation — is thus AC: the value, at free-trade prices, of consumption basket L is smaller by this size from the value of the free-trade consumption basket (G).

However, if the economy had been provided with the amount of resources OC, and free trade had still prevailed, the economy's budget constraint would have been the line *a'a'*, originating in C with the same slope as *aa*, and, this slope representing also the price faced by consumers, not L but a point like S would be selected as the consumption basket. To reach that level, the economy would have to possess an amount of goods equal to OT of the import goods, rather than OR. The difference, TR, is the loss from consumption diversion. In terms of the export good — the numeraire we are using here — this is equal, at free-market prices, to the size DE. This element should be added to AC to reach the aggregate loss to the economy from all three sources — trade destruction, trade dislocation, and consumption diversion.

The Impact of Economic Attributes

We now pose the basic question: given that a PTA leads to a loss, under what circumstance is this loss likely to be larger or smaller? We shall discuss attributes, which are the main concern of the Vinerian, second-best analysis.[6] To a large extent, we shall be assisted by the analytical framework just presented; however, inferences will not be confined to it, primarily when a multi-commodity world is addressed.

The Level of Initial Restrictions

When the general tariff level of the home country is high, prior to the PTA — which in our analysis translates into an imposition of a high tariff on ROW — the loss from a PTA (in comparison with free trade) is likely to be high. In terms of the analysis just sketched out, this would be easy to realize in the following way. First, take the range in which the discriminatory tariff is not sufficiently high to shift the source of supply of imports from ROW to the partner. The higher the tariff imposed, the higher will be the loss from it. (This could be easily shown by means of Fig. 4.1, but should be quite obvious without it.) Second, take the range (or point) at which the source of imports does shift. The higher the tariff level, which leads to this shift, the larger the price discrepancy of imports between the partner and ROW, and the bigger the loss from the shift. Beyond this level, further increases of the tariff are irrelevant — a "tariff redundancy" of a sort exists. At this range, thus, higher tariffs do not indicate bigger welfare losses — nor, however, do they indicate the opposite. More important, in a world of many goods, the higher the tariff level imposed, the more goods will shift from the column of trade with ROW to that of trade with the partner. Altogether, a higher tariff indicates a likelihood of a bigger welfare loss. This is probably the most important instance in which the present comparison yields a contrasting indication to that found in the second-best analysis. There, it will be recalled, a cardinal inference of the analysis states that the higher the initial tariff, the higher the likelihood of a gain, rather than a loss, from the conclusion of a PTA (in comparison, of course, with the continued maintenance of the overall restrictions). This contrast may, perhaps, help to explain some apparent contradictions between analytical inference and beliefs of policymakers. Over the last decade, since the introduction of radical trade liberalizations in many countries (particularly in Latin America), it is often stated that the lower level of trade restrictions makes the conclusion of PTAs (the so-called "second-generation" PTAs) a better proposition. While such statement patently runs contrary to the teaching of the second-best analysis, it may be potentially explained by a frame of mind in which the comparison made is not of a PTA with the maintenance of general restrictions, but of a PTA with a (further) general liberalization.

The Share of Trade in Income

When this share is large, the welfare loss from a PTA is likely to be high. This seems intuitively evident and may be demonstrated in a variety of ways. Suppose that, in two alternative situations, production possibilities are the same, but differences in demand patterns lead to different trade shares. In terms of Fig. 4.1, the transformation curve is given, hence also production locus F, under free trade. However, a larger preference for M, the importable good, leads the consumption locus to be above (and to the left of) G along line *aa*. The trade vector will be larger, constituting a larger share of the home country's income (which remains the value OA). With the imposition of tariffs on ROW, and the shift of the production locus to K, the new consumption locus — given the stronger preference for M — will likewise be to the left of L on *bb*: the vector of trade — now with the partner rather than with ROW — will be larger than in the alternative situation. The loss from trade destruction will remain the same (AB) as in the previous alternative; however, the loss from trade dislocation (not shown in Fig. 4.1, but easy to realize) will now be higher. Alternatively, take different production circumstances to be the source of different shares of trade in income. In Fig. 4.1, suppose the value of income stays at the size OA. However, a transformation curve more tilted toward X makes its tangency with AG — the new production locus — a point below (and to the right of) F. With given demand conditions, the consumption locus will stay at G, with a larger trade vector — hence, trade's share in income — than before. Again, it should be easy to see (but not shown) that the new production locus (on another transformation curve) will be to the left of line BK. Hence, the loss from the imposition of tariff will be higher, this time originating in a larger loss from trade destruction.[7] As before, this inference stands in contrast with that of the second-best analysis: the proposition drawn there is that a high share of trade in income is likely to increase the likelihood of a gain, rather than a loss, from the conclusion of a PTA (since the distortion removed, originating in the gap between foreign and home prices, is then more important).

The Partner's Share in the Home Country's Trade

The higher the share of the partner in the home country's aggregate trade (imports), the smaller the expected loss from a PTA. This cannot be demonstrated by means of an analysis represented by Fig. 4.1: with a single good, and fixed foreign prices, the share of the partner in home country's imports would be zero or one. But in a multi-good world, this proposition should be intuitively obvious. A larger share of the partner means that more goods, or goods of larger values (or, with variable foreign prices, larger fractions of trade in individual goods), are initially imported from the partner rather than from ROW. Hence, trade dislocation following the imposition of a tariff on imports from ROW will be less important. This time, the inference is similar to the one found in the second-best analysis: there, too, a high initial (relative) level of trade with the partner (an element we shall discuss at some length in Chapter 12) will increase the likelihood of a gain from a PTA.

Structural Attributes of the Partner

When the partner is a large country (or a large bloc of countries), and when its production and trade are highly diversified, the expected loss from a PTA with it is likely to be *small*. With a partner of these attributes, it is likely, first, that the imposition of a tariff on ROW will often not be relevant, since the goods involved are imported from the partner even without the tariff (this goes back to the point just discussed). Second, when the tariff does shift the source of imports from ROW to the partner, price differentials between the two sources are likely to be small in many goods — in contrast with a small partner, particularly one which specializes in a small range of goods. Thus, losses from both trade destruction and trade dislocation (as well as from consumption diversion) are likely to be small, and a PTA with such partner is likely to be less harmful. In this instance, too, the inference of this first-best comparison runs along the same lines as the second-best proposition, which states that a PTA is more likely to lead to a gain than to a loss — in comparison with the continuation of nondiscriminatory restrictions — the larger and more diversified the contemplated trade partner.

Cost Changes in the Home Country's Production

The more marginal costs (at home) tend to rise with an increase in the size of a good's production, the *larger* is the expected loss from a PTA. In terms of Fig. 4.1, suppose the starting locus to be as shown. A more rapidly rising schedule of marginal costs would be represented by a more convex (from the origin) transformation curve (which would still, by construction, be tangent to line *aa* at point F). An imposition of the specified tariff would now move the production locus to a point to the left of the line BK (this, as well as the new transformation curve itself, is not shown, but could be easily demonstrated). The loss from trade destruction, hence the aggregate loss from imposition of the tariff, would thus be higher. Intuitively, this should be easy to realize. The loss from trade destruction is, in substance, the loss involved in shifting the source of production from a more efficient economy (in production of the specific good) ROW, to a less efficient one (home), and this loss will be larger as the shift to the (relatively) inefficient source tends to increase its inefficiency. Once more, this inference is in full agreement with the one drawn in the second-best analysis: there, the analytical proposition states that the more rapid the increase of marginal costs when production (at home) expands, the more likely it is for a PTA to lead to a loss rather than a gain.

The Level of the Partner's Tariff

The higher, finally, the partner's tariff, the *smaller* the loss from a PTA with it. In fact, the introduction of the element of a PTA, which refers to the partner's removal of its restriction on imports from the home country, may even mean that the PTA will be, from the home country's point of view, a first-best solution, that is, the selection of a PTA instead of a general liberalization may involve a gain rather than a loss. Intuitively, this is easy to comprehend: the higher the tariff level, which the partner removes, in exchange for the home country's removal of its tariffs (or, in our analytical construct, in exchange for the home country's imposition of a tariff on imports from ROW), the more the home country will gain from improvement of its terms of trade. In terms of Fig. 4.1, the removal of the partner's tariff on its imports of X from the home country will be represented by a steeper *bb* line (a higher relative price of X); and the steeper this line, the more production locus K will tend to be to the right, and the lower the losses from both trade destruction and trade dislocation will be. In the extreme case, line *bb* will become steeper than *aa*, and the home country will gain from its imposition of tariff on ROW (reciprocated by the partner's removal of its tariffs on home country's goods).

Here, too, no contrast exists between the substance of the first-best and the second-best analyses: in the latter, too, a PTA with a partner whose trade regime is highly protective is more likely to lead to a gain (to the home country), rather than a loss, than a PTA with a partner whose regime is highly liberalized.

Conclusions

To sum up, we have addressed two elements in which the analytical inferences in the present, first-best comparison stand in contrast with the second-best analytical propositions. We have found that the loss from a PTA, in comparison with a nondiscriminating, free-trade policy, will be larger:

(i) the higher the level of trade restrictions imposed by the home country prior to a PTA;
(ii) the higher the share of trade in the home country's income.

We have also addressed four other elements, in which the inferences from the present analysis agree in substance with those of the second-best comparison. Namely, the loss from a PTA will tend to be larger:

(iii) the lower the share of the contemplated partner in the home country's aggregate trade;
(iv) the smaller the partner, and the less diversified its production and trade;
(v)   the more costs tend to rise in the home economy, with the expansion of production of a good; and, finally,

(vi) the lower the level of trade restrictions of the partner, which are designed to be removed upon conclusion of the PTA.

Notes

1. See Viner (1950).
2. The question whether the conclusion of a PTA would tend to come at the expense of a general liberalization (or, on the contrary, the former would facilitate the latter) has indeed been a central topic of analysis — particularly in recent years. However, this is a separate issue.
3. In fact, this component might be designated "trade diversion" here as well, except that this term is so strongly identified with the Vinerian element in the second-best comparison that confusion would be almost inevitable.
4. With this outcome, there would be no loss from "trade dislocation."
5. With variable, rather than constant, foreign prices, trade either with or without the tariff (within a certain range of prices) will be conducted with both foreign sources, rather than being directed exclusively to one or the other. The essence of the analysis, though, will be the same.
6. These have been introduced, beyond the analysis in Viner's (1950) foundation of the theory, primarily in the contributions of Meade (1955) and Lipsey (1960).
7. Still another possibility is to assume a given set of production possibilities, that is, a given transformation curve, and given demand patterns, but a lower price of M (a higher price of X) overall (that is, both in ROW and in the partner, maintaining the same price differential between the two). The initial share of trade in income, as well as the one established with the shift of trade to the partner, would be higher, and so would be the aggregate loss from the PTA — due again, in this instance, to a larger loss from trade destruction.

References

Lipsey, R G (1960). The theory of customs unions: A general survey. *Economic Journal*, 70, 496–513.

Meade, J E (1955). *The Theory of Customs Unions*. Amsterdam: North-Holland Publishing Company.

Viner, J (1950). *The Customs Union Issue*. New York: Carnegie Endowment for International Peace.

Chapter 5

Partners to a PTA: Implications of Varying Size

Introduction

The analysis of the welfare effect of a preferential trade agreement (PTA), like other analyses of trade policies, is mostly cast in the "small-country" framework. That is, the "home" country is assumed to be "small": it is a price taker, either in trade with its partner to the agreement or in its trade with the "third" country (the rest of the world ROW). For many purposes, the broad inferences of such analyses are indeed valid. However, in the view of the frequency with which preferential agreements are concluded (or at least contemplated) between a large home country and, *ipso facto*, a relatively small partner, attention should be paid to the particular implications of a possible deviation from the "small-country" framework.[1]

Essentially, the added element introduced when this deviation occurs is the impact of an agreement on and through the home country's terms of trade. Discussions of the terms-of-trade effect of a preferential agreement have long been part of customs-union theory[2]; however, this chapter intends to extend the analysis by focusing on the *changing size* of the potential trade partner, asking how a declining size of a partner may be expected to affect the welfare outcome of an agreement with it. This will be particularly relevant — hopefully helping to resolve apparent contradictions — to recent discussions of PTAs in which conventional, fundamental welfare propositions of the theory are sought to be overturned.[3]

The analysis will be restricted throughout to the free trade area of preferential treatment, that is, it will not cover the impact of a common external tariff conducted by a customs union. Before embarking on the main part of the analysis, it should be emphasized that it is confined to the outcome of the agreement through the impact of the trade of the home country on its terms of trade. A prior question is whether when such impact is absent (that is, when the home country is still considered "small"), an agreement with a large or with a small partner is preferable. The answer to this question is well known and unambiguous: the larger the partner, *ceteris paribus* (or, in other words, with no other specific knowledge), the more likely it is that a welfare gain will result to the home country from the agreement. A larger country is expected to be less specialized, less unique, more diversified, and closer in its relative price pattern to the ROW. Hence, the opening of trade with a larger country, following the conclusion of a preferential agreement with it, is likely to lead to smaller losses from trade diversion and larger gains from trade creation. This remains true, independent of the inferences of the following analysis.

Section 2 will present the analysis of welfare implications of the varying size of partners, while the following section will apply the findings to the recent dispute over the validity of salient propositions of orthodox theory of preferential trading agreements.

Analysis of Welfare Implication

The analysis of the role of smallness of the partner through the impact of an agreement on the terms of trade will be conducted diagrammatically with the aid of Fig. 5.1.[4] PQ is the transformation curve for the economy, with M being the importable good, and X the exportable. Take, first, the conventional case in which the home country is assumed to be "small," in relation to both the partner to the preferential agreement ("country B") and the ROW ("country C"), that is, to state the obverse, both the partner (B) and the "third" country (C) are assumed to be large in relation to the home country. The (given) price ratio in trade with C is represented by the slope of the line *cc*, whereas the price of imports in trade with the partner B, represented by the slope *bb*, is higher. Prior to the preferential agreement, trade will hence be with C. Under free trade, production would be at F, with trade taking place upward along the budget-constraint line *cc*. A (nonprohibitive) tariff exists, however, in the home country, which makes the home price of imports higher than under free trade: the price is represented by the slope of *tt*. Under this setup (that is, with a universal tariff imposed on imports from all sources), the home production locus will be at E (rather than at F, as it would have been under free trade), where

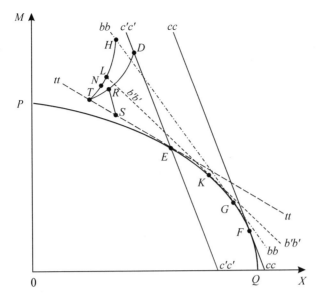

Figure 5.1:   A preferential agreement with partners of varying size.

the cum tariff price ratio (*tt*) is equal to the home cost of production. Trade (with country C) will take place along the line $c'c'$ — say, up to combination D, which will be the consumption locus. No trade will be conducted with country B.

Now introduce a free-trade-area agreement with B, under which no tariff is charged by the home country on its imports from B (while the previous tariff continues to be charged on imports from C). Assume — without this, the agreement would be meaningless — that the price of imports in trade with B, although higher than the price of imports from C, is lower than the latter when the tariff is added to it (that is, lower than the pre-agreement home price). Following the agreement, trade will switch from country C to country B, with the price both in trade and at home represented by *bb* (since no tariff exists now on imports from B). The new production locus will be at G, with trade taking place along *bb*, and the new consumption point will be somewhere on *bb* to the left of G — say, at point H. In the general case, the new consumption basket may be either superior or inferior to the pre-agreement basket D. This is the well-known uncertainty of the outcome of a customs union, due to conflicting impacts: positive trade creation and consumption effects, and a negative trade-diversion effect.

We shall now partially change the assumption about the size of countries and, instead of a generally "small" home country, assume that in relation to its partner it is "large": its trade with that country does have an effect on the price at which it is conducted.[5] For simplicity, we shall still assume that the home country is "small" in its trade with the nonmember country (C).[6] When, following the agreement, trade is diverted from C to B, the price the home country has to pay for its imports from B rises: it is no longer the price represented by bb, but a higher one (that is, bb becomes flatter).[7] Eventually, at an equilibrium, the price ratio is at some level such as that represented by line $b'b'$.[8] The production locus will now be at K (rather than G), and the consumption basket will be at, for instance, combination L. The latter is obviously inferior to basket H and is more likely than the outcome of the earlier case to represent a welfare loss, rather than a gain (or a bigger loss than before) from the preferential agreement. This is due, as can readily be seen, to a stronger (negative) trade diversion, a weaker (positive) trade creation, and, similarly, a weaker (positive) consumption effect. Thus, *ceteris paribus*, a PTA with a smaller country is more likely to lead to a loss than an agreement with a larger country.[9]

Next, take a smaller partner. Other things being equal, this smaller size will lead to a stronger deterioration of the home country's terms of trade, that is, to a larger price increase of imports at any given size of trade with the partner. Equilibrium will now be reached at a consumption point such as N, reflecting a higher price of imports and a smaller amount of trade. Similar to the argument made earlier, the new consumption basket will contain less of M, the import good, than before (with consumption basket L), whereas the direction of change of the amount consumed of X is ambiguous.

In a similar way, we may keep decreasing the size of the partner to the preferential agreement and keep getting different equilibrium consumption baskets. These are combined by the line HLNT, where the direction of the arrow indicates a decline of the size of the trade partner. T is the point at which the partner is just small enough to make the price at which it sells its goods to the home country reach the cum tariff level of the price paid for imports from country C (that is, to the price ratio represented by line tt). In this case imports will just be on the verge of being bought from both the partner and the "third" country, at the same price for the consumer (which is the home price prevailing prior to the agreement), but with a higher external price paid for imports from the partner than for the nonpreferred imports. Home production will be at E — the same combination as without the agreement (the home price having remained unchanged) — and exchange with the partner will be at the price ratio *tt*, up to point T. The latter is clearly inferior to any other consumption basket above it along the line HLNT.

Now, let us reduce the size of the partner still further. The price ratio at which the country trades remains, from this point on, unchanged: it is the price in trade with the third country (represented by line *cc*), which prevails also in trade with the partner country B. That is, no further price deterioration will take place from now on. On the other hand, the amount of imports bought from partner B will *fall* as the partner gets smaller: the amount its market is willing to supply as export to the home country becomes smaller (again, *ceteris paribus*) at the given price, where this market is smaller. Following an agreement with a smaller partner, the new equilibrium consumption basket will be at a point like R. Imports will now be bought from partner B only to the extent represented by trade from E to S rather than to T, and will be complemented by imports from country C, trade with which is represented by the vector SR (parallel to *cc*). Thus, the average price paid by the home country for its imports is now lower — more imports coming from the cheaper third country C, and less from the partner B, the expensive source; hence, an improvement in the home country's terms of trade. Point R will contain more of both M and X, with a higher real income in the home country and an unchanged price (to the consumer!). It clearly represents a higher welfare level than consumption basket T.

In a similar way, we may keep reducing the size of the partner to the preferential agreement, getting consumption combinations which will be on the line TRD; as before, the direction of the arrow indicates a reduction in the size of the partner. The extreme point of this line, D, is simply the pre-agreement consumption basket. It represents the case in which the partner country is so small that no imports will be forthcoming from it: in this instance, the PTA becomes irrelevant. Any movement along line TRD (with the arrow) represents an increase in welfare, resulting from a further decline of imports from the partner and hence a further decline of the average price the home country is paying for its imports. Line TRD must be below line HLNT. At any real income, the price of M (again, to the consumer) is higher here than in trade represented by line HLNT, where all imports were bought from the partner country at a price lower than the cum tariff price in trade with third country C (which prevails in trade along TRD).

For convenience, we may term a partner country of a size, which leads to consumption baskets along HLNT as "small," and one of a size, which leads to combinations along TRD as "ultra-small." The welfare implications (for the home country) of a reduction in the size of the partner country are thus *diametrically opposite* for partners classified into the two different groups. When the partners are just "small," a reduction in the size of the partner will lead, *ceteris paribus*, to a decline of the home country's welfare level, whereas where the partners are "ultra-small," the smaller the partner, the higher the home country's welfare level will be. The worst case, for the home country, is where the partner's size is just on the borderline between "small" and "ultra-small" (that is, where a preferential agreement with it would result in consumption basket T).

A preferential agreement with an "ultra-small" country must result in a welfare loss.[10] Any consumption basket along TRD (short of D itself) must be inferior to D, the pre-union consumption combination. We cannot be sure, on the other hand, what the consequences of a preferential agreement for the home country's welfare is when the partner country is just "small." "Smallness" starts at a point just below H (that is, at a size of country where trade with it, following a preferential agreement, just starts to have an impact on the terms of trade with it). We know that H could represent a welfare level either higher or lower than the pre-union basket D; hence, a point just below H could still represent a welfare improvement due to the agreement. On the other hand, we also know that combination T represents a welfare loss, in comparison with pre-union point D; hence, a combination just above T would also indicate a welfare loss. Somewhere along HLNT (going with the arrow), a welfare loss due to the preferential agreement turns from a possibility to a certainty; but where this is (that is, at what level of "smallness" of the partner) we cannot generally say.

Similarly, we cannot state in a general way whether it is preferable (that is, less costly) for the home country to conclude an agreement with a "small" or an "ultra-small" partner. We may expect the home country to be better off where an agreement with a "small" country results in a consumption combination close to H, on HLNT, than in an agreement with an "ultra-small" partner, which leads to a combination closer to T on TRD; but this, once more, does not suggest a general, unambiguous rule.

The analysis may be summed up by means of Fig. 5.2. On the horizontal axis, the size of partner countries is presented, whereas the vertical axis represents an *ordinal* measure of the home country's welfare. The diagram should be followed from right to left. The largest partner country — at

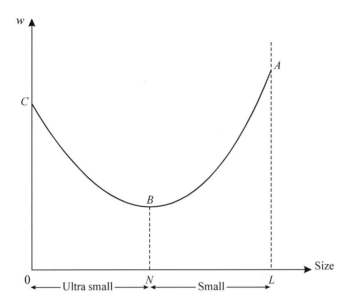

Figure 5.2:   Welfare levels and the size of the partner.

the point L — is just large enough to allow a potential trade with the home country no impact on its prices, and the home country's welfare level following a free trade agreement with that partner is LA. With a smaller partner, welfare will be lower, and will keep falling as the size of the partner keeps getting smaller, until it reaches the size represented by N: this is the size at which the partner just sells all the home country wants to buy at the pre-agreement, *cum* tariff price of imports. The welfare level following an agreement with a partner this size is NB, and it is the lowest possible level. From here onward, as the size of the partner keeps falling, the home country's welfare level keeps increasing.[11] At the limit, this welfare level is OC: this will be reached when the partner country is small enough to provide no imports at all at the pre-agreement home country's price, so that a preferential agreement with that partner becomes meaningless.

The welfare level represented by OC may be higher or lower than that of LA. With no specific knowledge, we likewise cannot rank the welfare levels of a point on AB and a point on BC. Countries of a size along the range represented by LN are "small," whereas those partners falling in the range NO are "ultra-small." Thus, while an agreement with an ultra-small partner is bound to result in a welfare loss (leading the home country to a welfare level somewhere on BC), it does not follow that an agreement with an ultra-small country is necessarily inferior to an agreement with a partner that is just small.

Application

The conventional customs-union theory (or the theory of PTAs, as it has, following Bhagwati, been recently designated) starts with Viner's distinction between trade creation and trade diversion. This results in the conclusion that "everything is possible" when inferences are made about the direction of the welfare impact of an agreement. But beyond this, propositions have been developed about the likelihood of one outcome or another[12]; we may refer to these as the "orthodox" propositions. Formulated from the point of view of a single country — the "home country" — they mainly state that an agreement is more likely to result in a gain rather than a loss (or a higher gain, or lower loss):

- the higher the initial (pre-agreement, universal) level of the home country's tariff on imports;
- the larger the economic size of the partner;
- the higher the initial share of the partner in the provision of the home country's imports;
- the higher the proportion of imports from the partner in the home country's aggregate production; and
- the more diversified the partner's exports.

The propositions are based on the analysis of the impact of an agreement through changes in the home country's imports, due to the removal of its *own* tariffs on imports from the partner. The added impact due to the removal of the *partner's* tariff on the home country's exports is ignored, in these inferences as well as in most of the "orthodox" analysis.[13]

Some of these fundamental propositions have been challenged recently by Bhagwati and Panagariya.[14] They argue, essentially, that trade diversion involves a heavier loss than the Vinerian analysis indicates. The home country does not just switch from a less expensive (the ROW) to a more expensive (the partner) source of imports: it will pay the partner the world price *plus* the tariff, thus losing (to the partner) the revenue imposed on its imports prior to the agreement. Following the agreement, the price to consumers will remain unchanged; but part of it will not consist of tariff revenues remaining in the home country, but of added payments to foreigners. This worsening of the terms of trade is likely, so the argument goes, to constitute the overwhelming element in the outcome of a PTA. From this inference follow *opposite* propositions[15] — we shall refer to them as "revisionist" — to those listed earlier about the attributes of a gain or loss producing PTA. To wit, a *loss* from a PTA is more likely and will be higher:

- the higher the initial (pre-agreement) tariff level on the home country's imports;
- the larger the economic size of the partner;
- the higher the initial level of imports from the partner; and, a corollary,
- the higher the share of imports from the partner in the home country's aggregate imports.

Since a PTA is bound to lead to a loss to the home country from its import trade, a mercantilist inference follows. A gain is ensured in the home country's *export* trade, due to the removal of the partner's tariffs on it, and a PTA will be beneficial only if this gain is larger than the loss on imports. The export gain will be higher, the higher the size of exports to the partner and the higher the initial level of tariffs imposed by the partner on its imports (hence the extent of reduction in tariffs on the home country's exports following the agreement).

The analysis of this chapter's earlier section provides a convenient framework for distinguishing circumstances in which either the "orthodox" or the "revisionist" set of propositions will be valid. To start with, the sign (positive or negative) of the effect on the home country's welfare of the *size of the partner* to a PTA is indeed ambiguous; but it is clear within any given range of the partner's size. When the home country is "small" and the partner is, hence, "large," the "orthodox" proposition definitely holds; this, of course, is the common frame of most of the Vinerian conventional analysis of a PTA. What may be less obvious, but is still true, is that the "orthodox" propositions are valid — and their "revisionist" counterparts must be rejected — also when the partner is what we have classified as "small." When the partner is "ultra-small," on the other hand, the tables are turned: the "orthodox" proposition loses validity and should be replaced by its "revisionist" counterpart. It is in this range of the partner's size that a PTA gets a mercantilist bent, where a benefit from a PTA may be expected only when the gain to the home country from its export trade more than outweighs a certain loss originating in the country's import trade.

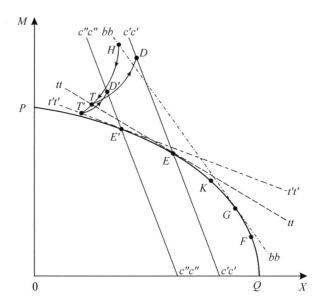

Figure 5.3:   Partner's size and the impact of initial tariff levels.

The effect of the *initial level* of the (uniform) tariff on the likelihood and size of a gain or a loss from a PTA is also ambiguous: again, ranges of size of the partner country may be distinguished, although this time the classification is somewhat more involved. Figure 5.3 reproduces the relevant parts of Fig. 5.1, and in addition compares the outcome of a PTA under two alternative initial levels; tariff t, as before, and a higher tariff t'. With the latter, the pre-agreement *cum* tariff home price is represented by $t't'$, rather than tt; the home production locus becomes E′, rather than E; and trade is conducted along $c''c''$, rather than $c'c'$, to a point like D′ — which obviously represents a lower welfare level than D. The conclusion of a PTA in the absence of an impact on prices in trade with the partner will lead to the consumption locus H — just as before, with the lower tariff t: this outcome is invariant to the level of the initial tariff. This is also true, as we keep lowering the size of the partners, for the curve HT. The difference is that this curve will now be extended down to T′: with the higher *cum* tariff home price, smaller partners will now be able to fully provide the home market's imports. When point T′ is reached, further reductions in the partner's size will result, as before, in smaller shares of the partner in the provision of the economy's imports. The new curve referring to this range of the "ultra-small" partners (a group, which now includes *smaller* countries than before) is T′D′ (rather than TD). A few observations may now be made; for brevity, we shall use the term "superior" to refer to an outcome with a higher likelihood of a welfare gain, a higher gain, or a lower loss, than its alternative.

(i) For "small" partner countries, with which a PTA results in the range HT, a higher initial tariff level clearly is superior to a lower level: the pre-agreement situation is worse, whereas the post-agreement outcome is identical.

(ii) For smaller, but still just "small," partners, with which a PTA leads to a point along TT′, the conclusion of the comparison is indeed ambiguous: the outcome with the higher initial tariff may be inferior to that of the lower tariff. However, this is not inevitable: even at the point T, the higher-tariff outcome may still be superior. This is probably counter to an intuitive conclusion, which would suggest that when all we get in concluding a PTA is worsening of the country's terms of trade, which will be larger the higher the country's tariff level, a higher initial tariff will be inferior. The reason why this is not necessarily so is, of course, the lower welfare level at which the economy starts with the higher tariff.

(iii) If, indeed, T′ represents an inferior outcome, so will points close to it on T′D′. This may hold, indeed, for the whole length of T′D′ (except for D′ itself, when the PTA ceases to be effective); but, once more, such inferiority is only a possibility rather than an inevitability.

In sum, for a certain range of "small" countries — the larger of these — the orthodox proposition (that with a higher initial level of tariff in the home country the likelihood and size of a gain from a PTA are higher) still holds. For smaller but still "small," as well as for "ultra-small" partners, the conclusion is ambiguous: the "revisionist," as well as the "orthodox," proposition may prove to be true.

Whether partners to a PTA are commonly in one range or another, or whether they are so in a specific potential PTA, may at best be a matter of conjecture. What still seems to be obvious is that the larger the partner, in terms of its income and trade, the more likely it is to be "large," or, at worst, "small," and the less likely to be "ultra-small." In a multi-product world, the degree of *diversification* of the partner's (actual or potential) exports is of major significance. The above-mentioned "orthodox" proposition, that the more diversified the partner's exports the more likely it is that there will be a gain to the home country from a PTA, has apparently not been

challenged by the "revisionists;" but it should. On the one hand — this is
the origin of the conventional wisdom — the more diversified the partner's
exports, the more its relative prices should resemble those of the ROW,
hence, the more likely are gains from trade creation and the less likely are
losses from trade diversion. However, on the other hand, a partner, which
specializes in only a few export goods, is more likely — given its aggregate
size — to be "large" in each of its export goods than an economy whose
exports are highly diversified, with each good being sold in a relatively
small amount. In one extreme case, though, a probable answer does suggest
itself. When the partner's exports are very highly concentrated, as they
still are in several LDCs — consisting mostly of one, two, or even three
goods — the partner is likely to have been the (or "a") provider of the
home country's imports of these goods even prior to the agreement (these
will normally be goods sold by the partner at a "world market price");
neither benefit nor loss should then be created by a PTA with reference to
these goods. In all of its other exports, this partner will probably be "ultra-
small;" hence, in the final account, a PTA with such a partner will probably
lead to a loss, at least so far as the impact on the home country's imports is
concerned.

Notes

1. A semantic issue, which might lead to some confusion, should be
   mentioned. When the home country is "small" (that is, a price taker)
   in its trade with a partner, the latter must be "large" (that is, it cannot
   also be a price taker). When, on the other hand, the home country is
   "large" — this attribute being of the essence in the present paper —
   will the partner be "small?" This is possible, but not inevitable: both
   countries could be "large." To avoid ambiguity, we should point out
   that reference in the paper to the partner as "small" will not indicate
   that it is a price taker — only that in trade with it, the home country
   is "large." Nor, for instance, will the indication of the partner as a
   "smaller" economy be taken to mean that it faces higher elasticities of
   supply and demand in its trade with the home country: it will rather
   mean, as we shall see in the analysis, a partner whose relative prices
   will be more heavily affected by trade with the home country.
2. In, for instance, the contribution of Vanek (1965), Arndt (1969), Kemp
   (1969), and Melvin (1969).
3. Elaboration and references will be provided in the last section.

4. This builds on Fig. 27 in Michaely (1977), with appropriate extensions for the purpose at hand.

5. We refer here to the home country as "large" and, as its obverse, to the partner as "small." But note, again, that the partner is not necessarily a "small country" in the sense of being a price taker.

6. Since the "third country" is actually the ROW, this assumption should not be too constraining. For an analysis of the terms of trade effects when the home country is "large" in relation to both its partner and to the third country see Michaely (1977, pp. 207–212).

7. Once the possibility of having an effect on B's price is admitted, it may be noted that some trade of the home country with B may have existed even prior to the agreement; but a larger trade would have raised B's price beyond that of C. The rest of the analysis is not affected by this possibility. I owe this observation to a referee's comment.

8. This is *not* a budget constraint: the home country cannot buy from country B any amount of M it wishes to at this price. It only represents the exchange ratio at the amount of exchange actually conducted.

9. This is due to the effect on the term of trade and should not be confused with the aforementioned superiority of a large partner; in terms of Fig. 5.1, regardless of any change in the terms of trade, the line *bb* may be expected to be closer to *cc* when the partner is a larger country.

10. We ignore, in this analysis, the effect of a reduction in (elimination of) the partner's tariff; this will be discussed in the following section.

11. The U-shaped effect of changes in the size of partners was first noted by Halevi and Kleiman (1995).

12. While the basic framework is that of Viner (1950), these propositions owe mostly to the analysis of Meade (1955) and have been further elaborated by Lipsey (1960). In more recent analyses — for instance, Summers (1991) and Krugman (1991) — some of these propositions, primarily those concerned with the partner's size, have appeared through the delineation of attributes of "natural trade partners." Other aspects of this issue will be addressed in Chapters 12, 13 and 14.

13. This component of a PTA is discussed by Meade (1955), but has been overlooked in most of the following literature. A notable exception is the contribution of Wonnacott and Wonnacott (1981).

14. See Bhagwati (1993), Bhagwati and Panagariya (1996a, 1996b), and Panagariya (1995, 1996).

15. These are either stated explicitly or clearly implied.

References

Arndt, S W (1969). Customs union and the theory of tariffs. *American Economic Review*, 59, 108–118.

Bhagwati, J (1993). Regionalism and multilateralism: An overview. In *New Dimensions in Regional Integration*, de Melo, J and Panagariya, A (eds.), pp. 22–51. Cambridge, Mass: Cambridge University Press.

Bhagwati, J and Panagariya, A (1996a). Preferential trading areas and multilateralism: Strangers, friends or foes? In *The Economies of Preferential Trade Agreements*, Bhagwati, J and Panagariya, A (eds.), pp. 1–78. Washington, DC: American Enterprise Institute.

Bhagwati, J and Panagariya, A (1996b). The theory of preferential trade agreements: Historical evolution and current trends. *American Economic Review*, 86, 82–87.

Halevi, N and Kleiman, E (1995). Regional versus non-regional integration: The case of the middle east, Hebrew University of Jerusalem (mimeo).

Kemp, M C (1969). *A Contribution to the General Equilibrium Theory of Preferential Trading*. Amsterdam: North-Holland Publishing Company.

Krugman, P (1991). The move to free trade zones. In *Policy Implications of Trade and Currency Zones*, pp. 7–41. Federal Reserve Bank of Kansas City.

Lipsey, R G (1960). The theory of customs unions: A general survey. *Economic Journal*, 70, 496–513.

Meade, J E (1955). *The Theory of Customs Unions*. Amsterdam: North-Holland Publishing Company.

Melvin, J R (1969). Comments on the theory of customs unions. *Manchester School of Economics and Social Studies*, 36, 161–168.

Michaely, M (1977). *Theory of Commercial Policy: Trade and Protection*. Oxford: Philip Allan, Chicago: University of Chicago Press.

Panagariya, A (1995). Rethinking the new regionalism, The World Bank Conference on Trade Expansion, Washington, DC: (mimeo).

Panagariya, A (1996). The free trade area of the Americas: Good for Latin America? *The World Economy*, 19, 495–515.

Summers, L (1991). Regionalism and the world trading system. In *Policy Implications of Trade and Currency Zones*, Federal Reserve, pp. 295–301, Bank of Kansas City.

Vanek, J (1965). *General Equilibrium of International Discrimination*. Cambridge, Mass.: Harvard University Press.

Viner, J (1950). *The Customs Union Issue*. New York: Carnegie Endowment for International Peace.

Wonnacott, P and Wonnacott, R (1981). Is unilateral tariff reduction preferable to a customs union? The curious case of the missing foreign tariffs. *American Economic Review*. 71. 704–714.

Chapter 6

Small Economies: Trade Liberalization, Trade Preferences, and Growth

Some 40 years ago, Simon Kuznets (1958, p. 10) made the empirical statement that "the challenge of economic growth has particular overtures for small nations and... in the current active concern with problems of economic growth more attention should be paid to the effect of size than has heretofore been the case." This applies with particular force to the specific concern of the relationship of size to the two major contemporary issues of trade policy, which occupy us here: trade liberalization and preferential trade agreements (PTAs).

Economic Attributes and Performance of Small Countries

What is a Small Nation?

"Smallness" can be defined by a number of criteria, and with each, the cutoff point between "small" and "large" will be determined by an arbitrary decision. An alternative approach is to study the effect of size as a continuous variable, rather than resort to the classification of countries into one category or another. When possible and helpful, this alternative approach will also be used here.

A major variable — one which requires practically no explanation — is the size of population. Kuznets (1958, p. 9) adopted this as the sole criterion for classification: "By a small nation I mean an independent sovereign state, with a population of ten million or less." He also ventured the proposition, based on demographic trends and forecasts, that "were I to draw it a hundred years hence, the dividing line would be far higher." In the forty years that have passed, the demographic trends anticipated then have indeed materialized, and almost all of the nations existing in the

71

1950s are now larger, usually much more so, in terms of population (Western European countries, as a group, are an obvious exception). On the other hand, the number of independent countries has almost doubled during this period, and the proportion of small countries is particularly high among the more recent entrants. Hence, raising the bar for the classification of "small" countries would leave a substantially higher proportion of "small" countries now than before. Thus, if population has to serve as a criterion, maintaining the bar at ten million may be the best option — although, needless to say, this would be an entirely arbitrary cutoff point, not subject to any defence as a logical inference.

Table 6.1 provides a classification of the world's countries, based on this criterion.[1] By this yardstick alone, using 1993 population data, over a half of today's independent nations would qualify as "small" — 112 out of a total of 183. This is roughly the same proportion as in Kuznets' classification where, in the world of 1955, 47 out of a total of 80 nations were defined as "small".[2]

The *size of territory* should also be used as a criterion of "smallness." It is an indicator — probably the best predictor if resort had to be made to a single variable — of the size and variability of natural resources. Thus, a country with a small population but with a very large territory may be expected to have different patterns of specialization, as well as other different attributes, from those of a small-territory nation. As it happens — this is evidently not a matter of accident — no small-population nation occupies a very large territory, although there is a large variance in the geographic size of such countries (from tiny islands to territories such as those of Bolivia, Libya, or Sweden).[3] A fuller study should probably pay separate attention to the role of the size of territory, but in the present context this will be dispensed with.

A third yardstick must be the economic size of a nation — best approached by its aggregate income, or aggregate product. For many purposes (such as for the "size of the market" in Adam Smith's statement that the size of the market determines the extent of specialization) this is probably the best indicator — more important than the size of population (although the two must be partly related). However, a problem may arise if countries that are large in terms of aggregate income and product (but small in population) are excluded from the list of "small" countries. Given their small population, these high aggregate-income countries must also constitute high per capita economies. Presumably, they are also (or must have been at some stage of their development) economies characterized by a high rate of growth of income. Excluding such countries from the category of "small" nations would thus tend, by definition, to bias this category toward the inclusion of poor, low-growth economies. To overcome this dilemma, a compromise has been adopted here: "small" countries will be defined by population alone; but the category will be subdivided into "low (aggregate) income" and "high income" countries. In fact, the latter group has been defined to include only 12 countries (out of a total of 112 small countries), ranging (in size of income) from Switzerland (with a 1993 GNP of $254 billion) to New Zealand (with a GNP of $45 billion).[4]

Attributes and Performance: **A Priori** *Considerations*

The small size of a nation may affect its attributes and performance in the following ways:

(i) If, as is sometimes argued, the limited ability of a small country to enjoy economies of scale constrains the efficiency of use of its resources, income levels should be lower, *ceteris paribus*, in smaller countries than in large ones.

(ii) Although this does not logically follow strictly from the former proposition, the restricted efficiency may (at least at some stage) also lead to a slower growth of the economy.

(iii) The limited size of the domestic market — both as a customer of the final product and as a provider of inputs — should grant a larger role in small countries to trade with the outside world. This is probably the most obvious proposition, and the one most often tested.

(iv) At the same time, the large exports (in relation to production and income) of a small country are expected to concentrate more heavily on a few commodities than the exports of a large country. This would be due to the small variety of national resources in the small economy, and the ability to reach an optimum scale of activity only in a limited range of goods. This proposition should hold for agricultural and mineral products, as well as for industrial activities.

(v) Given the (presumed) large role of exports and their high commodity concentration, a relatively high level of concentration may be expected also in the composition of production of a small economy.

(vi) Since a small economy exports a relatively small range of goods, and since it has less of an impact on the prices of its exports than a large economy (more on this later), its exports may also be expected to display a high level of geographical concentration.[5]

(vii) Small countries are more vulnerable to foreign fluctuations — which may be the consequences of either "objective" market forces or changes in policies of foreign governments (such as in tariffs or QRs). This is due to both the size and the composition of foreign trade. First, trade constitutes a higher proportion of income, so that any change will have larger impact on the typical small economy than on a large one. Second, due to the higher commodity (and possibly geographic) concentration of trade, particularly of exports, fluctuations of the terms of trade can be expected to be stronger for the smaller country. Hence, both the multiplier (the changes of prices) and the multiplicand (the proportion of trade) are higher in the small country, thus leading to an expected larger impact of foreign fluctuations on the country's fortunes.

(viii) Assuming that foreign investment is biased toward traded goods, and particularly toward export activities, the larger share of exports may be expected to lead to a relatively large share of foreign resources in financing the economy's investment. This would be reinforced if the presumption of a large concentration of production is valid: such concentration would make any given activity a larger borrower in terms of the country's financial system, and thus a higher risk. This would, in turn, lead to heavier reliance on a more global financial system.

(ix) Finally, small economies may share a pattern of policies. Specifically, they may be expected to have less autonomy in the conduct of macroeconomic (fiscal, monetary and exchange-rate) policies than large countries enjoy. A country with a high trade ratio is more likely to share a currency system with others, or, at least, to follow macroeconomic policies in concert with a large foreign country. One implication of such a presumption is that a small country is less likely than a large one to follow totally disruptive macroeconomic policies.

Empirical Verification

An empirical illustration or test of some of the attributes of structure and patterns of performance suggested here on *a priori* grounds would require excessive resources and time. For other attributes, though, such work is feasible and will be discussed here.

Table 6.1:   Economic attributes of countries, by category (in percent).

Attribute		Small countries, low income (1)	Small countries, high income (2)	Large countries (3)
Annual growth rate of	Average	3.2	3.4	3.3
aggregate GDP	Median	3.3	3.5	3.3
Annual growth rate of	Average	0.8	2.5	1.1
per capita GDP	Median	0.9	2.5	1.6
Share of investment in	Average	23.5	25.5	23.4
GDP	Median	23.8	25.0	22.0
Share of saving in GDP	Average	11.9	23.1	19.0
	Median	11.9	22.7	19.2
Ratio of long-term	Average	5.6	2.1	2.1
capital inflow to GDP	Median	4.5	2.4	2.5
Share of exports in GDP	Average	38.8	52.2	34.4
	Median	39.7	35.0	20.9
Coefficient of export	Average	0.446	0.216	0.287
concentration	Median	0.455	0.217	0.247
Annual rate of inflation	Average	47.1	14.2	52.9
(CPI)	Median	9.1	8.1	12.5
Annual rate of nominal	Average	7.2	7.2	49.6
devaluation	Median	1.4	1.5	8.3

Source: Variety of sources and estimates.

Table 6.1 presents "typical" levels of several variables of attributes and performance for, separately, the three categories of countries (large, small low-income, and small high-income countries). These data are not sufficient to provide a rigorous verification of propositions or establishment of patterns: for that, a much more ambitious work, in detail and method of analysis, would be required to separate out the effect of each factor.[6] Rather, the data suggest stylized facts and may indicate whether the *a priori* expectations would appear to be of much relevance.

The raw data used for the findings of Table 6.1 (as well as for others that will follow later) were annual observations for each individual country for the period from 1970 or 1971 through 1993 (in a few instances, data for the earliest or latest years may be missing).[7] These data were then averaged, to get a single observation for each country. For each category of countries, the table presents two summary statistics: the *average* (mean) and the *median*. Both are shown, despite a preference for the median over the mean: the latter is highly vulnerable to the effects of large deviations in extreme cases, whereas the median measure is free of such impacts. Thus, the median should be judged as a more reliable presentation of the "typical" or likely attribute of countries within each group.

One finding, which stands out in Table 6.1, is the *absence* of any distinction between the three categories of countries concerning the rate of growth of aggregate GDP: the rates are practically identical for the three when the averages of the groups are compared; and only slightly higher for small high-income countries than for others when the medians are observed.

The pattern is somewhat more involved when growth rates of *per capita* income are compared. Here, the three categories of countries appear to be distinctly different: the lowest growth rate is observed for the small low-income countries and the highest for the small high-income countries, with the large countries in-between. Thus, for large countries and small countries as a whole (i.e., both low and high income), the growth rates of per capita income are roughly equal; but they are distinctly different between low-income and high-income small countries. Causality could conceivably run either way. The high-income countries may have achieved that high level due to a faster rate of growth; or the reverse may be true: the high-income level — indicating a large market, a high per capita income, high skills, and a highly diversified economy — may have led to the high growth rate. Given that the high-income small countries have mostly been relatively rich for generations (Singapore and Hong Kong are the main exceptions), it is reasonable to assume that it is the latter chain of causality, rather than the former, which mainly explains the observed relationship.[8]

An interesting pattern may be observed in the behavior of saving and investment. To start with, the share of investment in GDP is practically equal for large and small low-income countries. It is somewhat higher for the third category — small high-income countries (about 25 percent, against approximately 22 percent for the other two groups).[9] The sources of financing this investment are, on the other hand, radically different between large and small high-income countries, on the one hand, and small low-income countries, on the other hand. Financing through long-term capital inflow from abroad is substantially higher (by about 2 percentage points of GDP) for the latter group. This supports our *a priori* hypothesis that foreign finance plays a larger role among small countries. A dramatic difference in the opposite direction appears, on the other hand, when the ratio of *domestic saving* is observed: the share of saving in income is only about 11.5 percent among the small low-income countries, as against almost

19 percent among large countries, and over 21 percent for small high-income countries.

The difference in domestic saving can partly be explained by the high ratio of foreign financing ("foreign saving") in the small low-income group, which must, at least to some extent, have displaced domestic saving. When foreign capital finances private activities in a free capital market, such displacement will take place through the lowering of interest rates, which discourages private saving (particularly business saving, but probably also saving by households, which tend to increase consumption). When foreign finance takes the form of unilateral transfers to the private household sector, this will definitely increase private consumption and lower the share of private saving in earned income. Finally, when foreign financing consists of unilateral transfers to the government — as is quite often the case — this flow to the government leads to an excess of public sector expenditures over taxes (through increased spending or lower taxation), creating once more a reduction in savings and a fall in the rate of national saving out of earned income (the GNP). Having said that, however, we have to recognize that, *as recorded*, foreign finance provides only a partial explanation of the low saving of small low-income countries: even an assumption of full displacement of domestic saving by capital inflow would assign a reduction of only 2 percent of GDP in the rate of saving, whereas the observed deficiency of saving in this group (that is, the degree by which it falls below that of the other two groups) is in the range of 7–10 percent of GDP. With the information we possess at this stage, we cannot advance a reasonable hypothesis to explain this difference.[10]

The most obvious difference between categories of countries is found, as would be expected, in the role of trade — represented, in Table 6.1, by the share of exports in GDP (exports and imports would most often be roughly similar). Interestingly, almost no difference is found, in this respect, between low-income and high-income small countries: in both, the typical share of exports in GDP is around 34–35 percent, in comparison with just over 20 percent among large countries.[11] It thus appears that the size of the country is a major determinant of the importance of trade in its economy, whereas the level of economic development is not. The latter does, however, play a predominant role in shaping the *structure* of exports, to which we now turn.

One of our presumptions, stated earlier, is that exports are much less diversified in the trade of a small country than in a large one.[12] In fact, the expected implications of changes in policy, which will be discussed later, depend to a large extent on the validity of this expected attribute. The presumption is indeed borne out by the estimates summarized in Table 6.1; but the pattern revealed there is more involved than would appear from just a "small–large" comparison.

For all small countries, export concentration is indeed typically higher than for large countries; this is indicated by both the mean and the median statistics. Thus, the median level of the concentration coefficient among large countries, shown in Table 6.1, is 0.247, whereas for *all* small countries together, the median (not shown in Table 6.1) is 0.368. It should be noted, however, that a radical difference exists among small countries between the "low-income" and the "high-income" groups: the median level of the coefficient is as high as 0.455 for the first, and as low as 0.217 for the second. Moreover, if we separate out the *large* countries into low and high per capita income groups,[13] we find there, too, a similar distinction (this is not shown in Table 6.1): the median coefficient would be 0.308 for the low-income group, and only 0.175 for the high-income countries. What stands out very clearly from these comparisons is that the level of commodity concentration of exports is indeed much higher among small countries than among large countries when our observation is confined to *less-developed* economies. Among the richer economies, size loses its impact: by and large, exports are as diversified among small rich countries as among large rich countries. It may be surmised that the reasons for this phenomenon are, first, the fact that a highly developed economy derives much less of its income from the product of natural resources — the small range of availability of which constrains diversification in the small economy. Second, in the rich economy, aggregate income and the size of the market are large enough to make the small size of population much less significant.

The last two comparisons of Table 6.1 address representations of macroeconomic policies, and they yield interesting findings. It appears that the "typical" rate of inflation is significantly lower among small countries, of both low- and high-income levels, than among the large countries. This seems to support the presumption that small countries have less room for independent macroeconomic (fiscal and monetary) policies than large countries possess. Quite often small countries maintain, formally or informally, a "currency board" set of rules, where the center country involved presumably conducts "responsible" fiscal and monetary policies; "excesses" are thus avoided by the peripheral, small countries. The observation of the rate of currency devaluation, in Table 6.1, is also consistent with this view of a pattern of dependence: the typical annual rate of (nominal) devaluation is substantially lower among small countries (of both low- and high-income levels) than among large countries. Whether such dependence of macroeconomic policies of small countries on major economic centers (or on the global situation) is a desirable attribute is an open issue, a discussion of the pros and cons of which is beyond the scope of the present analysis. The finding of a typically lower rate of inflation is probably the most important consideration in favor of such dependence, and it is relevant, as we shall see later, for the discussion of attributes of trade liberalization in small countries.[14]

Trade Liberalization in a Small Economy

The Gains from Trade

The gains from international trade should be expected to be doubly large for a small country, for two reasons. First — to belabor the obvious — the gains from specialization, which trade makes possible, will be particularly large. Without trade, the local production costs of the otherwise imported goods would be particularly high (in relation to the parallel comparison for a large country). Or, put differently, relative prices under autarky would be markedly different from what they are in the "world" (that is, in the potential partners for trade). Hence, there is a large gain from trade.

The other reason should be equally obvious, but for various reasons — partly understandable for some countries — may not be fully accepted. It is often argued that small countries get a raw deal in trade with large countries: it is the large country, which determines the price that will prevail in the exchanges between the two, fixing a set of prices most favorable to it (i.e., a high price for its export goods in terms of its imports from the small country), to the detriment of the small country. This viewpoint — still quite common in political rhetoric — is fallacious under most circumstances. It would apply where (i) "countries" (that is, normally governments), rather than private actors in each country, determine transactions and prices, or, alternatively, in each country (specifically, in the large country) trade is handled by one major monopolist; and (ii) the large country as a whole (that is, acting as a single unit) enjoys a monopolistic position in world trade (or at least in trade with the specific small country). Under such circumstances, the large country, acting as a monopolist (and, through the government, also introducing a wedge between prices in trade and in the home market) may indeed "dictate" prices, which are biased toward its own welfare, reaping

most or all of the gains from trade. These circumstances may have applied
in the past to parts of the colonial trade, biasing the outcome of trade to
the enrichment of the colonial power. Today (certainly since the middle of
the 20th century) such circumstances would be extremely rare. Normally,
trade is conducted among private agents, under conditions not too far from
full competition. In such a world, the scenario is entirely different, and
the consequences of the process of trade are exactly opposite to those just
described.

Suppose two autarkic economies open their borders to free trade
between them (and ignore, for the sake of simplicity, transportation costs).
Before trade is opened, relative prices are different in the two economies
(in the unlikely case that they are not, no trade will ensue). With trade,
relative prices (as well as absolute prices, given an exchange rate) must be
equalized. The common set of prices will be somewhere within the range
defined by the two autarkic sets. The larger the economy, however, the more
the common set will resemble its autarkic price set. In the extreme case, in
which one country is much smaller (in its market size) than the other, the
common prices would be fully equal to the larger country's set of relative
prices.[15] The "small" country would fully specialize, whereas the "large"
country would only partly specialize, producing for itself some of the goods
which it also imports from the small country. The small country would in
this case reap the entire benefit from the opening of trade, and the large
country — none.[16] In general, the smaller the country, the more it would
be a "price taker" (i.e., the more prices in its trade transactions would be
similar to the original prices in its partner's home market), and the *greater*
would be its gain from foreign trade.

Since its gains from trade are so obvious, so too should be the interest
of a small country in liberalizing its foreign trade when starting from a
regime of trade restrictions. The only qualification might originate from the
potential damage of "vulnerability" of a country engaged deeply in foreign
trade — indeed, this was a popular argument for constraining trade in the
heyday of restrictive regimes in the post-war world. However, even this
argument is not clear-cut. It depends, at least partly, on the presumption
of a highly concentrated trade (particularly exports) in the small country.
However, the degree of concentration itself, in a large measure, is a function
of trade policy: the more *open* the trade, the more *diversified* it should be
(this will be discussed in much detail in Chapter 8). This may be illustrated
by Chart 6.1 — greatly simplifying the nature of production and trade, but
nevertheless yielding the essential inferences.

Chart 6.1:   Impact of trade constraints on concentration.

Exportables				Nontradables			Importables		
a	b	c	d	e	f	g	h	i	j
Exports								Imports	

Take a world of 10 goods — a through j — arranged in the diagram from left to right according to the degree of comparative advantage, which the home country has, in the good, in relation to the rest of the world (ROW) (the "other" country).[17] Without further information, we can be sure only that the home country will export good a and import good j, and that whatever good is exported by the country, the goods to its left in the diagram would definitely be exported. Demand conditions will determine the precise cutoff between exported and imported goods, and, in the complete absence of transportation costs or other barriers to trade, any good will either be exported or be imported.

Suppose the actual cutoff is between f and g: goods a through f are exported, and g through j are imported. Now introduce transportation costs and assume, for simplicity, that they are proportional to the costs of production of each good, so that the ranking of goods remains unchanged.[18] This will make the exports and imports of some goods unprofitable. Suppose the cutoff points become, then, between d and e and between g and h: goods a through d are still exported and g through j are still imported — these are the "tradable" goods, "exportables," and "importables." Goods e through g become, on the other hand, "nontradables": they are produced in both the home and the foreign countries and are not traded between the two. At this stage, introduce also policy barriers to trade — say, tariffs, which will be assumed again to be uniform.[19] These are added costs to the movement of goods and will restrict further the range of actual exports (which will fall short of the range of "exportables") and imports (again, only a section of the range of "importables"). The cutoff points will then become between b and c and between h and i: a and b will be exported, and i and j will be imported. Goods c and d will be "exportables," which are not in fact exported — they are produced for sale only in the home market, whereas good h becomes an "importable," which is not in fact imported: it is locally produced, due to the protection afforded by the tariff.[20]

Thus, like transportation costs, barriers to trade serve to shorten the range of goods, which are actually exported and imported, that is, they work to lower diversification and increase the commodity concentration of the trade flows (concentration of exports, rather than of imports, will normally be the more important factor). In this way, they tend to make the country *more vulnerable* to fluctuations abroad. Trade liberalization will thus also have a *favorable* effect on the consequences of foreign trade: while increasing the (relative) size of trade would make the country more "vulnerable," increasing the dispersion in the commodity composition of trade (mainly of exports) would make it less "vulnerable" (consult, again, the analysis and findings of Chapter 8). Gauging the net impact is not a matter of logical deduction, but of the observation of experience. A guess may be ventured, though, that the effect of higher diversification will be dominant, so that freer trade will not only increase the "average" gains from trade but also reduce the loss due to foreign fluctuations.[21]

A separate point about the benefits of liberalization in small countries is concerned with the existence, prior to liberalization, of tariff duties on imported inputs. In the absence of a drawback scheme for such duties in export activities — and, indeed, such schemes are frequently absent or are highly imperfect — tariffs on inputs amount to taxation of exports. In small economies, as one of the manifestations of the large role of trade, the import component of exports (particularly exports of manufactured goods) would typically be higher than in large economies; hence, the element of tax on exports involved in input duties would be higher. Liberalization (which will almost always include the removal or drastic reduction in duties on imported inputs) should thus have a stronger promotion effect on exports — particularly of the "nontraditional" nature — in small economies than in large ones.

Trade liberalization thus seems to be even more desirable for the typical small nation than it is for a large one, in its long-term impact on the economy's welfare and growth. An issue that should be addressed, though, is whether the *transitional* costs of trade liberalization may not be different for the small economy than they are for others. To this issue we now turn.

The Cost of Adjustment

The transition costs of trade liberalization may indeed be expected to be different in a small economy, on several scores.

Since the gains from trade and the losses from trade restriction are more obvious in a small economy, trade barriers prior to liberalization may be expected to be lower in the "typical" small economy than in its large counterpart. If this is true, the extent of liberalization would be smaller for any given level of trade freedom maintained following the liberalization; hence, the cost of adjustment to the new trade regime would be smaller. However, by the same token, the longer-term gains from liberalization would also be smaller, since the extent of liberalization is smaller. A more meaningful question may hence be whether for any *given* size of liberalization (ignoring here the issue of what precisely this means, or how it is to be estimated), the process of adjustment may be more or less costly in a small economy.

A major consideration that may indeed indicate a presumption of higher adjustment costs is the high degree of commodity concentration of activities in a small economy, combined with the generally small number of firms engaged in each activity. This would imply stronger friction in the process of adjustment. The ability of each given firm to adjust to new circumstances by changing the composition of its production may be more limited than in the large economy, and indeed, empirical observation suggests that following liberalization, much of the adjustment takes place in the activities of existing firms.[22] Second, the activity of each firm tends to be highly localized, taking place in just one plant, in one specific location (or in a very small number of locations); naturally, this is more true for manufacturing activities and for minerals, and less so for agricultural production. And, in turn, the firm's activity is likely to form a major part of the economy in that specific location. The elimination, or drastic reduction, of the activity of the firm would thus create a need for the geographical mobility of factors (primarily of the labor force) — a particular painful element of the process of adjustment. In addition, the smaller variety of branches in which firms are presumably engaged in the small economy means that the activities, which are *encouraged* by the process of liberalization, are less likely to expand through the growth of an already existing branch of production: they are more likely than in a large economy to require the establishment of new firms in new lines of production — again, presumably a more difficult and slow process of adjustment. Thus, a presumption does exist that adjustment to a liberalization policy may carry higher transition costs in the small economy; hence, that a more gradual process of liberalization may be recommended in such an economy than, *ceteris paribus*, in a large economy.

An entirely different element of the "cost" of liberalization may be the *fiscal* cost: the loss of revenues from import duties (or, sometimes, from export taxes). Experience shows that most of the time this loss is absent, or is minimal: removal of highly protective tariffs does not significantly change the amount of revenues, which is low in any case, and import expansion following liberalization tends to increase tariff revenues. Where there is a loss, however, it tends to be relatively higher in small economies, which, due mainly to the relative size of foreign trade, tend to rely more on trade taxation than do large economies. If true, this indicates a need not so much for gradualism in reform as for the replacement of trade taxes by other taxes — such as value-added tax or general sales tax.

The Likelihood of Success

From general experience with trade liberalization — as well as *a priori* considerations — can any judgment be made about the question of whether liberalization is likely to be more or less sustainable in a small economy than in a large one?

To start with, when the question posed concerns not the fate of a single liberalization episode but the general drift of a country's trade policy, the size of nations does indeed seem to be a factor. In the findings of the World Bank's study of the liberalization experience,[23] small countries are distinguished by territory rather than by size of population. When, on the basis of long-term performance, countries are categorized as "liberalizers" vs "nonliberalizers," the size of territory is concluded to be related systematically to the policy trend: most of the "liberalizers" have been definitely small countries (Indonesia is the clearest exception), and most small countries have been "liberalizers," whereas, of the "nonliberalizers," only two — Portugal and Sri Lanka — have been small countries (in the present analysis Sri Lanka is defined as a "large" economy). On the other hand, classification of countries by income levels does not reveal a systematic difference: "the economy's *aggregate income*... appears to have little bearing on the long-term fate of liberalization... The median size of income in the two categories of countries ["liberalizers" vs "nonliberalizers"] is almost identical" Michaely *et al.* (1991, p. 122). The distinction by territory would agree with our *a priori* assumption that small countries would be more willing to adopt liberalization policies, due to the higher gains from trade — and from free rather than restricted trade — to be expected in a small economy.

Does the size of the country have any bearing on the likelihood that when liberalization is undertaken, it will be of a sustainable nature?

The overall experience of liberalization indicates that the following attributes contribute to the likelihood of sustained liberalization:[24]

- Trade liberalization should be introduced with a major move rather than a halting step.
- When trade liberalization is introduced under conditions of macro-economic instability, it must be accompanied by a (contemporaneous) stabilization policy.
- The initial move should normally be accompanied by a substantial nominal devaluation.
- A real depreciation and, particularly, a stable real exchange rate should be maintained for several years following the introduction of trade liberalization.
- This requires, above all, a restrictive monetary policy and, most important, a consistently tight fiscal policy.

In asking whether the size of a country might play a role in the likelihood of fulfilling these conditions, the degree of social coherence and political stability seems to be of crucial importance. The policies enumerated above are almost inevitably painful to one segment of the population or another, and they are more likely to be undertaken, and to be adhered to, where the socio-political system facilitates the adoption of policies, which are deemed desirable for the community as a whole. Kuznets (1958) postulated that small countries do indeed enjoy a higher measure of socio-political stability; however, this remains to be tested.

Beyond this, several specific considerations suggest themselves. One, concerning the strength of liberalization is implied by what already has been said. If adjustment is less smooth and transitional costs are higher in a small economy, it will be less likely for its government to adopt a strong liberalization policy, that is, one which starts with a major, bold first step. If true, this would lower the likelihood of an introduction of a sustainable liberalization policy in a small economy.

The set of issues concerned with macroeconomic conduct — fiscal, monetary, and exchange-rate policies — would seem to be relevant to the distinction of small vs large nations; however, considerations of contra-dictory directions are indicated. We recall the presumption — supported by empirical observation — that small countries, owing to their smaller scope for independent macroeconomic policies, are more likely to avoid the excesses of such policies. Hence, in the case of a typical small country, it is less likely that a thorough redressing of such policies will be required when trade liberalization is undertaken. Indeed, the empirical finding of a strong association of sustainability of liberalization with an initial nominal devaluation is drawn from experiences of countries with volatile macroeconomic policies, whereas such devaluation is not likely to be called for in a country following a "currency board" regime. When redirection of policies is required, on the other hand, it may prove to be more difficult. Specifically, if the small country shares with others a common currency — formally or at least effectively — it will not be possible to change its exchange rate when a nominal devaluation is indicated. Changing the real exchange rate will then have to be effected through a fall (relative to other nations) of domestic prices — normally a much more difficult and costly undertaking.

Lessons from Recent Experiences in Latin America

A thorough study of liberalization experiences to test the validity of the *a priori* considerations mentioned thus far would be a major project. An attempt has been made here, on the other hand, to study in a cursory manner the recent experience of countries in the region of Latin America and the Caribbean. Fortunately — from more than one viewpoint — in recent years almost all the region's countries have implemented at least some measure of trade liberalization, so that their combined experiences provide a reasonably large number of observations, sufficient to suggest at least some tentative conclusions.

To start with, dates (years) have been determined in which trade liberalization has been introduced in each country, and each liberalization experiment has been classified as strong or not.[25] This information is presented in Table 6.2.

Next, the pattern of behavior of several crucial variables during these episodes of liberalization is examined. This is done through a "before–during–after" observation, that is, by comparing the performance of each variable during: (i) the last three years prior to liberalization; (ii) the year of introduction of liberalization; and (iii) the three years following liberalization.[27] It should again be noted that an analysis along these lines does *not* constitute a rigorous test of causality; on the other hand, hopefully it suggests a pattern of "stylized facts" and offers some clues about the consequences of liberalization.

Table 6.2:   Episodes of trade liberalization, LAC countries.[26]

Country	Year of introduction of policy (1)	A "strong" policy package? (2)
Argentina	1989	Yes
Barbados	1991	No
Belize	1986	No
Bolivia	1985	Yes
Brazil	1990	Yes
Chile	1974	Yes
Colombia	1990	Yes
Costa Rica	1991	Yes
Ecuador	1990	No
El Salvador	1989	Yes
Guatemala	1991	Yes
Guyana	1989	Yes
Honduras	1990	No
Jamaica	1991	Yes
Mexico	1985	Yes
Nicaragua	1991	Yes
OECS	1991	No
Panama	1995	Yes
Paraguay	1989	Yes
Peru	1990	Yes
Trinidad and Tobago	1990	Yes
Uruguay	1989	Yes
Venezuela	1989	Yes

Source: Papageorgiou and Michaely (1995).

The variable that might have probably been the best indicator of transition costs of liberalization is the ratio of unemployment. Unfortunately, data of this measure of performance are hard to come by: they are often missing altogether, unreliable, or not comparable, so that their use could be misleading rather than illuminating. Consequently, the use of this variable has been dispensed with. Instead, two other variables of real performance are presented: the rate of growth of GDP, in Table 6.3, and the rate of expansion of exports,[28] in Table 6.4.

Starting with the rate of growth, a common pattern is apparent: it has several exceptions, but is nevertheless frequent enough to be considered "typical." During the year in which trade liberalization is introduced, a decline of the growth rate of income takes place. On occasion (particularly in the cases of Argentina, Nicaragua, and Venezuela), the drop is quite sharp. This may be interpreted as a transition cost of liberalization. However, from

Table 6.3:   Growth of GDP during episodes of liberalization, LAC countries.

Country	Year of liberalization	Average of three preceding years	Year of liberalization	Average of three following years
Small countries				
Belize	1986	−0.4	7.3	10.3
Bolivia	1985	−3.0	−2.8	2.4
Costa Rica	1991	5.0	3.6	6.1
El Salvador	1989	1.8	1.4	4.4
Grenada[b]	1991	4.5	5.1	0.4[a]
Honduras	1990	5.3	−0.6	3.3
Jamaica	1991	5.6	0.1	4.1[a]
Nicaragua	1991	−5.5	−10.6	1.8[a]
Paraguay	1989	3.3	7.0	2.1
St. Kitts and Nevis[b]	1991	5.8	0.3	4.1
Trinidad and Tobago	1990	−4.3	0.8	0.8
Uruguay	1989	6.7	1.0	5.6
Average		2.1	1.1	3.8
Large countries				
Argentina	1989	3.3	−10.3	8.3
Brazil	1990	2.7	−4.2	1.6
Chile	1974	1.7	0.1	1.8
Colombia	1990	4.2	3.8	4.0
Ecuador	1990	1.8	2.3	5.0
Guatemala	1991	3.6	4.4	4.6[a]
Mexico	1985	−0.9	3.8	0.1
Peru	1990	−4.2	−0.6	2.3
Venezuela	1989	5.7	−10.3	8.0
Average		2.0	−1.2	4.0

[a]Averages of only two years.
[b]These countries are components of the OECS group listed in Table 6.2.
Source: Elaboration of World Bank data.

other knowledge we possess, it would be safer to assign this fall of growth to restrictive macroeconomic policies, which have commonly been adopted concurrent with the introduction of trade liberalization (this is definitely true for the three aforementioned extreme cases). In fact, the presumed discouraging effect of trade liberalization on production can hardly be expected when the policy has just been introduced — when the expansion of imports and changes in decisions of entrepreneurs have barely begun. Be that as it may, we note that the decline of the rate of growth is *less* common among the small than among the large countries. On average, the growth rate falls by only one percent and remains positive for the group of small countries, whereas it turns negative, falling by three percent from

Table 6.4:   Export performance during episodes of liberalization, LAC countries.

Country	Year of liberalization	Average of three preceding years	Year of liberalization	Average of three following years
Small countries				
Belize	1986	−0.03	0.15	0.03
Bolivia	1985	−0.06	0.19	0.04
Costa Rica	1991	0.03	0.13	0.01[a]
El Salvador	1989	−0.10	−0.16	0.03
Grenada	1991	−0.02	0	0.01[a]
Guyana	1989	0.15	0.44	0.15
Honduras	1990	0.05	0.21	−0.02
Jamaica	1991	0.01	0.09	0.04[a]
Nicaragua	1991	0.37	−0.15	0[a]
Paraguay	1989	0.17	0.07	−0.14
St. Kitts and Nevis	1991	−0.07	0.13	—
Trinidad and Tobago	1990	0.09	0.02	−0.04
Uruguay	1989	0.03	0.07	−0.05
Average		0.06	0.08	0.02
Large countries				
Argentina	1989	−0.04	0.37	−0.02
Brazil	1990	−0.01	−0.13	0.06
Chile	1974	−0.01	0.49	0.02
Colombia	1990	−0.01	0.14	−0.06
Ecuador	1990	0.09	0.11	−0.07
Guatemala	1991	0.10	−0.13	−0.01[a]
Mexico	1985	0.21	−0.11	0.04
Peru	1990	0.04	−0.11	−0.08
Venezuela	1989	−0.05	0.62	−0.06
Average		0.04	0.20	−0.02

[a] Averages of only two years.
Source: Elaboration of World Bank data.

its pre-liberalization level, for the large countries. This difference may be related to differences in patterns of change of macroeconomic policies, which will be mentioned shortly.

Beyond the year in which liberalization is introduced, growth resumes its pre-liberalization pace and then exceeds it. In this, the groups of small and large countries behave, on average, remarkably alike: in both, the rate of growth about *doubles*, from a pre-liberalization level of two percent per year to around four percent. Partly, this compensates for the slack during the year of liberalization itself; however, even if this year is added to the three years following it, growth in the post-liberalization period still exceeds its pre-liberalization level, by about one percent. Thus, even in the short run, growth appears to accelerate following liberalization.[29] From this evidence, therefore, no transition costs appear to have been paid, and this, once again, applies to the small countries in LAC at least as much as to the large countries. So far as this evidence goes, it does not support our *a priori* presumption of higher transition costs of trade liberalization among small countries.

It may be expected that this absence of evidence for the presumed difference originates in liberalization policies having been less intensive among small countries. Indeed, some difference of this nature does exist. As may be gathered from column 2 of Table 6.2 above, the liberalization policies introduced were "strong" in only 8 out of 13 experiences among the small countries (they were "weak" in Belize, Grenada, Honduras, St. Kitts and Nevis, and Trinidad and Tobago), whereas among the eight experiences of large countries, in only one instance (Ecuador) was the policy judged to be "weak."

To what extent this does indeed bias the inferences about transition costs among small countries is hard to tell.[30] It is interesting to note, though, that the lower incidence of strong liberalization policies among the small LAC countries does give some support to another hypothesis postulated earlier, namely, that a presumed lower level of trade barriers among small countries (as well as a lower frequency of disruptive macroeconomic environment) would result in less intensive trade liberalization policies in the smaller countries.

The share of exports in GDP, recorded in Table 6.4, is another measure of performance. The pattern of change of this variable, which emerges from these data, is quite different from the one revealed for the rate of income growth, and it is rather disappointing for both small and large economies. In both categories, an acceleration of the rate of growth of exports (as a share of GDP) appears to take place in the year of liberalization — much more among large than among small countries.[31] It may be presumed that the main reason for this immediate reaction of exports is the slack domestic market at this time (indeed, we have seen that the contraction is more severe, typically, among the large economies).[32] Beyond that year, exports expand *less* than prior to the liberalization; this, once more, is true for both large countries (where export expansion becomes negative) and small countries. This pattern is remarkably different from that of earlier liberalization experiences, in which export growth appeared to have accelerated dramatically from the pre- to post-liberalization era.[33] The explanation for this difference must lie in the behavior of the real exchange rate.

In the earlier experiences, a real depreciation and a consequent growth of exports were necessary elements for the success and sustainability of trade liberalization. In the world of the early 1990s, on the other hand, with rather free- and large-scale capital movements, capital inflows into the liberalizing countries have helped to maintain low real exchange rates, with their discouraging impact on exports, without disrupting the sustainability of liberalizations. This pattern of behavior of the real exchange rate and of exports thus distinguishes the recent wave of trade liberalizations among LAC countries from the experience of preceding decades. However, *no* distinction is apparent, in this respect, between small and large countries.

The Small Country in a PTA

Gains and Losses: A Priori *Considerations*

Of the variety of forms of trade-preferential agreements, it is mainly the "free-trade-area" type that will be discussed here, that is, an agreement through which the partners completely remove tariffs and other barriers from their mutual trade, but follow separate policies concerning trade flows with nonpartners. At the end, a few words shall be said about the additional component contained in a "customs union" — the setting by the partners of a common external tariff (and common other barriers) on trade with the ROW.

We recall that on *a priori* grounds, a net welfare gain from a customs union becomes more likely (or a net loss, if there is one, becomes smaller):[34]

(i) The higher the initial level of tariffs (or NTBs) when the preferential agreement is introduced (a level which, following the agreement, continues to be applied to the ROW).

(ii) The higher the tariff level of the partner country, that is, the higher the concession the home country gets on exports to its partner(s).

(iii) The smaller the size of imports from the ROW (the nonpartners).

(iv) The higher the proportion of imports from the partner country, at any given level of the home country's aggregate imports.

(v) The closer the relative prices in trade with the partner country to those in the ROW.

(vi) The larger the economic size of the partner (measured by its income and trade).

(vii) The less unique the partner, that is, the more it resembles the ROW in its attributes. Absence of uniqueness leads, again, to similarity of relative prices.

To analyze the significance of smallness in a PTA, we shall start by looking at a small country as the potential *partner* to an agreement with a large country. What should the large country expect from such an agreement?

To start with, most of the propositions of the customs-union theory are based on the "small-country" assumption. They imply that the *home country* is small, in relation to its partner (and to the ROW): that it is a pure price taker, which can have no impact on the prices in its trade with foreign countries. In the case now examined, this is *not* true; the home country is large, and the partner is small, so that prices faced by the home country are no longer constant. This attribute, which was discussed extensively in Chapter 5, adds another dimension to the analysis.

When the partner country is small, and the home country large, the new imports from the partner (whether replacing home production — trade creation — or displacing imports from the ROW — trade diversion) will *not* take place at an existing, constant price; the added demand by the home country will serve to *increase* the price it pays for imports from its partner (due to an increased cost of production). This is an *added* loss — beyond the one conventionally defined as the loss from trade diversion (which is just the expression of a shift of imports from a less to a more expensive source, at *given* and unchanged foreign prices). In the extreme case, the price at the partner's market will reach the *cum tariff* price of the ROW, from which some imports will continue even after the agreement (alongside imports from the partner). The home price will then remain what it had been prior to the agreement. Thus, neither trade creation will take place nor any consumption effect so that the potential favorable impact of the agreement cannot materialize. Trade diversion, on the other hand, will not only be the sole consequence of the agreement but will be at its maximum height. This is thus a case of clear and definite loss to the home country.[35]

Examining the impact of small size of the country through the criteria indicated earlier — maintaining throughout the small size of the *partner* as defining the case in hand — the following inference may be drawn. The first criterion appears to be neutral (or irrelevant) to the phenomenon on hand: when the contemplated partner is small, there is no reason to expect — in the general case — the home country's initial tariff level to be either higher or lower than would be the case when the partner is a large country. There *may* be a reason — coming to the second criterion — why the *partner's* tariff level might initially be low; this would be true if it were found that small countries, due to higher losses from the imposition of trade barriers, tend to maintain lower levels of such barriers. In this case, the expected gain of the home country from the reduction of tariffs in the *partner's* market — the improved terms of trade coming from the source — will be smaller. However, whether such a presumption about initial tariff levels is valid must be established through empirical observations.

Criteria (iii) and (iv) may be combined, and they clearly point out a bias against the small partner. Trade with the small partner must itself be small, *ceteris paribus*. Hence, a stronger presumption of trade *diversion* exists when the contemplated partner is small, with a potentially larger loss on this score from the preferential agreement.

The indication of loss is probably strongest when we come to the next set of criteria — those relating to the similarity of the partner country to the ROW. This is of crucial importance. In the best case, the partner's attributes are identical with those of the ROW, leading to similar patterns of relative prices: under such circumstances, the trade-preferential agreement would be equivalent, from the home country's viewpoint, to a move to a universal and nondiscriminating free trade. This, for obvious reasons, is more likely the *larger* the partner country and — strongly related to it — the more diversified the structures of its production and exports. A small economy, with highly concentrated and specialized structures, would clearly be an undesirable partner, on this score — an agreement with it is likely to lead to a loss. The *level of development* of the economy should be highly relevant here: the more developed the economy and the higher its per capita and aggregate incomes, the more diversified will be the structure of its production and exports. If size is defined, as has been done here, by population, the best potential partner would be a large and highly developed economy (such as the US, the European Union, or Japan), whereas a small and poor economy would be the least desirable partner.

Thus, the most promising agreement is one concluded by a "small" country with a "large" partner. In having the least impact on its terms of trade through the country's own trade, in achieving maximum trade creation and trade expansion, a minimum level of trade diversion, and a minimum loss from any given level of such diversion, this would be the most promising preferential agreement. This by itself does *not* guarantee, however, that any agreement between a small country and a large one — even the largest — will be beneficial to the former; it merely states that, without further specific knowledge, the probability of a favorable outcome (from the point of view of the small partner) is higher than in any other partnership.

An agreement between a small economy and another small one is definitely less likely to be beneficial (to both small partners). The same considerations offered earlier to suggest that, for a large country, an agreement with a small one is likely to lead to a loss apply also to the case in which the "home" country is small rather than large — save one: the detrimental effect on the home country's terms of trade, found in the case of a large home country, does not exist here. Another way of stating this is to say that the terms-of-trade effect applies in such a case to *both* sides of the agreement — hence tending to cancel such an effect for each of them.

Finally — although this falls beyond the scope of this discussion — an agreement between two large economies is likely to be the most rewarding combination for the two partners *taken together*. For each of them, however, it would rank below the agreement of a small home economy with a large partner: in this case, too, the favorable impact of an agreement on the home country's terms of trade would be a matter of chance.[36]

This analysis may be summed up as follows. In a general way and with no knowledge of the specific elements of a PTA, an agreement between a small economy and a large one is the most promising for the former, and the larger the partner, the better. Making the obverse statement: an agreement between a large economy and a small partner is the least likely to be of benefit and is the most likely to lead to a loss to that economy. An agreement between two small countries is not likely to bring a gain to either — it will have the attributes of a losing proposition; it is also the agreement least likely to be of substantial consequence — a point we shall dwell upon shortly.

At this juncture, it should be recalled that these inferences have been derived for a PTA of the *free-trade-area* nature. For a *customs union*, however, an important qualification must be added. When a common external tariff is established, it is likely to reflect little, if at all, the desires and needs of the small country (at least as they are perceived by its government): it will predominantly reflect the tariff schedule (and other trade barriers) of the large partner. In a general way — again, with no access to the attributes and information of any specific case — it may be stated that for a small nation contemplating a PTA with a much larger partner, a free-trade-area form of association is likely to be preferable to a customs union.

Effectiveness of a Preferential Agreement: Compatibility of Trade Flows[37]

The considerations offered thus far indicate that a small economy is not a promising partner for a potential trade-preferential agreement, in the sense of presenting a high probability of a loss from the agreement and a low probability of a gain. Related to it is the issue of the *effectiveness* of a trade agreement — its potential to lead to extra trade between the partners. This can only be assessed in concrete terms on a case-by-case basis; however, a prior knowledge of the structural attributes of each country's trade flow may indicate the potential for trade expansion.

The tool employed for this purpose is the index of compatibility of trade flows.[38] This index will be higher the closer the two commodity structures of the trade flows (one country's imports and the other's exports). At one extreme, the partner country exports *none* of the goods the home country imports: in this case, the index will be zero. The other extreme is where the partner country exports goods in precisely the same proportions that the home country imports them, in which case the index will be unity. The more the exporting country offers goods in similar proportions to those demanded by the importing country — and thus the higher the index of compatibility between the two trade flows — the stronger the potential for trade expansion between the two economies, in the present context, as a response to a PTA. Related to our earlier analysis, it should be evident that the index will be higher the *less unique* the export structure of the exporting country — that is, the more it resembles the structure of major traders and of the world as a whole.[39] This, in turn, is closely related to the degree of commodity concentration of exports: the more diversified the exports, the more they should resemble the global structure of exports.[40]

The indices of compatibility of each country's exports with each other's imports have been estimated for close to 80 countries, for which the required data are available (1993 data have been estimated). It would be too cumbersome to present all the individual indices (the number of entries would exceed 6000!). Instead, Table 6.5 provides *averages* that are relevant in the present context. The countries are listed by groups, where the large countries are subdivided into two — the poorer and the richer

Table 6.5:   Country indices of trade compatibility.

Exporting country, by category	Small countries, low income (1)	Small countries, high income (2)	Large countries, low income (3)	Large countries, high income (4)	All countries (5)
(a) Small countries, low income					
Barbados	0.23	0.23	0.15	0.20	0.20
Belize	0.05	0.06	0.03	0.08	0.12
Bolivia	0.10	0.12	0.10	0.18	0.24
Costa Rica	0.26	0.26	0.20	0.28	0.22
Cyprus	0.28	0.25	0.15	0.22	0.26
El Salvador	0.29	0.29	0.22	0.26	0.03
Faroe Islands	0.03	0.03	0.02	0.02	0.12
Fiji	0.13	0.15	0.09	0.13	0.16
Guadeloupe	0.18	0.18	0.14	0.16	0.03
Greenland	0.04	0.04	0.03	0.04	0.03
Honduras	0.14	0.14	0.10	0.14	0.13
Iceland	0.06	0.07	0.05	0.07	0.06
Jordan	0.22	0.21	0.16	0.17	0.20
Martinique	0.24	0.19	0.17	0.17	0.20
Mauritius	0.13	0.16	0.10	0.14	0.13
Nicaragua	0.13	0.13	0.12	0.14	0.13
Panama	0.22	0.21	0.16	0.20	0.20
Papua–N. Guinea	0.06	0.07	0.07	0.08	0.07
Paraguay	0.10	0.09	0.09	0.10	0.09
Reunion	0.19	0.20	0.17	0.20	0.19
Senegal	0.22	0.17	0.18	0.16	0.19
Seychelles	0.02	0.02	0.02	0.02	0.02
Suriname	0.03	0.04	0.03	0.04	0.04
Trinidad & Tobago	0.23	0.17	0.21	0.19	0.21
Tunisia	0.28	0.31	0.26	0.30	0.28
Uruguay	0.26	0.26	0.20	0.25	0.24
(b) Small countries, high income					
Austria	0.51	0.60	0.47	0.56	0.51
Denmark	0.48	0.52	0.40	0.50	0.48
Finland	0.41	0.46	0.39	0.43	0.41
Hong Kong	0.26	0.38	0.24	0.33	0.29
Ireland	0.37	0.42	0.30	0.40	0.38
Israel	0.31	0.43	0.32	0.40	0.34
New Zealand	0.27	0.28	0.23	0.30	0.28
Norway	0.31	0.33	0.31	0.35	0.32
Portugal	0.39	0.44	0.33	0.42	0.39
Singapore	0.40	0.48	0.36	0.45	0.41
Sweden	0.49	0.50	0.46	0.55	0.49
Switzerland	0.40	0.48	0.39	0.45	0.41

Average index, by category of importing countries

(*Continued*)

Table 6.5:   (*Continued*)

Exporting country, by category	Average index, by category of importing countries				
	Small countries, low income (1)	Small countries, high income (2)	Large countries, low income (3)	Large countries, high income (4)	All countries (5)
(c) *Large countries, low income*					
Algeria	0.13	0.09	0.13	0.12	0.13
Bangladesh	0.08	0.11	0.06	0.09	0.08
China	0.39	0.47	0.33	0.44	0.39
Colombia	0.28	0.31	0.26	0.31	0.28
Ecuador	0.13	0.13	0.13	0.15	0.14
Egypt	0.28	0.28	0.28	0.29	0.28
Ghana	0.08	0.09	0.07	0.09	0.08
Guatemala	0.29	0.27	0.21	0.25	0.26
India	0.31	0.36	0.28	0.33	0.31
Indonesia	0.29	0.33	0.26	0.33	0.30
Kenya	0.22	0.18	0.18	0.17	0.19
Madagascar	0.16	0.17	0.13	0.16	0.15
Malaysia	0.32	0.41	0.31	0.40	0.34
Morocco	0.20	0.23	0.17	0.22	0.20
Nepal	0.06	0.08	0.05	0.08	0.07
Pakistan	0.13	0.18	0.11	0.14	0.14
Peru	0.16	0.17	0.14	0.16	0.16
Philippines	0.24	0.31	0.21	0.30	0.25
South Africa	0.23	0.27	0.26	0.28	0.25
Sri Lanka	0.14	0.20	0.12	0.18	0.15
Syrian Arab Rep.	0.17	0.15	0.16	0.18	0.17
Thailand	0.34	0.43	0.27	0.39	0.34
Turkey	0.31	0.33	0.27	0.30	0.30
Zimbabwe	0.20	0.22	0.18	0.22	0.20
(d) *Large countries, high income*					
Argentina	0.33	0.30	0.31	0.33	0.32
Australia	0.28	0.29	0.29	0.33	0.32
Belgium-Luxembourg	0.52	0.57	0.46	0.56	0.51
Brazil	0.39	0.43	0.38	0.45	0.40
Canada	0.42	0.46	0.41	0.53	0.45
Chile	0.17	0.19	0.15	0.20	0.17
Germany	0.54	0.66	0.52	0.66	0.57
Greece	0.32	0.32	0.28	0.30	0.30
Italy	0.52	0.62	0.47	0.53	0.53
Japan	0.41	0.53	0.48	0.53	0.45
Korea (Rep. of)	0.40	0.51	0.30	0.46	0.41
Mexico	0.45	0.54	0.41	0.56	0.47
Netherlands	0.53	0.59	0.46	0.56	0.52

(*Continued*)

Table 6.5:   (*Continued*)

	Average index, by category of importing countries				
Exporting country, by category	Small countries, low income (1)	Small countries, high income (2)	Large countries, low income (3)	Large countries, high income (4)	All countries (5)
Spain	0.52	0.58	0.45	0.56	0.52
UK	0.54	0.66	0.51	0.66	0.58
US	0.48	0.61	0.46	0.63	0.52
Venezuela	0.20	0.17	0.20	0.20	0.20

Method: see text.

(following the earlier discussion of the degree of commodity concentration). Thus, four groups are formed: (i) small countries of low aggregate income; (ii) small countries of high aggregate income; (iii) large countries of low per capita income; and (iv) large countries of high per capita income.[41] For each country, five *average* measures of the index of compatibility are presented: separate averages for the importing countries belonging to each of the four country categories, and an overall average for all (importing) countries. These findings are, in turn, summarized in Table 6.6, which presents a matrix of the averages of the indices of each group. Thus, for instance, the table shows the average index of compatibility of exports of small low-income countries with imports of small low-income countries;

Table 6.6:   Average indices of trade compatibility, by categories of size and income.

	Category of importing countries				
Category of exporting countries	Small countries, low income	Small countries, high income	Large countries, low income	Large countries, high income	All countries
Small countries, low income	0.16	0.15	0.12	0.15	0.15
Small countries, high income	0.38	0.45	0.35	0.43	0.39
Large countries, low income	0.21	0.24	0.19	0.23	0.22
Large countries, high income	0.41	0.47	0.39	0.48	0.42

Method: see text.

with, next, imports of small high-income countries; and so on, including the overall average index of this group (small low-income countries) will be all importing countries. Next, the table presents similar indices of compatibility of the exports of countries belonging to the small high-income group with the imports of countries belonging to the four categories, and so on.

The results are illuminating, and mostly conform with our *a priori* expectations — perhaps calling further attention to the role of income (as could already be gathered from the discussion of commodity concentration). It appears that small countries are indeed less promising as trade partners than large countries; but that a distinction by income is much more relevant than a mere distinction by size. The lowest indices are found for the exports of small low-income economies, and these indices are almost equally low whatever the attributes (size and income) of the importing countries. The next lowest indices are found for the exports of countries belonging to the group of large low-income economies: these are only somewhat higher than the indices of exports of countries in the former group. However, this distinction by size pales in comparison with the contrasts found when distinction is made by income levels. Among the high-income countries, it is again true that somewhat higher indices are found among the large nations than among the small nations; but both groups of high-income countries manifest much higher indices of compatibility of their exports than either group — large or small — of the low-income countries. The indices are particularly high when both the exporting and the importing countries are high-income countries — whether large or small: these indices range from 0.43 to 0.48 — in sharp contrast to the case in which both the exporters and the importers are low-income countries (again, large or small), where the indices range from 0.12 to 0.21.

These inferences are reinforced by tests of *significance* of the differences (not shown in the table). When we compare average indices of compatibility for low-income countries, all the relevant comparisons (that is, those made along the columns of Table 6.6) show *significantly* higher indices for the large than for the small countries, that is, the probability of these differences being a matter of accident is practically zero. When similar comparisons are made for the two categories of high-income countries, all indices are again higher for the large countries; however, the differences are, this time, of low significance. Thus, the probability of accidental results (that is, of the apparently different averages in fact representing samples drawn from the same population) lies in the range of 0.23 to 0.65. Once more, it appears that size matters a lot for low-income countries, but only little for the rich economies.

Thus, partnerships with high-income countries, *whether large or small,* promise to have a high potential of expanding the size of trade among the partners — especially (but not exclusively) when both partners are high-income nations. Conversely, only a low potential for trade expansion may be expected when the partner is a low-income country — and in particular when both countries are poor. Partnership with a small exporting country presents only a weak promise for trade expansion when it is a low-income country. When, on the other hand, the partner's aggregate income is high (also implying, most often, a high per capita income), the country's small size seems to lose most of its relevance: it is almost as promising a partner as a large, rich country, and it is definitely far superior, in this sense, to a large but poor economy.

Annex

Population and income (1993 data) of countries by category are given in Table 6.7.

Table 6.7: Countries by category: Population and income (1993 data).

Category and country	Population (millions) (1)	Aggregate GNP ($ billions) (2)	GNP per capita ($) (3)
(a) *Small countries, low income*			
Albania	3.4	1.2	340
Antigua and Barbuda	0.1	0.4	6390
Armenia	3.7	2.5	660
Azerbaijan	7.4	5.4	730
Bahamas	0.3	3.1	11,500
Bahrain	0.5	4.3	7870
Barbados	0.3	1.6	6740
Belize	0.2	0.5	2440
Benin	5.2	2.2	420
Bhutan	1.5	0.3	170
Bolivia	7.1	5.5	770
Bosnia and Herzegovina	4.4	n.a.	n.a.
Botswana	1.4	3.6	2590
Brunei	0.3	n.a.	n.a.
Bulgaria	8.5	9.8	1160
Burkina Faso	9.8	2.9	300
Burundi	6.0	1.1	180

(*Continued*)

Table 6.7:   (*Continued*)

Category and country	Population (millions) (1)	Aggregate GNP ($ billions) (2)	GNP per capita ($) (3)
Cambodia	9.6	n.a.	n.a.
Cape Verde	0.4	0.4	870
Central African Republic	3.3	1.3	390
Chad	6.1	1.3	200
Comoros	0.5	0.3	520
Congo	2.5	2.3	920
Costa Rica	3.3	7.0	2160
Croatia	4.8	n.a.	n.a.
Cyprus	0.7	7.5	10,380
Djibouti	0.6	0.5	780
Dominica	0.1	0.2	2680
Dominican Republic	7.5	8.0	1080
El Salvador	5.5	7.2	1320
Equatorial Guinea	0.5	0.2	360
Estonia	1.6	4.7	3040
Fiji	0.8	1.6	2140
Gabon	1.2	5.0	4050
Gambia	1.0	0.4	360
Georgia	5.5	3.1	560
Grenada	0.1	0.2	2410
Guadeloupe	0.4	n.a.	n.a.
Guinea	6.3	3.2	510
Guinea-Bissau	1.0	0.2	220
Guyana	0.8	0.3	350
Haiti	6.8	n.a.	n.a.
Honduras	5.6	3.2	580
Iceland	0.3	6.2	23,620
Jamaica	2.4	3.4	1360
Jordan	4.1	4.9	1190
Kuwait	1.5	34.1	23,350
Kyrgyz Republic	4.5	3.8	830
Lao PDR	4.5	1.3	290
Latvia	2.6	5.3	2030
Lebanon	3.9	n.a.	n.a.
Lesotho	1.9	1.3	660
Liberia	2.4	n.a.	n.a.
Libya	5.0	n.a.	n.a.
Lithuania	3.8	4.9	1310
Luxembourg	0.4	14.2	35,850
Macedonia	2.2	1.7	780
Malawi	9.3	2.0	220
Maldives	0.2	0.2	820
Mali	9.2	2.7	300
Malta	0.4	n.a.	n.a.

(*Continued*)

Table 6.7: (*Continued*)

Category and country	Population (millions) (1)	Aggregate GNP ($ billions) (2)	GNP per capita ($) (3)
Martinique	0.4	n.a.	n.a.
Mauritania	2.1	1.1	510
Mauritius	1.1	3.3	2980
Moldova	4.4	5.2	1180
Mongolia	2.4	0.9	400
Namibia	1.6	2.6	1660
Netherlands Antilles	0.2	n.a.	n.a.
New Caledonia	0.2	n.a.	n.a.
Nicaragua	4.0	1.4	360
Niger	8.4	2.3	270
Oman	1.7	9.6	5600
Panama	2.6	6.6	2580
Papua New Guinea	4.2	4.6	1120
Paraguay	4.7	7.0	1500
Qatar	0.5	n.a.	n.a.
Reunion	0.6	n.a.	n.a.
Rwanda	7.5	1.5	200
St. Kitts and Nevis	0.1	0.2	4470
St. Lucia	0.2	0.5	3040
St. Vincent	0.1	0.2	2130
Sao Tome and Principe	0.1	0.1	330
Senegal	8.1	5.9	730
Seychelles	0.1	0.4	6370
Sierra Leone	4.5	0.5	140
Slovak Republic	5.4	10.1	1900
Slovenia	2.0	12.6	6310
Solomon Islands	0.4	0.3	750
Somalia	8.5	n.a.	n.a.
Suriname	0.4	0.5	1210
Swaziland	0.8	0.9	1050
Tajikistan	5.7	2.7	470
Togo	4.0	1.3	330
Trinidad and Tobago	1.3	4.8	3730
Tunisia	8.6	15.3	1780
Turkmenistan	4.0	n.a.	n.a.
United Arab Emirates	1.7	38.7	22,470
Uruguay	3.2	12.3	3910
Western Samoa	0.2	0.2	980
Zambia	8.5	3.2	370
(b) *Small countries, high income*			
Austria	7.9	183.5	23,120
Denmark	5.2	137.6	26,510
Finland	5.1	96.2	18,970

(*Continued*)

Table 6.7:   (*Continued*)

Category and country	Population (millions) (1)	Aggregate GNP ($ billions) (2)	GNP per capita ($) (3)
Hong Kong	5.9	104.7	17,860
Ireland	3.6	44.9	12,580
Israel	5.3	72.7	13,760
New Zealand	3.5	44.7	12,900
Norway	4.3	113.5	26,340
Portugal	9.9	77.8	7890
Singapore	2.9	55.4	19,310
Sweden	8.7	216.3	24,830
Switzerland	7.0	254.1	36,410
(c) *Large countries*			
Afghanistan	22.1	n.a.	n.a.
Algeria	26.9	44.4	1650
Angola	10.0	n.a.	n.a.
Argentina	33.5	244.0	7290
Australia	17.7	310.0	17,510
Bangladesh	116.7	25.9	220
Belarus	10.3	29.3	2840
Belgium	10.1	213.4	21,210
Brazil	156.4	472.0	3020
Cameroon	12.6	9.7	770
Canada	27.8	574.9	20,670
Chile	13.8	42.5	3070
China	1175.4	581.1	490
Colombia	35.7	50.1	1400
Côte d'Ivoire	13.4	8.4	630
Cuba	10.9	n.a.	n.a.
Czech Republic	10.3	28.2	2730
Ecuador	11.2	13.2	1170
Egypt Arab Republic	55.8	36.7	660
Ethiopia	53.3	n.a.	n.a.
France	57.7	1289.2	22,360
Germany	80.8	1903.0	23,560
Ghana	16.3	7.0	430
Greece	10.4	76.7	7390
Guatemala	10.0	11.1	1130
Hungary	10.3	34.3	3330
India	900.5	262.8	290
Indonesia	187.2	137.0	730
Iran, Islamic Republic	61.4	n.a.	n.a.
Iraq	19.8	n.a.	n.a.
Italy	57.8	1135.0	19,620
Japan	124.9	3926.7	31,450
Kazakhstan	17.2	26.5	1540

(*Continued*)

Table 6.7:   (*Continued*)

Category and country	Population (millions) (1)	Aggregate GNP ($ billions) (2)	GNP per capita ($) (3)
Kenya	25.4	6.7	270
Korea Dem. Republic	23.1	n.a.	n.a.
Korea Republic	44.1	338.1	7670
Madagascar	12.7	3.0	240
Malaysia	19.0	60.1	3160
Mexico	86.7	325.0	3750
Morocco	26.7	27.2	1030
Mozambique	16.9	1.4	80
Myanmar	44.7	n.a.	n.a.
Nepal	20.4	3.2	160
Netherlands	15.3	316.4	20,170
Nigeria	104.9	33.0	310
Pakistan	122.8	53.3	430
Peru	22.8	34.0	1490
Philippines	65.8	54.6	830
Poland	38.5	87.3	2270
Romania	22.8	25.4	1120
Russian Federation	148.5	348.4	2350
Saudi Arabia	17.4	n.a.	n.a.
South Africa	40.7	117.1	2900
Spain	39.1	534.0	13,650
Sri Lanka	17.6	10.7	600
Sudan	27.3	n.a.	n.a.
Syrian Arab Republic	13.4	n.a.	n.a.
Tanzania	26.7	2.5	100
Thailand	58.8	120.2	2040
Turkey	59.5	126.3	2120
Uganda	18.0	3.5	190
Ukraine	52.1	99.7	1910
United Kingdom	58.0	1042.7	17,970
United States	258.1	6387.7	24,750
Uzbekistan	22.0	21.1	960
Venezuela	20.8	58.9	2840
Vietnam	70.9	12.0	170
Yemen Republic	13.4	n.a.	n.a.
Yugoslavia, Federal Rep.	10.7	n.a.	n.a.
Zaire	41.0	n.a.	n.a.
Zimbabwe	10.6	5.8	540

n.a.: Data not available
Source: The World Bank Atlas, 1995.

Notes

1. The tables include several territories, which are not fully "sovereign" nations. They are taken from the World Bank Atlas for 1995.

2. Chenery and Syrquin (1975) used a cutoff population point of 15 million. This definition would have added 14 more countries to the "small" category, bringing it to 126 out of 183. However, making this category of such proportions would reduce the uniqueness of the group and the scope for a separate study of its attributes. In a more recent study, Srinivasan (1986) used a cutoff point of a population of 5 million, adding a subcategory of "very small" countries with a population below 1.5 million people.

3. The most obvious case of a nation with a very large territory and a modest-sized population is Australia, a continent of 17.7 million people.

4. The next country, in terms of aggregate income, would be Tunisia, with a 1993 GNP of $15b. (and a per capita income of $1780, in comparison with $7890 in Portugal, the poorest of the list of twelve); a clear cutoff point is thus indicated. Note that the income level of the countries at the bottom of the list — around $45b. — is close to the *median* level of GNP of the "large" countries. Income considerations blur more the category (as defined by population) of "small" countries than of "large" countries. Thus, for instance, 10 of 96 "small" countries have an aggregate income, which exceeds the *median* income of "large" countries; whereas only 3 out of 57 "large" countries display an income level lower than the median of the "small" group.

5. This inference appeared to be validated in a study of a few decades ago. See Michaely (1962, Table 6, p. 25).

6. For instance, work along the lines of the analysis in Chenery and Syrquin (1975).

7. Export concentration is indicated by data of a single year, 1992. It is represented by the Gini-Hirschman coefficient of commodity concentration (see Michaely, 1962).

8. For the purpose in hand, we have separated the *large* countries into two income groups (this is not shown in Table 6.1): low per capita income (1993 level of per capita income below $2000 — 29 countries altogether) and high per capita income (19 countries). For the low-income group, the average annual rate of growth of per capita income is 0.6 percent, and the median is 0.9. These are quite similar to the statistics for small low-income economies (0.8 and 0.9, respectively).

Similarly, for the richer large countries the average growth rate is 2.0 percent, and the median 2.1 — quite close to the observations of the small high-income group of countries (2.5 percent for both the average and the median). Thus, for both large and small countries, per capita income grew substantially faster among the high-income than among the low-income countries. However, *no* clear distinction, for countries in the same income range, appears between large and small economies.

9. The higher investment share among small high-income countries provides at least a partial explanation of the higher rate of per capita income growth in this group. In addition, it should be noted that the richer the country, and the higher, presumably, its stock of capital in relation to other factors of production (such as labor), the higher the proportion of investment out of income, which would maintain a given rate of growth of income.

10. However, we underlined *as recorded*: an inadequate recording, particularly of the capital inflow, may be suspected. We note that for the two groups of large and small high-income groups, the addition of foreign capital inflow ("foreign saving") to domestic saving yields, roughly, the rate of investment — as, indeed, national-income identities would require. For the category of small low-income countries, on the other hand, such addition would fall short of investment by about 6 percent of GDP — a very large discrepancy indeed. It is likely that the recording of long-term financing is an understatement, missing much of the foreign financing, particularly the components originating in unilateral transfers. If this is true, the large inflow from abroad may still be found to provide a major explanation of the low rate of domestic saving among the small low-income economies.

11. This is based on comparisons of the *medians*. In this instance, a particular large deviation exists between the mean and the median for the group of small high-income countries: the former statistic is 35 (percent of exports in GDP), and the latter is 52. The size of the mean is very heavily influenced by two extreme observations: Singapore (where the export/GDP share is 160 percent!) and Hong Kong (where it is over 100 percent). In both economies — particularly in Singapore — exports include a heavy dose of transit trade.

12. Diversification of *imports* is quite similar among all countries, with only slight differences between small and large, or even between poor and rich economies. A coefficient of commodity concentration exceeding 0.200 is quite rare for imports.

13. Among small economies, the distinction was made by *aggregate* rather than per capita, income; however, using the latter yardstick would yield almost the same list of countries.

14. We have tried to test the *significance* of observed differences in the "typical" attributes among the separate categories of countries. In essence, the test consists of asking what is the probability that two sets of observations are actually samples drawn from the same population, so that the apparent difference between the means of the two sets is a matter of accident. The available statistical test can, unfortunately, be applied only to differences between *means* (averages), and not between medians. For this reason, the test has not been used for the two attributes of macroeconomic behavior — the rates of inflation and of devaluation — where the means are quite misleading as indicators of a "typical" level. It has also not been applied in those instances where the differences among groups of countries are so stark as to make a rigorous test redundant: this refers to differences in export shares and in export concentration.

For the rest, the results of the test are shown in the following table.

Attribute	Observed difference	Probability of an accidental outcome
Share of saving	*Lower for small low-income than for large countries.	0.00
	*Lower for small low-income than for small high-income countries.	0.00
Share of investment	*Lower for small low-income than for small high-income countries.	0.14
Share of capital inflow	*Lower for small low-income than for large countries.	0.00
	*Lower for small low-income than for small high-income countries.	0.00

Thus, the differences indicated in the text between the group of the small low-income countries and the other two groups are definitely not the result of accident. The only exception concerns the observed difference in the share of investment, which is in fact slight and which seems to be in some doubt.

15. An elementary exercise using the Marshallian "offer curves" would easily demonstrate this outcome.

16. This implicitly assumes a Ricardian world of constant costs. With increasing costs, this inference of the analysis should be qualified; however, the tenor of the argument will remain unchanged.

17. That is, in a Ricardian world: define units of the good so that a unit of each good requires for its production in the ROW the same basket of factors (units of "labor"). Good a will require in its production in the *home country* the smallest amount of resources; good b — the second smallest; and so on, through good j, which requires the largest amount of resources in home production.

18. Changing this assumption would invalidate the proposition that whatever good is exported, the goods to its left will definitely also be (and similarly for imports). It would make the presentation much more cumbersome, without affecting its central inferences.

19. We know from the "Lerner theorem" that import tariffs and export taxes are equivalent: the existence of one implies the existence of the other.

20. If tariffs are not uniform — and they mostly are not, before liberalization — it is likely that higher tariffs will be imposed on goods, which are most easily (i.e., at a lesser loss) replaced by local activity. These are the goods closer to the cutoff point; in the diagram, a higher tariff is likely to be imposed on good h than on goods further to its right. This only tends to reinforce the inference that the imports of h (rather than of i or j) will be discontinued.

    Whether import tariffs are uniform or not, if they are the trade barrier used, they imply a uniform rate of *export* taxes: these taxes will be "imposed" by an exchange-rate adjustment, which is equivalent (for the purpose on hand) to a uniform export tax. This statement obviously ignores complications such as those due to the existence of nonrefunded tariffs on imported inputs in exports.

21. Concrete estimates of such impacts would hardly be feasible. However, one proxy measure would be the extent to which trade liberalization leads heavily to the expansion of "traditional" or of "nontraditional" exports. The analysis of Chapter 8 will suggest that it is the latter.

22. See Chapter 6 in Michaely *et al.* (1991).

23. See Chapter 6 in Michaely *et al.* (1991).

24. See Chapter 6 in Michaely *et al.* (1991) mainly pp. 279–284. Only the attributes that may be relevant to the issue in hand are listed here.

25. The "strength" of liberalization, along with its other attributes, are discussed in Michaely *et al.* (1991, Chapter 3).

26. The delineation of liberalizations, as well as decisions about their intensities, is based primarily on judgments of country economists at the World Bank and the Inter-American Development Bank (IDB). Some modifications have been made by consulting other sources, primarily Edwards (1993), Alam (1992), and Papageorgiou and Michaely (1995).

27. This follows, again, the procedure used in Michaely *et al.* (1991). Since some liberalization episodes were introduced in 1991, and the data used here finish with 1993, the "last three years" sometimes means in fact only two.

28. To analyze export performance, *constant-price* estimates should have been used. However, these are scarce, or are of poor quality. Instead, we have examined changes in the *share* of exports in GDP. This measure still suffers, however, from being affected by changes in foreign prices, or, in a more general way, from the impact of changes in the relative price of exports.

29. This pattern roughly agrees with the findings of the aforementioned comprehensive study of experiences of trade liberalization prior to the 1980s (Michaely *et al.* 1991, Tables 7.2 and 7.3, pp. 88–89). The main difference is that in the analysis of earlier experiences, no decline of the rate of growth appears, on average, even during the year of introduction of trade liberalization. Interestingly, though, if we confine our observations to *Latin American* countries only, the same pattern appears for the earlier experience as we find now — with Colombia, where a sharp fall of growth occurring in the year *after* the year of introduction of liberalization is the only exception. In the combined observation of the earlier experiences of Argentina, Brazil, Chile, Peru, and Uruguay, the average rates of growth were as follows: pre-liberalization, 3.9 percent; year of liberalization, 1.1 percent; and post-liberalization, 4.8 percent.

30. Observing only the eight "strong" liberalization experiences among the small LAC countries, the pattern of change of the average rate of growth for the group looks as follows: pre-liberalization, 2.0 percent; year of liberalization, −0.4 percent; and post-liberalization, 3.8 percent. This is roughly the same pattern as for the group of small countries as a whole, except for a somewhat sharper drop of the rate of growth in

the year of liberalization. This pattern, again, does *not* indicate higher transition costs among the small economies.

31. However, the statistic of the average among large countries is heavily influenced by the extreme case of Venezuela, where export performance is determined in the short run primarily by external shocks in the oil market.

32. On the technical level, it should also be noted that we analyze the *share* of exports, which should go up whenever the denominator, the GDP, goes down.

33. See Michaely *et al.* (1991, Table 12.3, p. 191).

34. This set of rules is mentioned in this book on several occasions, primarily in Chapters 4 and 9.

35. This issue was analyzed at some length, and with more rigor, in Chapter 4.

36. There is likely to be some net impact on the terms of trade, one way or another, but we do not know which of the two partners will gain, and which will lose.

37. This is an application to the small-country issue of the general analysis of an *ex ante* assessment of a preferential agreement, which is elaborated in Chapter 9. For convenience, the essence of the "compatibility index" is re-stated here.

38. See the analysis and formulation of this index in Chapter 9.

39. In principle, this is true also for uniqueness of the *import* structure (of the importing country). However, as has been noted earlier, countries resemble each other — and the world as a whole — much more in import than in export structures.

40. Consult, again, the discussion in Chapter 9.

41. Note, again, that whereas small countries are classified by *aggregate* income; large countries are classified by per capita income. Classifying the former, too, by per capita income would yield largely the same list.

References

Alam, A (1992). Country trade profiles: Latin America and the Caribbean, The World Bank Washington DC (mimeo).

Chenery, H B and Syrquin, M (1975). *Patterns of Development 1950–1970*. London: Oxford University Press.

Edwards, S (1993). *Latin America and the Caribbean: A Decade after the Debt Crisis*. Washington DC: The World Bank.

Kuznets, S (1958). Economic growth of small nations. In *The Challenge of Development*, Chapter 2, Jerusalem: The Eliezer Kaplan School of Economics and Social Sciences, The Hebrew University. Reprinted in Robinson, EAG, (ed.) (1960). *Economic Consequences of the Size of Nations*. London: The Macmillan Press.

Michaely, M (1962). *Concentration in International Trade*. Amsterdam: North-Holland Publishing Company.

Michaely, M (1977). *Theory of Commercial Policy: Trade and Protection*. Oxford: Philip Allan, Chicago: University of Chicago Press.

Michaely, M, Papageorgiou, D and Choksi, A M (1991). In *Liberalizing Foreign Trade: Lessons of Experience in the Developing World*, Vol. 7, Papageorgiou, D, Michaely, M and Choksi, A M (eds.). Oxford: Basil Blackwell.

Papageorgiou, D, and Michaely, M (1995). Trade liberalization: The recent experience, The World Bank Washington, DC (mimeo).

Srinivasan, T N (1986). The costs and benefits of being a small, remote, island, landlocked, or ministate economy, *The World Bank Research Observer*, 1, 205–218.

Chapter 7

Preferential Agreements and Past Trade Patterns

The Issues

It is commonly accepted that a phenomenon of histerysis is manifested in determining geographic trade patterns: the existence of past trade between two partners leads to a larger present flow of trade between the two than would have existed had all other current trade-determining variables been the same, but past trade had been absent. This role of "history" may be large or small, and its origins may differ. In the simplest case, it may be due to "fundamental" variables that were more conducive to the relevant trade flow in the past than at present, or to past political circumstances, such as the existence of colonial relationships, and the like.[1] Whatever the source, the possibility that present trade is partly determined by "history" is relevant to the issue of the desirability of concluding a preferential trade agreement (PTA) in at least two ways. One question, partly related to the analysis of "natural trade partners," is whether trade determination through "history" should play a role in identifying more promising partners for a PTA. The other is whether this phenomenon is relevant to the order of policies, that is, to the stage at which a PTA is introduced. These two issues will be analyzed, in turn, in the following two sections.

"Historical" Trade and Partnership in a PTA

It may be convenient to start this analysis with reference to an interesting and, as far as I know, novel proposition made recently by Wonnacott.[2] He submitted that:

(i) "If, prior to the establishment of a free trade association, countries are close trading partners because of fundamental economic forces — those of classical comparative advantage and geographic proximity — the countries are natural trading partners, and discrimination against outsiders that any such agreement entails is likely to have relatively weak trade-diverting effects. In contrast, if the high level of trade is explained on the basis of historical accident, then discrimination against outsiders is more questionable ... "

(ii) "Fortifying traditional ties by discriminating against new outside competitors is less desirable than fortifying the natural advantages that come from geographical proximity or from comparative advantage in the traditional sense."[3]

This proposition may certainly be of concrete significance, and it merits a close look.

Past events, or "history," may best be considered an investment, or fixed cost. Whether these were indeed "costs" in the traditional sense, such as the establishment of a distributional organization, or advertisement, or whether they were events like the imposition of trade channels by a monopolist–monopsonist or a colonial power, is immaterial in the present context. Either way, a potential new entrant would have to make an investment (presumably, a substantial one) to overcome the advantage of the incumbent trader, and to gain equal (or more equal) footing — an element of cost absent in imports from the incumbent. We shall assume, for simplicity, that without making such investment, the potentially new provider cannot enter the home market at all, that is, that no imports from this ("third") country (or "the rest of the world," ROW) take place, and this is indeed the starting position, prior to the introduction of a PTA.[4]

Within this context, it is immediately evident that the first component of the proposition suggested by Wonnacott must be rejected. This should be clear even without recourse to a formal, rigorous analysis. In the circumstances of the "pure" case just laid out, no trade diversion whatsoever would be possible, since there is no trade at all with countries other than the contemplated partner to the PTA. Even if some trade is admitted, it will be small — otherwise, the situation under consideration is of no particular interest. Thus, with no scope (or almost none) for trade diversion, the contemplated PTA — expected to lead to some trade creation and trade expansion — will be beneficial. This will be true in this case just as it is in any other in which the partner to the PTA is the major source of the home country's imports.

However, the second component of the proposition at hand will look quite different, particularly if interpreted — as perhaps it was meant to be — not as a statement within the second-best frame of analysis, but in the context of our analysis in Chap. 4, that is, in a comparison of a PTA with a *first-best* situation, which is a multilateral, uniform liberalization or, at the extreme, with free trade. In this context, this element of the proposition does seem to be warranted.

We shall address the issue at hand through a partial equilibrium analysis, represented diagrammatically in Figs. 7.1 and 7.2. In both, subscripts p, r, and w designate, respectively, the partner, the ROW, and the world as a whole (that is, the combination of these two components); and S, S′, and S″ designate, respectively, supply curves prior to the PTA (with a tariff t imposed on imports from both sources), with a PTA (the tariff is removed just on imports from the partner), and with free trade (the tariff is removed also on imports from ROW). D_H stands for the home country's demand for imports.

Figure 7.1 presents the "normal" case, where the partner is a major source (prior to the PTA) — we show it here as the exclusive source — of the home country's imports due to some "natural" advantage, rather than to "history." This is indicated by S_P lying to the right, to a sufficient extent,

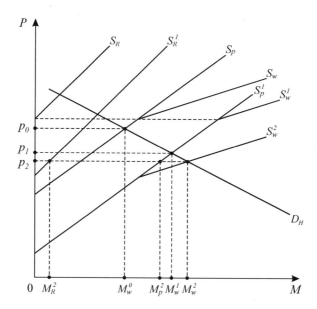

Figure 7.1:   A preferential agreement with a "natural advantage" partner.

of S_R, with S_W representing the (horizontal) aggregation of the two. Prior to the PTA, the equilibrium price is P_0, and the size of imports M_W^0 — all of it being provided by the (future) PTA partner. With the PTA, the tariff is removed on imports from the partner, and its supply curve (with the price axis standing for the home country's price[5]) becomes S_P', lying below the original supply curve S_P by the vertical distance of the tariff t. S_W' is the new aggregate, world supply of imports to the home country. The new equilibrium price becomes P^1, and the size of imports increases to M_W^1 (this is the source of the obvious benefit) — all of it originating, as before, from the partner country.

Now, moving to a universal free trade regime for the home country, the tariff is eliminated also on imports from ROW. Supply from this source increases from S_R to S_R', and the world supply from S_W' to S_W''. The equilibrium price falls to P^2. Imports increase from M_W^1 to M_W^2, and they are now provided by both sources: M_P^2 by the partner, and M_R^2 by ROW. The comparison of a PTA with free trade thus shows the following: with a PTA (notionally, the imposition of a tariff on ROW), the aggregate size of imports falls by M_W^2, M_W^1, this is a net change of a fall of imports from ROW (by the size M_R^2) and increase of imports from the partner (M_P^2, M_W^1). The welfare losses will not be shown in this diagram, but it should be clear that both trade contraction and trade dislocation are present.[6]

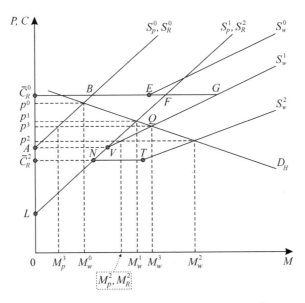

Figure 7.2: A preferential agreement with a "historical" partner.

Figure 7.2, to which we now move, represents the circumstances of a trade pattern determined by "history," rather than by inherent differences in (variable) costs of production. To make the distinction clear, we assume that in this case, variable costs are identical in the two potential sources of supply, so that marginal-cost schedules too are identical. The two supply curves, in turn, are the same — represented (with the existence of tariff t) by S_P^O, S_R^O. The ROW, however, has to make an investment to enter the home country's market and overcome the "historical" advantage of the partner. Hence, its level of minimum average costs, $\bar{C}_R^O$, is higher than that of the partner's (for convenience, we assume no fixed costs at all in production of the latter). Thus, the supply curve of ROW will start only at B, and go upwards from there. The aggregation of the two separate supply curves — the "world" supply curve to the home country — will thus be the broken line $ABES_W^O$. The equilibrium price will be P^0 — chosen to be below $\bar{C}_R^O$ — and the size of imports will be M_W^0, all of which is provided by the (future) partner. This is a clear case where the exclusivity (or, in less extreme circumstances, just the dominance) of a partner in providing the home country's imports owes nothing to "inherent" differences in costs, and everything to "history."

Now introduce a PTA, by which the tariff t is removed on imports from the partner. The latter's supply curve moves from S_P^0 to S_P^1, and the world supply curve — the (horizontal) aggregation of S_P^1 with S_R^0 — becomes $LFGS_W^1$. However, this aggregation is still not relevant, since all imports would still come from the partner country — and even more of it now. The equilibrium price will be lowered to P^1, and the size of imports will increase from M_W^0 to M_W^1 — all of it coming from the partner. No trade diversion is involved — only trade expansion — and the PTA must hence be welfare improving. So far, this is not different from the previous analysis of a "normal," comparative-advantage origin of trade patterns.

We move now to the situation of overall, nondiscriminating liberalization, i.e. (again, for simplicity) free trade. The tariff t is removed also on imports originating in ROW, and the latter's supply curve changes from S_R^0 to S_R^2. Its starting position, where the price equals the level of minimum average costs, also falls by the size of t — from $\bar{C}_R^O$ to $\bar{C}_R^2$. The new world, aggregated supply curve becomes $LNTS_W^2$. The sizes of movements have been selected so that imports from ROW now do become relevant, that is, so that the new equilibrium price exceeds the (new) level of minimum average costs in imports from ROW. With less than that, the outcome will be the same as with the PTA, and the overall liberalization will be irrelevant; that is, with free trade, imports will still be coming only from the (potential) PTA partner country. The new equilibrium price will be P^2, and the new aggregate size of imports M_W^2, now being provided from both the partner and ROW (by construction of the present case, the two sources will share equally in the aggregate, each exporting $M_P^2 = M_R^2$).

In comparing this outcome with that of a PTA, the difference is now substantial — due to the "step jumping" involved in moving between the two situations. The shift from free trade to a PTA will result in a large trade destruction (imports fall from M_W^2 to M_W^1), and, in particular, in a large size of trade dislocation — imports from ROW would fall from M_R^2 to nil. In comparing this outcome with that of Fig. 7.1 — the case of "comparative-advantage" origin of imports — we see that the impact of movement from free trade to a PTA are similar in sign: in both instances the changes involved would lower welfare. However, the outcome is more pronounced — that is, the welfare reduction is likely to be bigger — in the case in which the import pattern has been determined by "history." The proposition thus established is that, in comparison with a complete liberalization (a free trade situation), a PTA is more harmful, *ceteris paribus*, when concluded with a partner with which trade is due to "history."

Finally, let us go back to the second-best framework, and compare the outcomes of two alternative PTA tracks. One, which we have discussed thus far, is with the "partner"; the other is with the "other" country — the ROW.[7] Going back to Fig. 7.2, we recall that a PTA with the "partner" will result in the "world" supply curve moving from ABES_W^0 to LFGS_W^1, with equilibrium price P^1 and size of imports M_W^1 — all of it provided (as in the lack of a PTA) by the "partner." Consider now, instead of a PTA with this country, a PTA (again, a complete removal of the import tariff) with the other — the ROW. Designate this track, by superscript 3. It is now ROW's supply curve, rather than the partner's, which moves rightward to S_R^2 — with the "partner's" supply curve remaining at S_P^0, and the minimum average cost level in ROW's supply goes down (as under free trade) from the level $\bar{C}_R^0$ to $\bar{C}_R^2$. The new "world" supply curve now becomes $\bar{C}_R^2 \text{NVS}_W^1$. The new equilibrium position becomes Q, with price P^3, and the size of imports increases from M_W^0 to M_W^3, with M_P^3 being provided by the partner and M_R^3 by ROW.

This outcome is clearly superior to that of a PTA with the "partner." The volume of imports is larger — hence a larger size of trade creation. Trade diversion does take place now: imports from the "partner" fall from M_W^0 (with no PTA) to M_P^3. However, in this instance, trade diversion is beneficial: it diverts trade toward a cheaper source of imports. This unconventional outcome is due to the fact that the preferential treatment accorded to ROW serves to enable that country to break the barrier "history" has created, and join the market as a supplier of imports to the home country.

This is an interesting inference — and one which is probably not entirely obvious intuitively. The analysis carried out here demonstrates that a PTA with a "nontraditional" trade partner, although inferior to universal free trade, is superior to both the continued existence of overall, nondiscriminatory restrictions and to the conclusion of a PTA with a "traditional" trade partner. *Ceteris paribus* — on these grounds alone — if a PTA is contemplated by the home country, a "nontraditional" trade partner will be a better candidate for it.[8]

General Liberalization and a PTA: The Order of Introduction

Once the possibility that past trade patterns affect present (and future) geographic composition of trade is admitted, the *order* of introduction of policies becomes relevant. Specifically, assuming that a general, nondiscriminatory trade liberalization is eventually achieved, the interim introduction of a PTA — a "two-step" implementation of a general liberalization — may have a long-term consequence.

This is analyzed with the aid of Fig. 7.3, which is similar in nature to those used in the previous section. In this figure, S_P^0 and S_R^0 represent the tariff-ridden supply curves of M to the home country of, respectively, the "partner" to the (future) PTA and the ROW; the two are taken as equal — dissimilarity between the two, as will be indicated later, will either reinforce or weaken the probability of the outcome addressed here. The "world" supply curve, S_W^0, is the (horizontal) aggregation of the two separate supply curves. At this initial position, the equilibrium price is P^0; and the equilibrium size of imports is M^0, shared equally by the two exporting countries.

Now introduce a PTA with the "partner," by which the tariff (at the level AF) is eliminated — with the tariff on imports from ROW remaining intact. The partner's supply curve (with the price axis representing the *home* price) moves to the right, becoming S_P^1. At any price below OA, this is also the "world" supply curve, since nothing will be offered then by ROW. As drawn here, the new equilibrium price, P', is indeed within

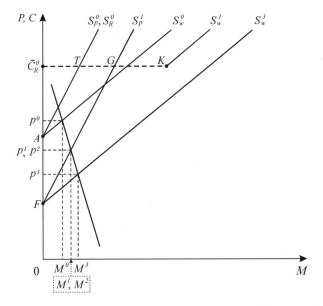

Figure 7.3: The order of introduction of a multilateral liberalization and a PTA.

this range. Imports will increase to M^1, all of it now supplied by the "partner," with imports of ROW disappearing completely. Now, a crucial (in the present context) assumption is made, namely this disappearance creates some (fixed) costs to any future re-appearance of exports from ROW to the home country, requiring some investment (of the nature discussed earlier) for such re-introduction. This element of fixed costs raises (as in our earlier analysis) the level of minimum average costs by the size $A\bar{C}_R^1$. $\bar{C}_R^1$ thus becomes the lowest price at which any exports from ROW will be forthcoming: ROW's supply curve becomes $\bar{C}_R^1 TS_R^0$, and the "world" supply — $FGKS_W^1$.

At this moment (*after* the disappearance of ROW's exports and liquidation of the past investment in it), introduce a *full* liberalization, eliminating the geographic discrimination: the tariff is fully removed also on imports from ROW. The latter's supply curve shifts to the right to the same extent as the earlier shift of the "partner's" supply; however, it is still bound from below by the level $\bar{C}_R^1$. That is, ROW's supply now becomes $\bar{C}_R^1 GS_P^1$. The "world" supply (not shown) also moves to the right, at the range above $\bar{C}_R^1$. However, this — as drawn here — is immaterial: the equilibrium price and quantity of imports remain unchanged ($P^2 = P^1$, $M^2 = M^1$) since nothing has changed in the *relevant range*. We thus get a result by which the general liberalization becomes irrelevant: the ROW stays excluded from the home country's market, even though it is no longer discriminated against.

The outcome is quite different with a general liberalization, which has *not* been preceded by a PTA, that is, where the process does not incorporate a stage in which geographic discrimination is involved. In Fig. 7.3, starting from general restriction and moving straight to general liberalization, the world supply curve will become the straight line FS^3_W. P^3 will be the equilibrium price, and M^3 will be the equilibrium size of imports — shared equally, as under a universal restriction, between the "partner" and ROW. This is evidently a superior outcome, for the home country, in comparison with the two-step liberalization. A larger amount of imports materializes at a lower price.

Thus, admitting the possibility of the long-term impact of a PTA through the elimination of some trade flows and the cost involved in restarting them, we get an inference indicating that the introduction of a stage of geographic discrimination into the process of liberalization may lead to an inferior outcome, even beyond the transition — beyond, that is, the completion of a universal liberalization. This is, evidently, a *possible* outcome, not an inevitable one. Its likelihood — as may be gathered by looking at Fig. 7.3 — will be higher the lower the home country's elasticity of demand for imports: the lower this elasticity, the larger will be the price fall following the PTA, and thus the likelihood of imports from ROW being driven out. Also, recalling that we have assumed so far two equal trading partners, it should be easy to see how changing this assumption will affect the outcome. Thus, for instance, if the "partner" were a cheaper producer of imports, or if it were a larger economy, so that its supply curve *without discrimination* would lie further to the right of that of ROW, the outcome inferred here would become *more probable* (although of *lesser consequence*), and vice versa.

Notes

1. A recent empirical analysis of the role of "history" in determining trade patterns is conducted in Eichengreen and Irwin (1998) — where references to earlier contributions may also be found. The specific role of a history of colonial relationships is analyzed extensively in Kleiman (1976).
2. See Wonnacott (1998). This was a comment on the contribution of Eichengreen and Irwin (1998).

3. Separation of the proposition into two parts and indication by small roman numerals are added by the present author.

4. This is not a crucial assumption: the analysis, and its inferences, will be basically similar when some imports from the "third" country exist even without the required investment. However, the "pure" case makes the analysis better focused.

5. Most often, the analysis would be technically less cumbersome if the *supplier's* price were to be represented on this axis, and tariff changes shown through movements of the demand curve. This is, however, not feasible when a discriminatory policy is practiced — different tariffs apply to different source of supply.

6. See Chap. 4 for the terms.

7. To avoid confusion — may be, at the expense of creating confusion in a different way — we shall refer in this comparison too to the country with "historic" trade relations with the home country as the "partner," though the contemplated PTA in one of the alternatives is with the *other* country, to which we refer as the ROW.

8. This is a somewhat different proposition from the one suggested by Wonnacott, with which we opened the discussion of the present chapter. However, in spirit, the two are similar.

References

Eichengreen, B and Irwin, D A (1998). The role of history in bilateral trade flows. In *The Regionalization of the World Economy*, Frankel, J A (ed.), pp. 33–57. Chicago: University of Chicago Press.

Kleiman, E (1976). Trade and the decline of colonialism. *Economic Journal*, 86, 450–480.

Wonnacott, P (1998). The role of history in bilateral trade flows: Comment. In *The Regionalization of the World Economy*, Frankel, J A (ed.), pp. 59–62.

Chapter 8

The Impact of Liberalization on Trade Structure

Issue and Manifestations

The Issue

It is commonly accepted that a sustainable trade liberalization should lead to the expansion of the country's foreign trade, both its imports and exports, and both in absolute levels and as proportions of the country's product. The effect of liberalization on trade *structure*, however, is probably of no lesser consequence than its impact on *size*: it should be of crucial importance in assessing some salient outcomes of trade liberalization. One is the implication of liberalization for the degree of the liberalizing economy's dependence on foreign markets: while trade expansion implies a stronger dependence, trade diversification — if that happens — would tend to lower it. Of at least equal importance is the impact of increased integration of the economy in the world market on employment, or on inequality in income distribution. Such issues are certainly related to the degree to which trade expands only in very few sectors or, to the contrary, spreads over a variety of the economy's activities. Another issue is the extent to which trade liberalization encourages new fields of activity and intensifies entrepreneurship rather than increasing rents in old-established branches of production. Still another issue, raised recently in the literature, is the welfare impact of an increased range of traded goods.[1]

This aspect of the outcome of trade liberalization — its impact on trade structure — has not attracted much attention as a subject of empirical investigation.[2] It made an appearance, once in a while, as one of the issues in individual country studies, but has not benefited from a comparative, multi-country study.[3] The present chapter intends to provide such a wide-scale investigation.

The basic *a priori* hypothesis of this study is that trade liberalization should change the commodity structure of trade.[4] Analytically, this follows very easily, even without resort to any elaborate model. Any relaxation of restrictions on trade — be they man-made like tariffs, or "natural" like transportation costs — should expand the *range* of traded goods (this point has been elaborated in the discussion of Chapter 6). The exception would be a case in which the removal of restrictions is selective in a certain direction, being applied strongly to (imported or exported) goods which are particularly heavily traded prior to liberalization. The general experience indicates the opposite: goods that are lightly traded (or not at all) are normally subject — not incidentally, of course — to higher trade barriers and are thus likely to be the goods on which trade liberalization falls most.

Manifestations of Structural Change

Structural changes may, obviously, have almost infinite dimensions. Here we select four salient attributes, or manifestations, which seem to be most relevant to the issue at hand. Of these, two are overall descriptions of structure, with no reference to the specific nature of traded goods, whereas the other two describe the changing shares of goods of certain attributes.

(i) *The extent of commodity diversification.* This relates, of course, directly to the presumption that trade liberalization should expand the range of traded goods. The extent of commodity diversification — or its inverse commodity concentration — is known empirically to differ more, among countries, in exports than in imports. Hence, changes in it may presumably be larger in export than in import flows. Yet, since expanding the range of traded goods should be expressed in both imports and exports, we should look at both flows.

(ii) Another manifestation of a changed structure, still without a specific content, is the degree of *similarity* of the trade structure following liberalization to that preceding it. The stronger the impact of liberalization on the commodity structure of trade, the less similar to each other should be the structures of trade prior to and following liberalization. Once more, this expectation would seem to be particularly relevant to the export trade.[5]

We now move to the two indices that indicate structural changes of a specific content.

(iii) *The share of nonprimary goods.* Suppose trade barriers are uniform (and, of course, effective). It should be expected that the barrier is less restrictive the larger is the intensity of comparative advantage of the economy in the good on hand (this is clearly the case when the barrier is prohibitive), and this advantage would most often be strongest where it is determined by natural forces, i.e., in primary goods. This, again, should hold for both exports and imports. Hence, the relaxation of barriers should lead to greater trade expansion in nonprimary goods, that is, their share should increase in both exports and imports flow. This should *a fortiori* be the case when the (relaxed) trade barriers are nonuniform, being imposed at higher levels when comparative advantage is lowest — as is most often the case.

(iv) Of a somewhat different nature would be the exploration of what I have termed the income level of trade, that is, of the (average) income level of countries which export, or import, the goods in the trade of which the economy concerned tends to specialize. Once more, this would *a priori* seem to be particularly relevant to the flow of exports. The liberalizing countries that will be investigated here are commonly low-income or, at best, middle-income economies. Earlier observations show — this should not be a surprise — that such economies also export, by and large, goods, which are commonly exported by other lower-income countries (this will be seen again in the present study). Following liberalization and expanded trade, does the liberalizing economy move toward trading more of the goods, which tend to be traded by higher income economies?

Method

Indicators of Structural Changes: Definition of Indices

The variables just surveyed, of a structural change, will each be represented by an index (or coefficient). Definitions of these indexes are presented below. The symbols used in each index derive from the following list of symbols:

X_{ij} = Exports of good i by country j
$X_{.j}$ = Total exports of country j
X_i = World exports of good i
M_{ij} = Total imports of country j
$M_{.j}$ = World imports of good i
$\bar{Y}_j$ = Per-capita income of country j
$\bar{Y}_u$ = Per-capita US income
$\hat{y}_j$ = $\bar{Y}_j/\bar{Y}_u$.

(i) *Commodity diversification.* The extent of commodity diversification is gathered by observing its complement, namely, by an index of commodity concentration.[6] This index will be the Gini–Hirschman coefficient of concentration, C_j.

For exports, this is defined as

$$C_{jx} = \sqrt{\sum_i \left(\frac{X_{ij}}{X_{\cdot j}} \right)^2}.$$

And similarly, for imports,

$$C_{jm} = \sqrt{\sum_i \left(\frac{M_{ij}}{M_{\cdot j}} \right)^2}.$$

This index ranges from zero — its size when the aggregate flow consists of an infinitely large number of goods, each of infinitely small share in the aggregate — to unity — its value when the aggregate trade flow consists of a single good.

(ii) *Dissimilarity of trade flows.* The index of dissimilarity, designated by D, is applied here for changes over time; however, it could obviously address, *mutates mutandis*, geographical comparisons.[7] It compares point 1, the end of a period, with a starting point 0. Starting with exports, the index is defined, for country j, as

$$D_{jx} = \frac{\sum_i |x^1_{ij} - x^0_{ij}|}{2},$$

where $x_{ij} = \frac{X_{ij}}{X_{\cdot j}}$, $|\ldots|$ indicates *absolute* size (i.e., regardless of sign), and superscripts 0, 1, indicate values for, respectively, periods 0 and 1. Similarly, for imports

$$D_{jm} = \frac{\sum_i |m^1_{ij} - m^0_{ij}|}{2}.$$

The index will range potentially from zero to unity. It would be zero when absolutely no structural change takes place between the two points of time: the shares of individual goods in the aggregate flows are identical in the two points. The index will be unity, on the other extreme, with a complete transformation, that is, when no good traded at one point of time is also traded at the other.

(iii) *The share of nonprimary goods in trade.* The classification of goods into "primaries" and "nonprimaries" used here is presented in Table 8.14.

The share of nonprimaries in the aggregate trade flow of country j is, for exports,

$$S_{jx} = \sum_f \frac{X_{nj}}{X_{\cdot j}},$$

where X_{nj} are country j's exports of each nonprimary good. Similarly, for imports,

$$S_{jm} = \sum_f \frac{M_{fj}}{M_{\cdot j}}.$$

(iv) *The income level of trade.* This index is defined in two stages: first, the income level of any traded good is estimated. Then, based on it, the income level of a country's trade is derived.[8] Take first, again, *exports.*

(1) *The income level of the exports of a good.* For any good i, at a specified period, this measure is a weighted average of the incomes of the exporting countries. Weights are assigned by the shares of countries in world exports of the good, and per capita incomes are specified as a ratio of US (per capita) income.

Thus, $\hat{Y}_{ix}$ the income level of exports of good i is

$$\hat{Y}_{ix} = \sum_j \hat{y}_j \frac{X_{ij}}{X_{iw}},$$

where $\hat{Y}_j$ is the per capita income level of country j, X_{ij} the (as before) exports of good i by country j, and X_{iw} the world exports of good i.

(2) *The income level of a country's exports.* This is defined as the weighted average of the income levels of the goods which the country exports, with weights determined by the share of each good in country j's aggregate exports. Thus, this index for exports Y_{jx} is

$$Y_{jx} = \sum_i \hat{Y}_{ix} \frac{X_{ij}}{X_{\cdot j}}.$$

The indices for imports are defined, *mutatis mutandis*, in a parallel manner. The index of a country's income level of a trade flow ranges, potentially, from the (relative) income level of the poorest to that of the richest countries. If the latter is the US — as would be most often approximately true — the upper bound of the index is *unity*.

Liberalizing Countries and Liberalization Episodes

The investigation will address, in principle, all countries in which some significant trade liberalization took place since the 1960s and was sustained for at least several years (it thus does not refer to the European post-war liberalization experience).[9] Using evidence available in the literature of the last 15–20 years, "liberalization episodes" have been identified in each of the liberalizing economies. In two countries — Israel and Sri Lanka — two episodes have been defined in each, whereas the majority of countries are represented by just a single episode. For each such episode, a span of years (most often 3, but ranging all the way to 8) is identified as the period in which the policy was introduced and mostly implemented. The countries and episodes identified are provided in Table 8.1.

Table 8.1:   Episodes of liberalization.

Country	Years of implementation
Argentina	1989–1991
Bolivia	1985–1990
Brazil	1990–1994
Chile	1974–1981
Colombia	1989–1991
Ecuador	1990–1992
India	1991–1995
Indonesia	1966–1972
Israel I	1966–1968
Israel II	1992–1994
Mexico	1985–1989
New Zealand	1982–1984
Peru	1990–1991
Philippines	1962–1965
Singapore	1966–1972
Spain	1977–1980
Sri Lanka I	1977–1979
Sri Lanka II	1989–1990
Thailand	1986–1988
Turkey	1980–1984
Uruguay	1989–1991

Method of Analysis

Most of the inferences of the study will be drawn through observations of changes of trade structures between points of time. These points are determined as follows.

First, each "point of time" will be defined here as the average of three years. This, rather than the adoption of a single year as a "point," is done in order to diminish the likelihood of confusing accidental, very short-term developments with those of a longer-term nature. In particular, it should help, partly at least, to avoid the confusion of price movements with those of changes of real magnitudes: it is the latter which must be the object of a study like the present one.

Second, the period of implementation of liberalization (e.g., 1989–1991 in Argentina) is abstracted from altogether. The "base" period with which comparisons are made will thus be the point just prior to the introduction of liberalization (e.g., 1986–1988 in Argentina).

Third, following this, a point distant five years from the end of the implementation of liberalization (e.g., in Argentina, the average of the period 1996–1998) is defined as the "post-liberalization" period (an earlier point may be adopted for recent liberalizations, where the definition at hand would require data which are not yet available). Observation of the changes from the "base" to the "post-liberalization" period will be the essential subject matter of the study. Selecting this point is necessarily an arbitrary decision. It is presumed that a period of five–seven years is long enough for the more fundamental impact of the liberalization policy to show up. Since the length of the period of implementation of liberalization varies from one experience to another, so must be the time difference between the "base" and the "post-liberalization" periods. However, it may be hoped that even in the extreme cases, in which this distance amounts to a dozen years, it is not long enough to allow the impact of other factors, not related to liberalization, to dominate.

Finally, a "past" point of time is defined, to be able to compare the movements following liberalization with movements which preceded it, and see whether the two differ substantially from each other. The "past" period is determined so that it is equi-distant from the base period as the post-liberalization period is, but in the opposite direction (in the case of Argentina, the past period will be 1976–1978, being equi-distant from the base period 1986–1988 as the post-liberalization period 1996–1998 is). In the case selected for illustration, Argentina, this is summed up in the following table.

Past period	Base period	Liberalization period	Post-liberalization period
1976–1978	1986–1988	1989–1991	1996–1998

The inferences of the study will thus be based on, first, the observation of changes from the base period to the post-liberalization period, *per se*; then, on comparing these observations with the changes prior to liberalization, that is, from the past to the base periods.

I have entertained the idea of supporting the time-period analysis by a cross-section comparison, that is, by contrasting the experiences following liberalization with those of nonliberalizing countries over roughly the same chronological periods. Unfortunately (just for this purpose!) the size of the group of nonliberalizers is small: excluding countries for which appropriate data are absent or in which exports of oil are a major component, only seven such countries were identified: El Salvador, Guatemala, Kenya, Malawi, Morocco, Tunisia, and Zimbabwe. Thus, a comparison with such a small group would be of little significance. Nevertheless, parallel estimates of performance were made for these countries (analyzing changes between 1984–1986 and 1994–1996) contrasting this performance with that of the liberalizing countries following liberalization. The inferences yielded are often, but not always, similar to those of the time-series analysis. In view of the very limited significance of such exercise, though, its inferences are not presented here.

Data

Data on trade structure are classified through the SITC at the three-digit level. The data are taken from COMTRADE. This is also the source for the data on income levels of countries.

Of special concern is trade in oil and oil products. Oil is, obviously, a "temperamental" product. The real size of its trade may vary frequently due to reasons that have little to do with "normal" economic responses, and, probably of even more importance, the recorded amount of trade is heavily determined by substantial fluctuations of price. Hence, observations of recorded trade structures, which include trade in oil, would tend to suffer from distortions if the target is — as in the present study — finding inferences about responses to policy changes. This might be true also for several other commodities; however, none is nearly as important as oil. The distortion introduced by the inclusion of oil would also be present when *imports* are observed; however, it is much smaller than that which must exist in observations of *export* flows. For this reason, the export of oil and its products is excluded here altogether. Following such decision, it would make little sense to include countries in which oil exports are a major component of the aggregate. On these grounds, Venezuela is excluded from the study.

Findings

The basic findings of the study are presented in a series of tables in Tables 8.4–8.13. This is a set of 10 tables, which describe five variables — each, separately, for exports and for imports. The variables are as follows: (i) the share of trade (exports or imports) in GDP; (ii) the commodity concentration of trade (exports or imports); (iii) the index of dissimilarity of trade structures (exports or imports); (iv) the share of nonprimary goods in trade (exports or imports); and (v) the income level of trade (exports or imports). For each variable, the following findings are provided: (i) its level in the "past," comparator period (denoted by "A"); (ii) its level in the "base" period on the eve of liberalization (a period denoted by "B"); (iii) its level in the "post-liberalization" period (denoted by "C"); (iv) the ratio of the level of the variable in the base period ("B") to its level in the past period ("A"); (v) similarly, the ratio of the level following liberalization (in "C") to that found on the eve of liberalization (in "B"); and (vi) finally, the ratio of the latter ratio (v) to its predecessor (iv). The pattern of presentation differs somewhat in the table referring to the dissimilarity index, due to the nature of this measure (which in itself refers to *changes*, rather than to levels). The following discussion will summarize these findings, basing these summaries on some elementary manipulations of the data.

Trade Expansion

To start with, Tables 8.4 and 8.5 present the performance of trade (exports and imports) following liberalization. This performance, by itself, is not part of the subject matter of the present study — which addresses, we recall, the *structure* of trade rather than its size. However, the existence and intensity of trade expansion is important as an indication of the extent to which trade liberalization was indeed effective. Trade expansion is obviously not a perfect, or complete, indicator of effectiveness; however, it is probably the best single yardstick, which could be employed in a multi-country study. Put differently: one may assume, on *a priori* grounds, that the prevalence of changes in trade structure should be related to the degree of trade expansion. This hypothesis will in fact be tested here on various occasions.

It appears that trade has indeed commonly expanded strongly following liberalization. In exports, expansion appears in sixteen out of twenty-one episodes; in imports, even more emphatically, this applies to all but two episodes. On average, the export share in GDP following liberalization was over 70 percent higher than its level prior to liberalization, with a median ratio of expansion of 40 percent. In imports, the average expansion was by 87 percent, and the median — 73 percent. In the movements prior to liberalization, on the other hand, no such trade expansion took place at all: in both exports and imports, declines slightly outnumbered increase; on average, imports failed to increase — they even declined somewhat. It may thus be safely concluded that the liberalization episodes with which the findings of this study are engaged were indeed effective in leading to strong expansion of trade (as a ratio to the economy's income).

The Degree of Commodity Concentration

In examining changes in commodity concentration, it is *a priori* the *exports* trade flow, which should look as the more promising observation. This follows from the simple fact that to start with, differences among countries and changes over time are more frequent and intensive in export than in import flows: the latter is more uniformly low and has commonly been so for many years.

It appears, from Table 8.6, that commodity concentration of *exports* did, indeed, decline as a rule following liberalization: this was true in 16 out of the 21 observations. However, this trend of decline is only roughly similar to the one observed in the comparator period prior to liberalization. By this evidence, a conclusion that liberalization *per se* contributed to a decline of commodity concentration would not be warranted. A more important observation, however, is the following. It appears that commodity concentration of exports tended emphatically to decline, following liberalization, where it was particularly high on the eve of liberalization. This is true both in itself and in comparison with developments in the comparator, pre-liberalization period. Outstanding cases are those of Chile, Indonesia,

Bolivia, or Colombia. If one looks at the five countries with the highest initial coefficients of concentration, the average ratio of decline of the coefficient, following liberalization, would be by 35 percent, whereas in the other 16 instances, the average coefficient remained practically unchanged (an average decline of 2 percent). Another representation of this relationship is the (Spearman) rank-correlation coefficient between the initial level of the coefficient and the extent of its decline, following liberalization, which amounts to 0.644 (significant at practically any desired level). This finding should in fact not be surprising. It states that commodity concentration of exports declined indeed, following liberalization, where it counted, that is, where it was high to start with.

In *imports*, in which commodity concentration was commonly much lower than in exports, it appears from Table 8.7 that not much happened following liberalization — as might have been expected. It is still true, though, that in countries in which import concentration was particularly high on the eve of liberalization, it did tend to decline following liberalization. Thus, on average for the five countries with the highest pre-liberalization concentration (Indonesia, Sri Lanka, Uruguay, Brazil, and Spain), the coefficient of concentration declined by 36 percent, whereas in the other 16 cases, no such tendency is observed (the average coefficient increased by less than 3 percent — that is, remained practically unchanged).

Dissimilarity in Structures of Trade Flows

Like its predecessor, the coefficient of concentration, the index of dissimilarity of a trade flow (in comparisons at different points of time) is a synthetic representation of change, with no reference to the commodity specifics of such change, and, again like its predecessor, it has no inherent meaning or interpretation except in a comparative context. Thus, Tables 8.8 and 8.9 present the dissimilarity index of exports and imports in the movement from the base point, on the eve of liberalization, to the post-liberalization point, and contracts it with the index of dissimilarity in the comparator movement — that is, from the "past," pre-liberalization point to the "base" point on the eve of liberalization.

In both exports and imports, it appears the index of dissimilarity tended to increase following liberalization; however, the pattern of this change was different in the two trade flows. In exports, dissimilarity increased dramatically in a few countries (Indonesia, Bolivia, the Philippines, and Chile). In the rest — most of the group — changes were more moderate, and no trend appears (the average index for these 16 countries is roughly the same in the two movements). In imports, on the other hand, only a single country (Indonesia) shows a remarkable increase in dissimilarity following liberalization. However, a trend does appear for the group as a whole. In 14 out of the 20 observations, the index of dissimilarity increased; on average, it was over 20 percent higher than in the period preceding liberalization; and the median level of the index, too, was 16 percent higher in the post-liberalization change.

The Share of Nonprimary Goods in Trade

The earlier two indices — the coefficient of commodity concentration and the index of dissimilarity in the structures of trade flows — addressed changes in structure in an index form, with no reference to the specific content of a trade flow. We now move, on the other hand, to two indicators, which focus on the specific commodity content of trade. The first of these is the share of nonprimary goods in trade, which is presented in Table 8.10 and 8.11.

Paying attention, first, to *exports*, it appears very clearly that the share at hand increased, often substantially, following liberalization. In only 4 instances out of 21 observations did this share decline, whereas in 16 instances it increased (in one case there was no change). On average, this share increased by as much as nearly 60 percent (the median level increased by close to 30 percent). In the earlier, comparator period too, the share of nonprimary goods tended to increase; however, this tendency was substantially weaker. Increases outnumbered declines then by 12 to 8 (there are only 20 observations for this period). The average share increased by close to 30 percent in this period (in comparison to twice as much in the period following liberalization); the median level, though, increased about as much in the comparator period as it did following liberalization. Altogether, the weight of the evidence clearly indicates an expansion of the share of nonprimary goods in aggregate exports following liberalization.

In *imports*, the conclusion is similar, and the evidence is as compelling. Once more, the share at hand increased in 17 instances, declining in only 4 of the 21 observations. On average, this share increased by 26 percent, and the median — by 23 percent. That is, the increase in the share was smaller, but more evenly spread, than in exports. The increase of the share in imports looks as remarkable as in exports when placed in comparison with developments in the earlier, comparator, period. In the latter, the share increased about as often as it declined — in 9 out of 20 observations. On average, it remained practically unchanged; so, too, did its median level. Thus, the share at hand increased more (often substantially so) in the post-liberalization period than in the comparator period in 15 out of 20 observations (on average, the excess of one increase over the other was by 36 percent). The evidence thus clearly indicates a substantial increase in the share of nonprimary goods in imports following liberalization.

The Income Level of Trade

We recall that the index of the income level of trade indicates the extent to which a country trades in goods which are traded by richer or poorer countries. This applies, evidently, also to the *change* in the index. Thus, for instance, an increased level of the income level of exports, from one period to the next, indicates a shift in the country's exports toward goods exported by richer countries.

Looking first, in Table 8.12, at the index of income level of *exports*, it appears that a general shift did indeed take place, following liberalization, toward goods exported by higher-income economies. Only in 2 instances out of 19 did the index decline; in one of these (Peru) the change was minute; and in the other (Philippines) it was also moderate. On average, the index increased by about 9 percent: this is substantial, in view of the fact that the index of countries with very high level of income level of exports exceeds the average of the group at hand only by a range of some 40 percent.[10]

In the comparator, pre-liberalization period this trend is also evident, but it is somewhat weaker. The index declined in 4 out of the 19 observations, though in two of these the decline was minimal (by 1 percent). The average index increased by 6 percent (in comparison with a 9.1 percent increase following liberalization). Thus, a somewhat stronger tendency of increase of the index of income level of exports is apparent, following liberalization; however, the difference from the earlier period is only moderate. It should be noted that for the *world* as a whole, the average level of the index remained practically unchanged, during the decade roughly corresponding to most post-liberalization periods. That is, the increased income level of the group of liberalizing countries does *not* follow from the world as a whole moving to export goods characterized by a higher-income level. However, the fact that in the countries at hand income level of exports tended to increase also prior to liberalization, although less than following it, would indicate that the income level performance is at least partly due to some attributes of the group, which are not revealed in this study, and only partly due to the impact of liberalization.

Parenthetically, it may be noted that a strong relationship exists, as may be expected (although this is not logically inevitable) between a country's per capita income level, at any point of time, and the income level of its exports: the Spearman rank-correlation coefficient of the two, for a very large number of observations, is over 0.700. It may thus be guessed that the general increase in income level of exports following liberalization is associated with increased levels of the per capita incomes of the countries concerned. However, being outside the focus of the present study, this hypothesis has not been tested here.

A very similar pattern appears, from the findings presented in Table 8.13, when the income level of *imports* is observed, though this might have been less expected by *a priori* guesses. Most remarkably, in *all* 21 observations in the table — with no single exception — the income level of imports increased following liberalization. On average, the index shows an increase of about 6 percent. Moreover — and here this change seems to be even more convincing than in the case of exports — no similar increase appears to have taken place prior to liberalization. In the pre-liberalization, comparator period the index did increase in the majority of cases, but it failed to do so in one third of the cases — 7 out of 21; and the average level of the index increased by a mere 1.3 percent.

As might have been expected from the observation of a group of countries which, by and large, tend to be lower-income economies, the income level of imports tends to be *higher* than that of exports: on the eve of liberalization: this is true for *all* 20 observations for which findings are available for both exports and imports. That is, these economies all tend to import goods characterized by being exported by high-income countries, in contrast with exporting goods, which largely originate from low-income economies. Following liberalization we noted, the income levels of both imports and exports tended to rise; however, the gap between the two remains. The rise of the income level of imports is, apparently, another consequence of an increased income level of the economy following liberalization.

Inter-Relationships of Manifestations of Change

Since the indices, or measurements, assessing movements all address the changing structures of trade flows, it might be expected that at least some of them should be related to each other. This expectation is tested here through the estimates of Spearman rank-correlation coefficients between any pair of variables. Five variables are involved: the four indices used here to observe structural changes — the extent of commodity concentration, the dissimilarity of structures, the share on nonprimary goods in aggregate trade, and the income level of a trade flow, and the intensity of expansion of trade (represented by its share in GDP), to which presumably the change in trade structure should be related. These coefficients are presented in Table 8.1, for exports, and in Table 8.2, for imports.

Starting with exports, observe first their expansion (i.e., the change in the ratio of exports to GDP). The intensity of indications of changing structure should be expected to be positively associated with it. This appears indeed to be the case for the measure of dissimilarity of export structures before and after liberalization (a particularly strong association) and for the increase in the share of nonprimary goods in exports. No such relationship is found for the change in commodity concentration — as might indeed have been expected from the earlier discussion of this measure, and, perhaps more surprisingly, for the change in the country's income level of exports.

Table 8.2: Rank correlation of changes in coefficients: Exports.[a]

	Share of exports in GDP (1)	Coefficient of commodity concentration (2)	Index of dissimilarity (3)	Share of nonprimary exports (4)	Income level of exports (5)
1. Share of exports in GDP	—				
2. Coefficient of commodity concentration	0.149	—			
3. Index of dissimilarity	**0.628**	**0.515**	—		
4. Share of nonprimary exports	**0.499**	**0.586**	**0.371**	—	
5. Income level of exports	0.243	0.194	0.341	0.321	—

[a]The number of observations, both here and in Table 8.3, is either 20 or 21. For 20 observations, the 0.05 level of significance is reached with a coefficient of 0.377; and the 0.01 level — with a coefficient of 0.534. Coefficients with (at least) the 0.05 level of significance are indicated in the table by a **bold** type.

The increased share of nonprimary exports is associated, in addition, quite strongly with the reduction of commodity concentration; this should be less evident on *a priori* grounds. It is also associated, as might have been guessed, with the intensity of dissimilarity of export structures prior to liberalization and following it. Finally, a positive association exists between this dissimilarity and the extent of decline of commodity concentration of exports.

On the other hand, no association is found between the extent of increase of the income level of exports and either the intensity of expansion of exports — and this would probably not agree with prior expectations, or with the decline of commodity concentration. A weak association (significance of the rank correlation coefficients just weaker than the 0.05 level) is found between this variable (the income level) and either the intensity of dissimilarity or, as might indeed be expected, the increasing share of nonprimary goods in exports (Table 8.3).

Turning to *imports*, it appears that some of the inter-relationships of performance variables are similar to those revealed when exports were observed; but not all. As in exports, the index of dissimilarity of import structures is clearly associated with the intensity of expansion of imports (as a share of the GDP); however, somewhat surprisingly, the share of nonprimary imports in the aggregate does *not* seem to be related to the expansion of aggregate imports. Similar to exports, again, the increased share of nonprimary imports is seen to be clearly related to the lowering

Table 8.3:　Rank correlation of changes in coefficients: Imports.

	Share of imports in GDP (1)	Coefficient of commodity concentration (2)	Index of dissimilarity (3)	Share of nonprimary imports (4)	Income level of imports (5)
1. Share of imports in GDP	—				
2. Coefficient of commodity concentration	0.224	—			
3. Index of dissimilarity	**0.526**	0.143	—		
4. Share of nonprimary imports	0.175	**0.531**	0.345	—	
5. Income level of imports	**0.449**	−0.96	0.182	**0.445**	—

degree of commodity concentration of imports. The relationship of the share of nonprimary goods to the degree of dissimilarity of import structure is just on the verge of the 0.05 level of significance. Other significant inter-relationships are those of the index of income level of imports to the expansion of aggregate imports, and, as might have been presumed beforehand, to the share of nonprimary goods in aggregate imports.

Conclusions and Further Research

A priori expectations about the impact of trade liberalization on the structural attributes of trade flows are, by and large, borne out by the findings of this study. The evidence is always there, though it is sometimes less than overwhelming (as might have actually been expected in a study of only 21 observations). Specifically, it is indicated that:

- Trade liberalization is followed by an increased range of traded goods, whether in exports or, of lesser importance, in imports. This is pointed out by the measure of commodity concentration of trade, which tends to fall after liberalization. However, this tendency exists almost only where the trade flow exhibits intensive commodity concentration to start with, that is, prior to the introduction of a liberalization policy.
- Changes in the commodity structure of trade, as indicated by the extent of dissimilarity between the structures prior to and following liberalization, are widespread.
- Most of the liberalization policies covered here were undertaken by less-developed (though not least developed) economies. It appears that following liberalization the trade flows of these economies tended to display attributes more similar to those of richer countries. This is manifested in increased shares of trade (exports and imports) in nonprimary goods — hence higher shares of final (or semi-manufactured) goods — and, in a less specific way, in increased indices of income level of trade, that is, in a tendency to trade more in goods in which richer countries specialize.

All these outcomes tend to increase in intensity with the extent of expansion of trade (relative to income) following liberalization. In other words, the impact of trade liberalization on trade structure depends distinctly on the effectiveness of the former.

The pattern of structural changes of trade, following liberalization, carries a variety of inferences. It would imply, for instance, a lesser impact of a country's trade expansion (mainly its exports) on world prices; hence, a smaller deterioration of its terms of trade following such expansion. In a similar way, it will signify a lesser vulnerability to disturbances in the outside world — partly, at least, offsetting the stronger vulnerability and higher dependence, involved in the trade expansion itself. In the impact of liberalization on the domestic economy, such change in structure would imply influences on employment, which are more widespread, among sectors and activities, rather than having an incidence only on a narrow segment of the economy. Similarly, the push given to expanding activities should carry, with the structural changes, a higher likelihood of real expansion rather than just an increase of rent in old-established activities. Finally, as theory indicates it would mean a stronger impact of trade liberalization on an increased level of welfare.

This study should be viewed as providing some tentative conclusions, rather than firm answers. Its inferences should be supported — or refuted — by further research. Beside the impact of relying, at the end, on only a limited range of experiences, some deficiencies of the present analysis should be obvious. For one, as has been noted earlier, trade structures are observed here when shares of goods in aggregate trade flows are recorded in *money* values, whereas what should actually be looked for are shares of *real* flows, which would generally be different due to changes in relative prices of traded goods. Abstraction from price changes would require a massive work, which would be feasible in studies of single countries, or of a small group of countries, rather than in a more universal study.

Related to it is the impact of very large expansion of trade (normally, exports) of a single good, which may be taken as exogenous (i.e., not dependent on current policies) and may be due to either a real physical expansion or to a price increase. Exports of oil are obviously the most important case in point — though once in a while other commodities may play the role (say, exports of copper by Chile in earlier generations). As was mentioned earlier, this was the reason for excluding oil here from aggregate exports and for the exclusion altogether from the study of an oil-exporting country (Venezuela). However, this solution is not fully satisfactory: large changes in exports of oil *do* have an impact on the structure of the economy, and of other exports, which do not disappear with the exclusion of oil from our observations. That is, a study that aims to relate structural changes to liberalization should actually try to abstract from the *impact* of changes in oil exports. This, again, would be feasible only in the analysis of a single country, or of a small group.

Beyond these comments, it might be noted that the impact of trade liberalization on the structure of *production* (and, to a lesser extent, consumption) should probably be even more important than its impact on trade structure; hence, should be a tempting subject of analysis. However, this calls naturally for another study altogether.

Annex A

Table 8.4:   Export share (X/GDP).

	A (1)	B (2)	C (3)	(2)/(1) (4)	(3)/(2) (5)	(5)/(4) (6)
Argentina	6.9	6.4	7.9	0.93	1.23	1.32
Bolivia	18.8	6.4	13.1	0.34	2.05	6.03
Brazil	4.9	10.0	9.7	2.04	0.97	0.48
Chile	55.2	7.6	22.6	0.14	2.97	21.21
Colombia	10.1	9.4	8.2	0.93	0.87	0.94
Ecuador	10.0	11.3	15.6	1.13	1.38	1.22
India	5.0	5.1	9.3	1.18	1.61	1.36
Indonesia	n.a.	5.0	8.4	—	1.68	—
Israel I	n.a.	12.8	13.4	—	1.05	—
Israel II	21.8	20.3	26.4	0.93	1.30	1.40
Mexico	3.2	4.5	20.1	1.41	4.47	3.17
New Zealand	19.1	28.0	21.8	1.21	0.95	0.79
Peru	9.1	6.3	8.7	0.69	1.38	2.00
Philippines	10.5	9.8	14.5	0.93	1.48	1.59
Singapore	n.a.	74.8	112.4	—	1.50	—
Spain	4.6	7.1	11.2	1.54	1.58	1.03
Sri Lanka I	22.7	14.4	20.2	0.63	1.40	2.22
Sri Lanka II	23.4	19.8	18.2	0.85	0.92	1.08
Thailand	15.5	27.1	41.4	1.75	1.83	1.05
Turkey	5.3	2.9	18.4	0.55	4.62	8.40
Uruguay	10.3	18.5	11.8	1.82	0.64	0.36
Mean		14.3	20.4		1.72	
w/o three [n.a.]	14.2	11.5		1.05	1.72	3.09
Median		9.8	13.4		1.40	
w/o three [n.a.]	10.2	9.9		0.93	1.38	1.34

In this and in the following tables, "A" stands for the "past" period, "B" for the "base" period, and "C" for the "post-liberalization" period.
The mean and median figures (and similarly in the following tables) are of the *column* above.

Table 8.5:   Import share (M/GDP).

	A (1)	B (2)	C (3)	(2)/(1) (4)	(3)/(2) (5)	(5)/(4) (6)
Argentina	4.8	4.7	9.9	0.98	2.11	2.15
Bolivia	16.0	7.2	22.1	0.44	3.16	7.18
Brazil	6.4	5.5	10.3	0.86	1.87	2.17
Chile	46.6	7.5	16.5	0.16	2.20	13.75
Colombia	9.5	10.0	14.5	1.05	1.45	1.38
Ecuador	15.4	17.1	20.6	1.11	1.20	1.08
India	5.3	7.1	10.4	1.34	1.46	1.09
Indonesia	n.a.	2.8	13.5	—	4.82	—
Israel I	n.a.	30.3	28.8	—	0.95	—
Israel II	34.1	26.3	29.3	0.77	1.11	1.44
Mexico	5.8	7.5	23.2	1.29	3.09	2.40
New Zealand	18.2	23.2	20.8	1.27	0.90	0.71
Peru	13.3	7.5	14.5	0.56	1.93	3.45
Philippines	13.0	9.4	17.7	0.72	1.88	2.61
Singapore	n.a.	121.5	182.6	—	1.50	—
Spain	12.9	15.5	16.0	1.20	1.03	0.86
Sri Lanka I	22.7	17.7	30.6	0.78	1.73	2.22
Sri Lanka II	50.8	31.0	45.8	0.61	1.48	2.43
Thailand	21.5	39.0	50.9	1.81	1.31	0.72
Turkey	7.7	6.8	20.7	0.88	3.04	3.45
Uruguay	27.0	15.2	16.8	0.56	1.11	1.98
Mean		19.6	29.3		1.87	
w/o three [n.a.]	18.4	14.3		0.91	1.78	2.84
Median		10.0	20.6		1.73	
w/o three [n.a.]	14.4	20.1	—	1.62	2.07	2.16

Table 8.6: Commodity concentration of exports (C_x).

	A (1)	B (2)	C (3)	(2)/(1) (4)	(3)/(2) (5)	(5)/(4) (6)
Argentina	0.216	0.229	0.216	0.93	1.23	1.32
Bolivia	0.599	0.567	0.297	0.95	0.52	0.55
Brazil	0.269	0.177	0.167	0.66	0.94	1.42
Chile	0.722	0.695	0.413	0.96	0.59	0.61
Colombia	0.641	0.523	0.302	0.82	0.58	0.71
Ecuador	0.472	0.462	0.444	0.98	0.96	0.98
India	0.188	0.253	0.227	1.35	0.90	0.67
Indonesia	n.a.	0.601	0.370	—	0.62	—
Israel I	n.a.	0.411	0.390	—	0.95	—
Israel II	0.381	0.323	0.371	0.85	1.15	1.35
Mexico	0.183	0.179	0.243	0.98	1.36	1.39
New Zealand	0.406	0.314	0.230	0.77	0.73	0.95
Peru	0.297	0.335	0.303	1.13	0.90	0.80
Philippines	n.a.	0.405	0.365	—	0.90	—
Singapore	0.460	0.311	0.235	0.69	0.76	1.10
Spain	0.253	0.160	0.198	0.63	1.24	1.97
Sri Lanka I	0.649	0.506	0.472	0.78	0.93	1.19
Sri Lanka II	0.258	0.182	0.187	0.71	1.03	1.45
Thailand	0.276	0.233	0.195	0.84	0.83	0.99
Turkey	0.371	0.287	0.276	0.77	0.96	1.25
Uruguay	0.398	0.294	0.240	0.74	0.82	1.11
Mean		0.355	0.292		0.90	
w/o three [n.a.]	0.391	0.335		0.86	0.91	1.10
Median		0.311	0.276		0.90	
w/o three [n.a.]	0.376	0.303		0.83	0.90	1.10

Table 8.7: Commodity concentration of imports (C_m).

	A (1)	B (2)	C (3)	(2)/(1) (4)	(3)/(2) (5)	(5)/(4) (6)
Argentina	0.180	0.187	0.208	1.04	1.09	1.05
Bolivia	0.178	0.208	0.226	1.17	1.09	0.93
Brazil	0.299	0.268	0.185	0.90	0.69	0.77
Chile	0.260	0.169	0.194	0.65	1.15	1.77
Colombia	0.187	0.187	0.169	1.00	0.90	0.90
Ecuador	0.216	0.186	0.168	0.86	0.90	1.05
India	0.283	0.214	0.320	0.76	1.50	1.97
Indonesia	n.a.	0.538	0.191	—	0.36	—
Israel I	n.a.	0.197	0.219	—	1.11	—
Israel II	0.267	0.241	0.250	0.90	1.04	1.16
Mexico	0.185	0.177	0.187	0.96	1.06	1.10
New Zealand	0.171	0.198	0.173	1.16	0.87	0.75
Peru	0.193	0.189	0.171	0.98	0.90	0.92
Philippines	n.a.	0.202	0.192	—	0.95	—
Singapore	0.382	0.203	0.250	0.53	1.23	2.32
Spain	0.162	0.260	0.233	1.60	0.90	0.56
Sri Lanka I	0.228	0.324	0.223	1.42	0.69	0.49
Sri Lanka II	0.258	0.182	0.187	0.71	1.03	1.45
Thailand	0.205	0.213	0.185	1.04	0.87	0.84
Turkey	0.212	0.271	0.196	1.28	0.72	0.56
Uruguay	0.299	0.301	0.175	1.01	0.58	0.57
Mean		0.234	0.239		0.93	
w/o three [n.a.]	0.231	0.221		1.00	0.96	1.06
Median		0.203	0.192		0.95	
w/o three [n.a.]	0.214	0.205		0.99	0.96	0.93

Table 8.8:   Dissimilarity index of exports (D_x).

	From A to B (1)	From B to C (2)	(2)/(1) (3)
Argentina	0.266	0.226	0.85
Bolivia	0.156	0.508	3.26
Brazil	0.314	0.191	0.61
Chile	0.131	0.358	2.73
Colombia	0.217	0.311	1.43
Ecuador	0.328	0.263	0.80
India	0.307	0.192	0.63
Indonesia	0.120	0.602	5.02
Israel I	—	—	—
Israel II	0.214	0.198	0.93
Mexico	0.337	0.423	1.26
New Zealand	0.188	0.196	1.04
Peru	0.300	0.243	0.81
Philippines	0.109	0.308	2.83
Singapore	0.442	0.389	0.88
Spain	0.379	0.237	0.68
Sri Lanka I	0.194	0.312	1.61
Sri Lanka II	0.464	0.154	0.33
Thailand	0.282	0.436	1.55
Turkey	0.358	0.547	1.53
Uruguay	0.338	0.232	0.69
Mean	0.272	0.316	1.47
Median	0.291	0.286	0.99

Table 8.9: Dissimilarity index of imports (D_m).

	From A to B (1)	From B to C (2)	(2)/(1) (3)
Argentina	0.204	0.301 (7)	1.48
Bolivia	0.284	0.294 (9)	1.04
Brazil	0.237	0.259	1.09
Chile	0.260	0.287	1.10
Colombia	0.159	0.225	1.42
Ecuador	0.210	0.195	0.93
India	0.362	0.212	0.59
Indonesia	0.692	0.687	0.99
Israel I	—	—	—
Israel II	0.189	0.169	0.89
Mexico	0.222	0.350	1.58
New Zealand	0.121	0.193	1.60
Peru	0.290	0.303	1.04
Philippines	0.217	0.616	2.84
Singapore	0.481	0.330	0.69
Spain	0.182	0.191	1.05
Sri Lanka I	0.284	0.498	1.75
Sri Lanka II	0.260	0.108	0.42
Thailand	0.191	0.217	1.14
Turkey	0.218	0.284	1.33
Uruguay	0.262	0.297	1.13
Mean	0.266	0.301	1.21
Median	0.249	0.288	1.10

Table 8.10:   Share of nonprimary goods in aggregate exports (S_x).

	A (1)	B (2)	C (3)	(2)/(1) (4)	(3)/(2) (5)	(5)/(4) (6)
Argentina	46.2	38.8	54.4	0.84	1.40	1.67
Bolivia	3.4	7.0	30.2	2.06	4.31	2.09
Brazil	57.9	48.9	56.1	0.84	1.15	1.37
Chile	3.6	4.9	21.3	1.36	4.35	3.20
Colombia	20.0	25.2	38.2	1.26	1.52	1.21
Ecuador	32.3	67.7	31.3	2.10	1.20	0.57
India	50.1	67.3	68.5	1.34	1.02	0.76
Indonesia	13.7	13.3	10.0	0.97	0.75	0.77
Israel I	n.a.	78.2	77.9	—	1.00	—
Israel II	79.1	78.4	83.9	0.99	1.07	1.08
Mexico	57.1	86.6	78.9	1.52	0.91	0.60
New Zealand	62.6	56.4	58.6	0.93	1.04	1.16
Peru	18.6	15.5	24.6	0.83	1.59	1.62
Philippines	27.0	33.1	31.6	0.89	0.95	1.07
Singapore	40.0	45.0	64.4	1.13	1.43	1.27
Spain	73.0	72.0	68.1	0.99	0.95	0.96
Sri Lanka I	14.8	21.8	80.8	1.47	3.71	2.52
Sri Lanka II	23.4	54.1	73.9	2.31	1.37	0.59
Thailand	52.6	68.8	84.5	1.31	1.23	0.94
Turkey	33.0	36.4	43.3	1.10	1.19	1.08
Uruguay	37.9	57.2	62.9	1.51	1.10	0.73
Mean		45.1	54.4		1.58	
[w/o Israel I]	37.3	43.4		1.29	1.61	1.28
Median		48.9	62.9		1.20	
[w/o Israel I]	37.0	47.0		1.20	1.20	1.08

Table 8.11: Share of nonprimary goods in aggregate imports (S_m).

	A (1)	B (2)	C (3)	(2)/(1) (4)	(3)/(2) (5)	(5)/(4) (6)
Argentina	46.0	49.0	69.3	1.07	1.41	1.32
Bolivia	61.9	58.8	67.1	0.95	1.14	1.20
Brazil	37.5	39.7	58.8	1.06	1.48	1.40
Chile	59.3	57.5	56.7	0.97	0.99	1.02
Colombia	56.2	52.4	62.0	0.93	1.18	1.27
Ecuador	67.3	55.1	60.3	0.82	1.09	1.33
India	38.9	44.6	42.5	1.15	0.95	0.83
Indonesia	42.0	25.6	55.8	0.61	2.18	3.57
Israel I	n.a.	56.2	52.3	—	0.93	—
Israel II	55.2	65.4	71.8	1.18	1.10	0.93
Mexico	65.2	59.6	74.1	0.91	1.24	1.36
New Zealand	32.9	49.0	67.6	1.49	1.38	0.93
Peru	63.3	55.9	62.2	0.88	1.11	1.26
Philippines	43.9	45.7	51.6	1.04	1.18	1.13
Singapore	33.0	46.7	48.0	1.42	1.03	0.73
Spain	45.0	36.2	47.5	0.80	1.31	1.64
Sri Lanka I	60.0	38.0	45.5	0.63	1.20	1.90
Sri Lanka II	83.3	83.7	82.0	1.00	0.98	0.98
Thailand	46.1	44.9	62.2	0.97	1.39	1.43
Turkey	49.3	44.4	57.7	0.90	1.30	1.44
Uruguay	28.5	35.3	64.4	1.24	1.82	1.17
Mean		49.7	60.0		1.26	
[w/o Israel I]	50.7	49.4		1.00	1.27	1.34
Median		49.0	60.3		1.18	
[w/o Israel I]	47.7	47.9		0.97	1.19	1.27

Table 8.12: Income level of exports (Y_x).

	A (1)	B (2)	C (3)	(2)/(1) (4)	(3)/(2) (5)	(5)/(4) (6)
Argentina	0.584	0.565	0.568	0.97	1.01	1.04
Bolivia	34.9	0.346	0.485	0.99	1.40	1.41
Brazil	0.443	0.523	0.551	1.18	1.05	0.89
Chile	0.376	0.390	0.445	1.04	1.14	1.10
Colombia	0.283	0.338	0.438	1.09	1.30	1.09
Ecuador	0.349	0.394	0.431	1.13	1.09	0.96
India	0.461	0.484	0.502	1.05	1.04	0.99
Indonesia	0.406	0.373	0.416	0.92	1.12	1.22
Israel I	n.a.	n.a.	n.a.	—	—	—
Israel II	0.552	0.573	0.597	1.04	1.04	1.00
Mexico	0.504	0.544	0.612	1.08	1.13	1.05
New Zealand	0.568	0.568	0.566	1.00	1.00	1.00
Peru	0.443	0.447	0.444	1.01	0.99	0.98
Philippines	0.509	0.504	0.485	0.99	0.96	0.97
Singapore	0.443	0.483	0.541	1.09	1.12	1.03
Spain	0.497	0.537	0.567	1.08	1.06	0.98
Sri Lanka I	0.215	0.293	0.300	1.36	1.02	0.75
Sri Lanka II	0.295	0.346	0.398	1.17	1.15	0.98
Thailand	0.455	0.470	0.528	1.03	1.12	1.09
Turkey	0.454	0.475	0.495	1.05	1.04	0.99
Uruguay	0.519	0.505	0.527	0.97	1.04	1.07
Mean	0.435	0.458	0.495	1.06	1.09	1.03
Median	0.449	0.479	0.499	1.05	1.06	1.00

Table 8.13:   Income level of imports (Y_m).

	A (1)	B (2)	C (3)	(2)/(1) (4)	(3)/(2) (5)	(5)/(4) (6)
Argentina	0.560	0.574	0.601	1.025	1.047	1.022
Bolivia	0.537	0.539	0.589	1.004	1.093	1.089
Brazil	0.544	0.561	0.578	1.031	1.030	0.999
Chile	0.557	0.541	0.569	0.971	1.052	1.083
Colombia	0.563	0.565	0.579	1.004	1.025	1.021
Ecuador	0.567	0.556	0.573	0.981	1.031	1.051
India	0.497	0.565	0.581	1.197	1.028	0.859
Indonesia	0.484	0.440	0.540	0.909	1.227	1.350
Israel I	0.536	0.568	0.575	1.060	1.012	0.955
Israel II	0.593	0.602	0.614	1.015	1.020	1.005
Mexico	0.576	0.560	0.598	0.969	1.068	1.102
New Zealand	0.580	0.580	0.605	1.000	1.043	1.043
Peru	0.559	0.542	0.570	0.970	1.052	1.085
Philippines	0.537	0.537	0.543	1.000	1.011	1.011
Singapore	0.525	0.569	0.576	1.084	1.012	0.934
Spain	0.543	0.559	0.589	1.029	1.054	1.024
Sri Lanka I	0.502	0.423	0.550	0.843	1.300	1.542
Sri Lanka II	0.477	0.541	0.559	1.134	1.033	0.911
Thailand	0.559	0.567	0.585	1.014	1.032	1.018
Turkey	0.546	0.539	0.546	0.987	1.013	1.026
Uruguay	0.531	0.550	0.596	1.036	1.084	1.046
Mean	0.542	0.547	0.577	1.013	1.060	1.056
Median	0.544	0.559	0.578	1.004	1.033	1.024

Annex B

Table 8.14:　Classification of Three-Digit SITC Groups into "Primary" and "Nonprimary" Goods.[a]

Category	Primary goods		Nonprimary goods	
Category 0				
Food and live animals	001	045	All other groups	
	041	046		
	043	047		
	044	081		
Category 1				
Beverages and tobacco		121	All other groups	
Category 2				
Crude materials, inedible	All groups			
Category 3				
Mineral fuels	All groups			
Category 4				
Animal and vegetable oil			All groups	
Category 5				
Chemicals	All other groups		541	553
			551	554
Category 6				
Manufactured goods	All other groups		612	656
			613	657
			624	665
			629	666
			642	667
			654	697
			655	698
Category 7				
Machinery and transport equipment			All groups	
Category 8				
Miscellaneous manufactured articles			All groups	

[a]Adopted from Michaely (1984, p. 50).

Notes

1. An important contribution to this topic is made in Romer (1994). In this paper, Romer introduces a model in which trade liberalization adds new goods to the economy's trade flow (in his formulation it is the obverse movement — imposition of trade barriers leading to the withdrawal of

goods from trade). In comparison with the conventional model, in which freedom of trade (or its restriction) leads to the expansion (contraction) of trade in existing goods, Romer demonstrates that in the adjusted model the impact of trade policy on welfare increases dramatically. Since in practice it is impossible to identify "new goods" — not only empirically, but even conceptually — one may interpret the appearance of "new goods" as the expansion of the *range* of traded goods. For work related to this approach, see Collie and Su (1998). Another contribution relevant to the issue is Chan (1991). Using a game-theoretic approach, it is found there that the more diversified the country's trade options, the more it stands to gain from a bilateral trade agreement with a partner country.

2. One impact related to the structure of trade is the factor content of trade expansion and its impact on income distribution. This has been a frequent topic of research and will not be addressed here.

3. A partially related analysis may be found in Athukorala and Jayasuriya (2000), Galiani and Sanguinetti (2003), Harrison and Hanson (1999), Hoekman and Djankov (1997), Pigato *et al.* (1997), and De Pinieres *et al.* (1997).

4. A partly related issue is the implication of liberalization for the geographic direction of a country's trade; but this will remain beyond the scope of the present paper.

5. I have also examined another measure of a structural change: the changing share of "nontraditional" goods in trade — specifically, in exports — expecting this share to increase following liberalization. This measure is similar, in essence, to the description of changing shares through an index of dissimilarity. Indeed, the findings indicate a very close resemblance of the two (the rank correlation coefficient of the two measures exceeds 0.800). Given, moreover, that the measure of the share of "nontraditional" goods suffers from a degree of arbitrariness (in defining the content of this group), I have selected not to include this measure in the presentation of the study. The findings may, however, be obtained from the author upon request.

6. See Michaely (1962). A typical coefficient of concentration of a trade flow would be much below one half — say, around one quarter. Hence, if its complement — a coefficient of diversification — were to be used, most changes in the degree of diversification would appear as (relatively) rather small.

7. The index was first developed in Michaely (1962).

8. The index has been first formulated in Michaely (1981), and further discussed in Michaely (1984).
9. Very few appropriate candidates for the study are excluded for scarcity of data.
10. In 1973, the five countries with the highest indexes of the income level of exports were Austria (0.689), Sweden (0.690), Finland (0.695), the US (0.639), and Germany (0.639). The average of these five indices was thus 0.652 — exceeding the average of the group of liberalizing countries on the eve of liberalization (0.458) by 42 percent. See Table 7.6 in Michaely (1984).

References

Athukorala, P-C and Jayasuriya, S (2000). Trade policy reforms and industrial adjustment in Sri Lanka. *The World Economy*, 33(3), 387–404.

Chan, K S (1991). Bilateral trade negotiations and trade diversification. *Journal of Development Economics*, 36(2), 243–257.

Collie, D R and Su, Y-T (1998). Trade policy and product variety: When is a VER superior to tariff. *Journal of Development Economics*, 55(1), 249–255.

de Pineres, S, Gutierez, A and Ferrantino, M (1997). Export diversification and structural dynamics in the growth process: The case of Chile. *Journal of Development Economics*, 52(2), 375–391.

Dodzin, S and Vamvakidis, A (2004). Trade and industrialization in developing economies. *Journal of Development Economics*, 75(1), 319–328.

Galiani, S and Sanguinetti, P (2003). The impact of trade liberalization on wage inequality: Evidence from Argentina. *Journal of Development Economics*, 73(2), 497–513.

Harrison, A and Hanson, G (1999). Who gains from trade reform? Some remaining puzzles. *Journal of Development Economics*, 59(1), 125–156.

Hoekman, B and Djankar, S (1997). Determinants of the export structure of countries in Central and Eastern Europe. *World Bank Economic Review*, 11(3), 471–487.

Michaely, M (1962). *Concentration in International Trade*. Amsterdam: North-Holland.

Michaely, M (1981). Income levels and the structure of trade. In *The World Economic Order: Past and Prospects*, Grassman, S and Lundberg, E (eds.), London: The Macmillan Press, pp. 121–161.

Michaely, M (1984). *Trade, Income Levels and Dependence*. Amsterdam, New-York: North-Holland.

Pigato, M, Farah, C, Itakura, K, Jun, K, Martin, W, Murell, K and Srinivasan, T G (1997). *South Asia's Integration into the World Economy*, Washington, DC: The World Bank.

Romer, P (1994). New goods, old theory, and the welfare costs of trade restriction. *Journal of Development Economics*, 42(1), 5–38.

Chapter 9

Ex-Ante Assessment
of a Preferential Agreement: Methods

Introduction

This chapter intends to contribute to the methodology of assessing *ex-ante* the potential for welfare expansion of a contemplated preferential trade agreement (PTA): to analyze salient issues involved in such assessment, and, in view of this analysis, to clarify the meaning of some conventional yardsticks used for the purpose and suggest a number of new tools.

The discussion will take place predominantly within the Vinerian framework, that is, it will address the issue of the impact of a PTA through changes in trade flows and, in conjunction with them, in domestic economic activity. It is probably worthwhile to be explicit on what the analysis will not do: (i) By implicitly assuming a free trade area rather than a customs union, it will avoid the issue of establishment of a common external tariff. Yet, as a matter of convenience and focus, it will also ignore the issue of the rules of origin, which are inherent in a free trade area and which may distort its operation (see Krueger, 1993). (ii) It is a "static" analysis, referring to the impact of a PTA within an existing system and avoiding "dynamic" issues, which have formed a substantial part of recent discussions. It also overlooks potential economies of scale. (iii) It will not go into "political-economy" considerations — again, an important element of recent analyses that refer to the extent and direction in which the conclusion of a PTA affects other trade-policy decisions (such as the introduction of multilateral or unilateral tariff changes, or the conclusion of other PTAs). (iv) Finally, the analysis will refer strictly to trade, and not to issues such as free labor mobility, integration of capital markets, harmonization of taxation systems or monetary policies, and the like. In addition, although the analysis applies in principle to trade in services as well as in goods, many of the issues involved refer in fact only to the latter.

In the rest of this section, the conventional list of attributes involved in the assessment of a PTA will be briefly re-stated. Following this, the plan of the discussion will be laid out.

Viner's (1950) pioneering analysis concluded, roughly, that so far as the welfare outcome of a PTA is concerned, anything is possible. Viner's followers, primarily Meade (1955) and Lipsey (1960), have developed the major considerations by which the likelihood of one outcome rather than another should be judged. The Meade–Lipsey criteria, which have long been the conventional wisdom, will be listed here in the briefest way, since their rationale is only too well known. Some of these criteria are not entirely independent; they may be related to others or even be components of others. The order in which the list is organized does not necessarily reflect importance; rather, it is intended to suit the order of the following discussions.

A home country welfare expansion rather than a contraction, following a PTA, is more likely:

(i) The higher the level of the home country's (geographically uniform) tariffs prior to the agreement.

(ii) The higher the tariff level of the contemplated partner.[1]

(iii) The larger the economic size of the partner.

(iv) The higher the share of the partner in providing the home country's imports.

(v) The lower the ratio of imports from the rest of the world (ROW) to the home country's aggregate economic activity.

(vi) The closer the relative prices in the partner's economy are to those of the ROW. This is partly related to (iii) above — economic size — and to the following criterion.

(vii) The more similar the partner is to the ROW in the structure of its economic activity.[2]

The first three attributes listed here — (i), (ii), and (iii) — will be addressed in the following section: "Clarification of criteria and indication for measurement."[3] The third section, "Indices of Assessment," will then propose measures that are related to the criteria, which have just been analyzed. The final section will draw some conclusions.

Clarification of Criteria and Indication for Measurement

We shall now turn to the analysis of the first three criteria just listed: clarify them where clarification is needed and specify the concepts in some detail, in view of the principles by which the criteria have been formulated. Part of this analysis will not reveal much that is new; however, in other parts, issues will be exposed to which little attention has been paid and whose consideration should make the application of the criteria involved more meaningful.

Level of the Home Country's Pre-Agreement Tariffs

The higher the tariff level, the more likely it is for trade creation rather than trade diversion to follow a PTA, and the stronger the (favorable) consumption effect will be, due to the reduction of the home price to the consumer.[4] However, a few issues must be raised:

(i) What is the home country's (aggregate) "tariff level"? The term is, as is rather well known, far from straightforward and a considerable amount of attention has been paid in the literature to its ramifications.[5] Using a weighted average to indicate the aggregate level in which import values of the individual goods are used for weights will yield an outcome, which, for well known reasons, is biased downwards — in most cases, probably drastically so. A nonweighted average, on the other hand, though free of bias, will resemble the "true" average only by accident. For the purpose at hand, however, the relevant question is not primarily whether the definition, or index, used is a good approximation of the "true" concept but whether a bias is introduced, in some way, by the use of one index or another for the assessment of a PTA. That is, when we compare aggregate tariff levels in the context of the statement that starting from a higher tariff level makes a PTA more promising, does the use of a proposed index lead to bias? The answer appears to be in the negative. Although either a weighted average (by imports) or a simple arithmetic mean is poor approximation of the "true" average level, the absence of bias should make the use of either of these indices legitimate for *ordering* alternative starting levels of tariffs.

(ii) A related issue arises in this context — namely, the degree of *dispersion* in the home country's tariff system. Suppose, for simplicity, that we use an unweighted, arithmetic mean as our index of aggregate tariff level, and that by this measure two tariff systems are found to be equal. However, one system involves a higher level of dispersion of individual tariff levels than the other. The promise of a welfare expansion rather than contraction, following a PTA, should be higher when the more-dispersed tariff system is involved. This can be seen from the following reasoning. It is well known that the welfare loss from the existence of a tariff system is a function not just of the average tariff level but also of the degree of dispersion in it.[6] Hence, the gain from trade creation, as well as the (positive) consumption effect following a PTA, will be higher the higher the dispersion (given the average level). The loss from trade diversion, on the other hand (again, of course, *ceteris paribus*), is a function of the tariff level alone and not of the dispersion. Hence, taken together, these considerations should lead to a higher expectation for a welfare improvement when the tariff system is more highly dispersed. We thus reach the conclusion that in assessing the significance of the pre-agreement (home country's) tariff system, levels should be indicated not just of the average tariff but also of the system's degree of *dispersion*.

(iii) Yet another issue should be raised in this context — namely, whether a tariff level *specific* to the partner should be used. Although by assumption the home country's tariffs are *geographically* uniform prior to the PTA, no uniformity by *commodities* will be found (except by chance, so rare as to have never been observed — and if these were to happen, all the discussion of averages and dispersion would become redundant). Unless — again by chance, whose probability must be zero — the commodity structure of imports from the partner happens to be identical to that of the home country's imports from the ROW, the average tariff level of the former will be different from that of the latter. Is it of any relevance, in the present context that such a difference exists? Consequently, should we be concerned only with the home country's aggregate tariff level or also with the average tariff level on imports from the partner?

The answer is that the latter tariff level is of much significance, although we do not know whether particularly low or particularly high tariffs on the partner's imports are a factor more conducive to welfare expansion or its contraction.[7] When, say, this particular tariff level is low, it can be presumed that: (1) to the extent that trade creation takes place, the gain from it will be low; (2) when trade diversion is the outcome, its loss will, again, be low; and (3) finally, the (favorable) consumption effect will also be low. Thus, all welfare effects — positive and negative — are likely to be low. Hence (this is not, though, a logical inevitability), the agreement is likely to be of smaller consequence — one way or another — than if the tariff level under consideration had been high. To cite an extreme case, when this tariff level is zero, the agreement will be meaningless (but with a proviso to be specified shortly). We do not, however, know whether in the general case this (smaller) impact is more or less likely to be positive or negative.[8]

The discussion thus far suggests that "the" level of the home country's tariffs prior to the PTA should be represented by a specific average concerned with tariffs on imports from the partner.[9] This, however, should be qualified: it may be expected that following the PTA import patterns will change — and even that new imports altogether will be forthcoming from the partner (once more, in the Vinerian context this is the *only* way in which imports change!). Hence, other tariffs on goods, which are not imported from the partner, or not to any significant extent, will also be relevant. Thus, the attribute in question, namely the home country's tariff level prior to the PTA, should be indicated by *both* the aggregate level and by a measure specific to the partner.

(iv) Finally, an issue exists as to which type of tariffs should be the subject of observation. Specifically, should it be *nominal* tariffs — nominal rates of protection — or *effective* protection rates? The answer is that both sets of protection rates are relevant. For the extent of a potential trade diversion, it is the set of *nominal* tariff rates, which matters.[10] For the potential for trade creation, the nominal rate is again the relevant variable. However, once trade creation does take place in any given activity, it is the effective protection rate, which will determine the size of the gain from it to the economy. For the consumption gain, the nominal tariff rate is applicable. Both sets of rates should hence be used. (This also applies — as can be seen, even more forcefully — to the specific average tariff level related to the structure of imports from the partner.) In pragmatic terms, one should probably construct two indices. One, to represent the level of nominal tariffs, will be an arithmetic, unweighted average of tariff rates. The other — certainly more difficult to construct — will be a weighted average of effective protection rates where the size of *value added* should be used as the weight of each activity.

The Level of the Partner's Tariffs

In considering this factor, no ambiguity is involved. Removal (or reduction) of these tariffs will definitely be a source of gain to the home country — whether trade creation or trade diversion follows for the partner, and whether it leads to a net gain or loss for it. And, again unambiguously, the gain to the home country will be higher the higher the size of removal of the partner's tariffs (whether due to a higher initial tariff level or, when the tariff is only lowered rather than fully eliminated, to a higher proportion of tariff reduction).[11] With complete tariff elimination, the gain per unit of trade translates simply to the rate of tariff imposed by the partner on any good imported from the home country.

As in the earlier case discussed, *two* separate "average levels" of tariffs are relevant. The first applies to *existing* exports of the home country to the partner. Here, unlike other instances discussed thus far, the index used will be both *precise* and provide a *cardinal* outcome.[12] It should be a weighted average of tariff levels where the values of exports of each good to the partner are used for weights.[13] The use of this measure in the present context will be free of the biases normally involved in estimating the "average" tariff level. Combining the use of this measure with the total value of the trade flow involved — multiplying one by the other — will yield the aggregate gain, in money terms, of the home country from the partner's tariff removal.[14] To give it any meaning, this size should be presented as a ratio of the country's aggregate economic activity.

Another index belongs again to the family of indicators of an ordinal outcome. This will be an average (once more, perhaps a simple arithmetic average will serve) of the partner's tariffs on its imports in general (that is, not specifically from the home country). This will be an indication of the potential of expansion of the home country's exports through displacement of the partner's imports from others, not necessarily where imports from the home country already exist (or, where they do, beyond their present size).

It should be noted that in this instance — that is, when the partner's tariffs are discussed — it is only the *nominal* tariff rates, which are of concern: effective rates of protection are relevant to the welfare impact of the agreement on the partner, but not on the home country.

The Partner's Size and Economic Diversification

It had been considered an important and undisputed criterion of assessment for many years that the larger the economy of a partner, the more successful a PTA is likely to be. Recently, however, doubts have been raised; hence, a need exists for some clarification on this matter.[15]

The rationale for this criterion is rather simple and is related to criteria (v) and (vi) in the list presented in the introduction. The larger the size of the partner (whether this is due to a large size of a single economy or to a large number of countries, which constitute the partner), the less distinct it is likely to be. That is, the more its economic structure will resemble that of the ROW (unless the "ROW" itself becomes only a small fraction of the world) and the more relative prices in its tradable sector will resemble those of the ROW. Hence, trade diversion toward it will be less costly and the fall of domestic prices of imports in the home country will be larger following the agreement. In an extreme case in which the partner is large enough to constitute most of the world (in terms of economic activity), a PTA will become almost identical with a complete move of the home country to free trade.

An objection to this line of reasoning has been raised in recent years by Bhagwati and Panagariya — both separately and jointly.[16] They argue, on the contrary, that "small is beautiful" for a partner: the smaller the partner, the less will be the deterioration of the home country's terms of trade following the PTA and hence the smaller its (certain) loss.

This, indeed, is a valid argument when the partner country falls in the range of what I have termed (see Chap. 5) "ultra-small" economies, that is, when the partner is small enough for the home country to fully absorb the partner's exports, following the agreement, and still import some of the good from others. Thus, this becomes a valid and relevant consideration when agreements are contemplated among the world's smaller economies.

"Size" may obviously be interpreted in more than one way. In the present context both the (partner) country's *trade* and its aggregate economic activity should be considered (the two should be different in the general case — unless the ratios of trade to aggregate activity happen to be similar between economies). The sizes of both aggregate activity and trade provide an indication of the ease with which the partner's goods may potentially replace imports from others as well as the home country's own production.

Diversification of the partner's economy is strongly related to its size — and is, indeed, a major element in leading one to consider size as an important attribute. Diversification of economic structures must be predominantly a function of two factors: size of the economy and its level of development. And the more diversified the economy, the less "unique" it will be, that is, the more it will resemble the ROW and, hence, the more promising a PTA with it will be.

Although this inference has not, apparently, been disputed in the literature, the just-discussed qualification concerning size should hold true here as well. When the partner's economy is both small and highly diversified, its actual and potential export goods thus being many, rather than few, it is more likely to become "ultra-small" with reference to the markets of its individual goods. Thus, when the partner is a small economy, diversification beyond a certain range will make an agreement with it less rather than more promising.

Indices of Assessment

The Intensity of Trade Flows

For the assessment of a concrete (contemplated) PTA, the observed size of trade with a partner (that is, its share in the home country's aggregate flow) — referring to criterion (iv) above — is sufficient, with no need to go beyond it and inquire about the origins of this size. For generalizations, on the other hand (such as for assessing the role of "regionalism"), a separation of contributing factors is required.

The simplest, and most common, instrument used for such separation is the "intensity ratio" of trade flows. This is defined — say, for country j's imports from country k — as

$$I_{jk} = \frac{M_{jk}}{M_j} \bigg/ \frac{X_k}{X_w},$$

where j is the home country, k the partner country, I_{jk} the intensity ratio of the partner's provision of the home country's imports, M_{jk} the country j's imports from country k, M_j the aggregate imports of country j, X_k the aggregate exports of country k, and X_w the aggregate world exports.[17]

An index of unity indicates a perfect "neutrality": the share of the partner in providing the home country's imports is identical with the former's share in world exports (hence in world imports). An index above unity indicates a "preference" in favor of the partner — the stronger, the higher the index — whereas an index below unity will indicate, on the contrary, some constraining element. The intensity ratio is thus a summary measure of all factors other than the partner's size (that is, its share in world trade), which contribute to the bilateral trade flow.

The "intensity ratio" is a rather straightforward instrument of assessment. However, two issues deserve some consideration. First, as it is presented here, the share of one country in the trade of the other is fully explained — by definition — by its size and by the intensity ratio of the trade flows involved (that is, by a multiplication of the two measures). In recent literature, a measure appears, which does not have this attribute. This has been suggested by Summers (1991), whose (implied) definition of the intensity ratio is $I_{jk}^s = (M_{jk}/M_j)/(G_k/G_w)$, where G_k and G_w stand, respectively, for the partner's and the world's incomes (GDP) rather than, as before, the respective trade flows. The difference between the two measures lies, of course, in the fact that trade ratios (the share of trade in income) differ between economies (as well as over time in any given economy). Hence, to fully explain (in the accounting sense) the size (that is, share) of a given bilateral trade flow, one would have to add to the suggested intensity ratio another factor — the "internal" trade share (in income). It is hard to see why this index should be used, rather than the one defined in its conventional manner.

An interesting issue is concerned with the possible relationship of the geographic pattern of a country's trade with its commodity structure. With a given size (of trade) of two economies, their bilateral trade flows may be large or small not because of factors (such as proximity, common language, and the like), which facilitate one country's trade with another but (or additionally) due to the commodity structure of these flows. Thus, if one country's imports consist in a particularly high proportion of a good of which the other country exports a large quantity and of which it is (proportionately) a large world supplier, imports of the former from the latter will tend to be high, regardless of proximity or distance. Hence, if the intensity ratio is presumed to indicate just the impact of factors, which facilitate (or constrain) trade between two partners, it has to be abstracted from or standardized for the impact of commodity composition of the trade flows of the countries involved — the imports of the one and the exports of the other. This is done through an adjusted index in which the intensity ratios are calculated separately for each good, then aggregated using the appropriate weights.

Thus, the adjusted intensity ratio in country j's imports from country k is defined as

$$\bar{I}_{jk} = \sum_i \left[\frac{M_{jk}^i}{M_j^i} \Big/ \frac{X_k^i}{X_w^i} \right] \frac{X_k^i}{X_k} = \frac{1}{X_k} \sum_i \left[\frac{M_{jk}^i}{M_j^i} X_w^i \right],$$

where $\bar{I}_{jk}$ is the commodity-adjusted intensity ratio of country j's imports from country k, M_{jk}^i the imports of good i by country j from country k,

M_j^i the aggregate imports of good i by country j, X_k^i the aggregate exports of good i by country k, X_k the aggregate exports of country k, and X_w^i the aggregate world exports of good i. Note that the weights used are the shares of each good in the exports of country k — the *partner* country.

The adjusted intensity ratio will, indeed, be an indicator of the impact of factors, which have a geographic interpretation. The two indices — the adjusted and the unadjusted ratios — will differ from each other in the general case and either one could be larger or smaller than the other. The two will tend to be more similar when both the import structure of one country and the export structure of the other resemble those of the world flows. The two will thus tend to be far from each other when commodity structures of the two flows involved are more distinct. The adjusted ratio will be far below the unadjusted when both trade flows (one country's imports, the other's exports) are heavily concentrated in the same good. The reverse relationship will be observed when the two flows are concentrated in different goods. Be that as it may, if our interest lies in geographic explanations the adjusted rather than the unadjusted intensity ratio should be used as an appropriate instrument for assessment.[18]

Indices of Compatibility

Purpose of the indices. The "indices of compatibility" to which we shall now turn are designed to address the prospects of trade expansion between two partners on the basis of the commodity structures of the countries involved — a feature which has been referred to repeatedly in our earlier discussions. They incorporate the effects of a variety of elements. Some of these are mentioned in or implied by the list of attributes presented in the introduction: in particular, the degree of similarity of a partner — as well as of the home country — to the ROW, and the level of commodity diversification in the partner country's trade and production flows. These are general attributes of an economy. However, in addition the indices of compatibility, like the index of trade intensity we have just discussed, refer to the specific relationship of two concrete economies to each other. In other words, a knowledge of the general attributes of two economies will give us a clue as to what levels may be expected for the indices of compatibility between them; but, the indices will still be materially different between different pairs of countries possessing the same attributes.

We shall suggest here three different indices, all of which have the same basic structure.[19] First their definitions and formulations will be presented, following which their meaning and implications will be explored. All three indices are designed to describe the similarity — or its absence — between the commodity structure of two flows, of either trade or production, between two partners for which the prospects of a PTA would be of concern.

Formulation. The first index refers to compatibility of the trade flows of the two partners — the imports of the one and the exports of the other. It is defined as

$$Sm_jx_k = 1 - \frac{\sum\limits_i |m_{ij} - x_{ik}|}{2} \quad \text{and} \quad Sx_jm_k = 1 - \frac{\sum\limits_i |x_{ij} - m_{ik}|}{2},$$

where Sm_jx_k is the index of compatibility of imports of country j with exports of country k (partner), Sx_jm_k the index of compatibility of exports of country j with imports of country k, $|\ |$ indicates absolute values (that is, regardless of sign), x_{ij} the share of good i in total exports of country j, m_{ij} the share of good i in total imports of country j, x_{ik} the share of good i in total exports of country k, and m_{ik} the share of good i in total imports of country k.

The range of values of this index of compatibility (say, between j's imports and k's exports) is between zero and unity. It will be zero when the trade flows have no similarity whatsoever: there is no good imported at all by one country (j), which is exported to any extent by the other (k). On the other hand, the index will reach unity, its maximum level, when the structures of the two trade flows are identical: in proportion of each aggregate, one country exports precisely what the other imports.

Second, the index of compatibility between the home country's production and the partner country's exports is defined as

$$Cx_jq_k = 1 - \frac{\sum\limits_i |x_{ij} - q_{ik}|}{2},$$

where Cx_jq_k is the index of compatibility of exports of country j with production of country k, x_{ij} (as before) the share of good i in total exports of country j, and q_{ik} the share of good i in total production of tradables of country k.

Once more, the index ranges potentially from zero to unity. It will be zero when one country exports none of what the other country is producing and unity when the structure of one country's exports is identical with that of the other's production.

The third index describes the compatibility of the structures of the two export flows — one of the home country and the other of its partner. It is defined as

$$Tx_jx_k = 1 - \frac{\sum_i |x_{ij} - x_{ik}|}{2},$$

where $X_w \equiv M_w$, Tx_jx_k is the index of compatibility of exports of country j with exports of country k, x_{ij} (as before) the share of good i in total exports of country j, and x_{ik} (as before) the share of good i in total exports of country k.

As is self-evident by now, the index ranges from zero — where no good is exported jointly by the two countries — to unity, where the structures of exports of the two countries are identical.

Interpretation and implications. We shall now address the meaning of the three proposed indices, each in its turn.

The first index of compatibility (S), which matches the import flow of one country (home) with the export flow of the other (the partner), yields important information about the potential of a PTA for trade diversion (of the home country's trade toward the partner). The higher the index, the more similar the structure of the partner's exports to that of the home country's imports; hence, the stronger the potential of displacement of imports from the ROW by imports from the partner. Also, presumably, the less costly such displacement (for any given amount of it) — that is, the smaller the welfare loss to the home country from any given size of trade diversion.

As stated earlier, the match-up of these two trade flows will be *partly* a reflection of the peculiarities of the two economies involved and will thus be specifically related to these two economies: one country's exports may just happen to fit well with the import requirements of another and be a poor match with the imports of a different partner. However, in another part, the degree of compatibility should reflect some fundamental economic attributes affecting the partner equally in its relationships with any other economy. In terms of our criteria, the less of an exception the partner is — that is, the more alike it is to the ROW — the better the match of its exports should be with the import structure of any other country. The absence of uniqueness should in turn primarily reflect several attributes, partly related to each other, some of which we have already addressed: the size of the economy — the larger it is, the closer it should be to the ROW; the degree of *diversification* of the structure of economic activity and, in particular, of the economy's trade flows; the degree of the economy's *industrialization*

Table 9.1:   Determinants of the Index of Export–Import Compatibility.

Explanatory variable	Regression coefficient	T-statistic
Constant	0.326	4.748
Aggregate GDP	1.46 E-14	1.167
Concentration of exports	−0.587	−5.417
Per capita GDP	8.22 E-06	5.383
Share of manufacturing	0.461	2.168
Adjusted R^2	0.807	
D-W statistic	2.137	

(which must, in turn, also be an important determinant of the degree of diversification) — the larger the role of manufacturing (and services) and the weaker the reliance on raw materials and other primary goods, the less distinct the economy's features will be; and finally (again, partly related to other attributes), the level of economic wealth — the richer the economy, the fewer its unique attributes.

All these assertions make strong *a priori* sense; however, an empirical verification is also attempted. Table 9.1 presents the findings of a study of a large sample of countries.[20] The level of the index of compatibility is the dependent variable and four attributes are the independent explanatory variable: (i) the country's size — represented by aggregate GDP; (ii) the commodity diversification of its exports;[21] (iii) the economy's wealth, represented by the level of per capita GDP; and (iv) the level of industrialization, represented by the share of the manufacturing sector in aggregate GDP.

The findings of Table 9.1 indicate that: (i) taken together, the four attributes presumed to explain the level of the index of compatibility do, indeed (with an R^2 around 0.8) provide a major explanation; (ii) all four attributes have an impact in the expected directions: the index is negatively related to the intensity of commodity concentration (that is positively related to the level of diversification) and positively related to all other variables; and (iii) the confidence levels of the estimates suggest, however, that only three of these inferences have strong credibility, whereas the fourth, concerning the impact of the variable of *aggregate* GDP, received (with a confidence level of 0.25 for this regression coefficient) only more hedged support. The latter finding seems to imply that when an economy is highly developed — rich, industrialized and with a highly diversified economic structure — its *size* does not matter much. This does agree with the inferences presented earlier in Chapter 6.

The second index of compatibility suggested here addresses the similarity of the structures of the home country's *production* (rather than its imports) and the partner's *exports*. Although its interpretation is less self-evident than that of the earlier index, it will be clear, upon reflection, that this index provides an indication of the potential of a PTA for trade *creation*. The creation of trade is, by definition in the present context, a replacement of home production by imports from the partner, and this should be easier the more similar the pattern of the partner's exports is to that of the home country's own production (with a proviso to be mentioned shortly). To cite an extreme case, when the partner exports nothing which the home country produces, no displacement of production by imports could take place at all.[22] At the other extreme, replacement should be easiest — *ceteris paribus*, of course, including a given size of the partner — when the partner's export structure perfectly matches the home country's own production pattern.

Like the earlier index, the one discussed now reflects some element of chance, concerned with specific and unique features of both the home country and its partner. However, beyond it, like its predecessor, it originates again from basic economic features of the partner, all contributing to the absence of "uniqueness" of the structures of its production and trade: large economic size, wealth, degree of diversification, and intensity of industrialization. In other words, the same attributes that make a partner country a candidate for providing a large amount of trade of a diverting character will also make it a potentially large provider of trade of a creating nature. These same attributes make the partner's production and trade appropriate for displacing either imports from the ROW or the home country's own production.[23]

The third index (T), which matches the *export* structures of both countries, is actually of an auxiliary nature — without, that is, much life of its own. It mostly serves to qualify inferences drawn by the use of the other two indices: in particular, those based on the just-discussed index of production–exports compatibility. The higher the exports–exports compatibility, the *less* a PTA is likely to lead to new trade between the two partners through either trade creation or trade diversion. When the two economies are found to specialize in their export flows in the same range of goods, neither partner should be expected to provide much of the imports of the other; hence, a PTA discriminating in favor of such partner would not lead to much displacement of either imports from the ROW or of the home country's own production. This inference should be of particular strength if the two countries display a high degree of commodity concentration of their exports and, *a fortiori*, when these exports consist mainly of primary rather than manufactured goods — intra-industry trade being much less likely in the trade among economies specializing in the former category of goods.

Concluding Remarks

Following a discussion of the criteria by which an idea of the likely outcome of a PTA can be formed, methods of constructing an assessment have been suggested and analyzed. A few concluding remarks about the nature of this assessment, and its limitations, are now in order.

First, it should be emphasized again that the focus of this analysis is the *ex-ante* evaluation of the *promise* of a contemplated PTA. Thus, the methods developed and discussed here are not appropriate for the analysis of the *outcome* of an agreement. The latter, discussed in Chapter 11, is, needless to say, an important issue and it involves several elements common with the *ex-ante* analysis; however, it is nevertheless a separate matter.

Second, a *variety* of indices, or instruments of measurement, has been discussed here. Some of these refer to different aspects altogether of the general issue; others have areas of tangency, referring (partly and implicitly) to the same basic criteria. All of these instruments are, hopefully, of some use (as will be others that may come up) and all should be applied *in conjunction* with others. A warning should be sounded against the endeavor — always tempting — to make some composite index out of the separate instruments to provide a single number, which might be used for the assessment at hand. Even more than Fisher's now-defunct "ideal" index, any averaging of the separate measures, done in one way or another, will lack an appropriate economic interpretation. Desirable as it would be, a short-cut is not available. This also implies that *judgment* must, in the end, play a part: with the same set of measurements, different users may reach different conclusions. This is unfortunate, but at least the use of the "objective" measurements such as those discussed here will make the inferences less arbitrary.

Third, all the yardsticks analyzed here are intended to suggest potential sizes of trade flows — trade creation, trade diversion, or trade expansion. Although this knowledge is required, at some point, in order to draw welfare implications, the latter are definitely not measured by any of the methods discussed here. Moving from changes in quantities (and prices) to welfare gains or losses is a topic loaded with potential hazards and is, in any case, beyond the scope of the present discussion.

Finally, and related to the last point, we should not even make the claim that the analysis is designed to provide estimates of trade flows; it is less than that. The measurements analyzed here will not provide cardinal answers, only *ordinal*. They will not tell us whether a contemplated agreement would lead to one or another change in trade flows (and certainly not whether the agreement would be "good" or "bad"). They will, instead, tell us whether, given a certain set of circumstances, a potential agreement is more or less likely than other (actual or potential) agreements to be of consequence; hence, whether it is more or less worthy — if at all — of being concluded.

Notes

1. This consideration has been absent in Viner's analysis as well as in most of the following literature, since only imports were analyzed as the source of change; it is thus not strictly a "Meade–Lipsey" criterion, although Meade did pay passing attention to the export side. A major contribution to the incorporation of exports into the analysis is that of Wonnacott and Wonnacott (1981). See also Michaely (1977, pp. 216–217).

2. Another attribute, which will not be addressed here directly but will be implied in some of the analysis, is the degree to which the home country's and the partner's economies are complementary rather than competitive. This issue has not been fully resolved in the literature (see Michaely, 1977, pp. 205–207).

3. A fuller discussion of criteria (iv) and (v) — which is often conducted today under the term of "natural trade partners" — is provided in Chapters 12 and 13.

4. This has been an undisputed element of the conventional wisdom: in fact, many of the other criteria are strongly related to this attribute. Yet it runs counter to the perception expressed quite commonly in recent years — both in deliberations of policy makers and in the professional literature — which asserts that PTAs contemplated at present (say, in Latin America) stand a better chance of success in comparison with those of a generation ago because they start from a more favorable position: they come on the heels of a major (unilateral nondiscriminatory) trade liberalization, with a dramatic reduction of trade barriers (tariffs and NTBs alike). See the discussion in the following chapter.

5. A thorough discussion of the concept may already be found in Haberler's (1936) classic. See also Corden (1966) and Michaely (1977, Chap. 5).

6. For one exposition, see again Michaely (1977).

7. The analysis here is suggestive and intuitive, rather than formal. The Vinerian context assumes that prior to the PTA no imports from the partner exist (or, put differently, where they do exist, the PTA is immaterial). Hence, implicitly, here we step out of this context.

8. Deviating somewhat from the present context, we may note that the inferences just drawn apply also to the case in which a low tariff level on imports from the partner originates not from the latter's specialization in goods, which carry low tariff tags in the home country but, instead, to discrimination in favor of the (future) partner prior to the PTA: it is immaterial for the outcome whether the initial level of tariffs is low due to dispersion of the tariff system or to geographic discrimination. The latter possibility will be referred to again below.

9. In symbolic terms, this index is

$$T_{jk} = \sum_t t_j^i m_{jk}^i,$$

where T_{jk} is the average level of tariffs imposed by country j ("home") on imports from country k ("partner'), t_j^i the rate of tariff imposed in country j on imports of good i, and m_{jk}^i the share of good i in country j's aggregate imports from country k.

10. It should be noted, though, to avoid confusion, that once trade diversion does take place, the size of the loss from it, for a unit of diversion — the terms-of-trade deterioration — is not a function of the tariff level but only of the price differential between imports from the partner and those from the ROW.

11. The relationship between the extent of tariff removal by the partner and the home country's gain should be understood as follows (assuming, for simplicity, constant costs: that is, a fixed supply price of the home country of exports to its partner). First, over some range, when the rate of tariff removal is small enough the preference given by the agreement will be ineffective — no change will take place. With a tariff reduction beyond this range, exports from the home country will replace the partner's imports from the ROW: when just this takes place, no gain to the home country is yet involved. From here onwards, any further tariff reduction by the partner will be a source of further gain to the

home country. With reference to existing imports (by the partner from the home country) prior to the PTA, it is obviously just the latter range, which is relevant. If the supply price of either the home country or the partner is not fixed, the analysis will become more complicated and the inferences should be hedged.

12. Strictly speaking, this statement applies again to the case in which the home country's supply price is fixed.

13. Similarly to the index of the home country's level of tariffs on imports from its partners, this will be defined as

$$T_{kj} = \sum_i t_k^i m_{jk}^i,$$

where T_{jk} is the average level of tariffs imposed by country j ("home") on imports from country k ("partner"), t_j^i the rate of tariff imposed in country j on imports of good i, and m_{jk}^i the share of good i in country j's aggregate imports from country k.

14. This outcome could obviously be yielded by foregoing any estimate of an "average": by instead estimating, separately, the gain for each tariff item and aggregating the results.

15. The discussion here of the impact of size is very concise; for a fuller analysis, see Chaps. 5 and 6.

16. See Bhagwati (1993), Panagariya (1995, 1996), and Bhagwati and Panagariya (1996a, 1996b).

17. In principle, $X_{kj} = M_{jk}$, but in concrete estimates, the two will normally differ somewhat from each other.

18. To illustrate the difference between the two indicators, Table 9.2 provides an example of two alternative trade structures. In one, the commodity composition of the two trade flows is "atypical" and the two are concentrated in the same commodities (good A); in the other, commodity structures are "typical" (that is, close to those of the world at large).

We see that in the atypical case, the adjusted ratio is far below the unadjusted; in comparisons involving many countries, the two could provide entirely different indications. In the typical case, the two measures are practically identical.

19. The indices of compatibility have been developed in my recent paper (Michaely, 1996). They are, however, a modification of the "index of similarity" I designed, many years ago (Michaely, 1962a), to assess the chance of diverging price movements of a country's exports and imports. I then applied it, with a slight variation (Michaely, 1962b),

Table 9.2: Trade flows of two partners (j, k): Alternative commodity structures.

Common data to two alternatives

X_w = world exports (= imports) consists of

Value		
100	=	Good A
600	=	Good B
900	=	Good C
1600	=	Total
100	=	M_i (aggregate imports of j)
150	=	X_k (aggregate exports of k)
80	=	M_{jk} (aggregate imports of j from k)

Case 1

k's exports to		j's import from				Good
Total	ROW	j	Total	ROW	k	
88	10	78	80	2	78	A
21	20	1	10	9	1	B
41	40	1	10	9	1	C
150	70	80	100	20	80	TOTAL

Case 2

k's exports to		j's import from				Good
Total	ROW	j	Total	ROW	k	
7	3	4	5	1	4	A
50	22	28	35	7	28	B
93	45	48	60	12	48	C
150	70	80	100	20	80	TOTAL

I_{jk} = Intensity ratio (unadjusted) = 8.53.

$\bar{I}_{jk}$ = Commodity-adjusted intensity ratio: Case 1 = 1.65 and Case 2 = 8.53.

to the geographic rather than the commodity structure of trade flows, as a measure of the intensity of multilateral balancing of trade (this index has been adopted by Grubel and Lloyd (1975) to refer again to commodity structures and to indicate the extent of intra-industry trade). As a tool of predicting future trade flows following a radical policy change, I first used the index for the purpose at hand, roughly in the way it is presented here, in a paper (1980, in Hebrew) analyzing the trade implications of the peace agreement between Egypt and Israel.

20. This is taken from my earlier-noted recent paper (1996). The data cover 44 countries, as follows: Argentina, Australia, Belgium, Bolivia, Brazil,

Canada, Chile, China, Colombia, Costa Rica, Denmark, Ecuador, El Salvador, Finland, France, Germany, Greece, Guatemala, Honduras, Hong Kong, Indonesia, Italy, Jamaica, Japan, Korea, Malaysia, Mexico, The Netherlands, New Zealand, Nicaragua, Norway, Panama, Paraguay, Peru, the Philippines, Portugal, Singapore, Spain, Sweden, Thailand, UK, USA, Uruguay, and Venezuela. For each of these countries, the index of compatibility of its exports with the imports of, separately, all the other 43 countries was estimated. Following that an unweighted average of the 43 indices was taken, to represent "the" index of compatibility of the country's exports with the imports of foreign countries. This index served, then, to represent the country's observation as the dependent variable in the regression run here (that is, the regression is based on 44 observations).

21. Represented here by its inverse — the level of commodity concentration — which is, in turn, measured by the Gini–Hirschman index of concentration and is based, like the index of compatibility itself, on the three-digit level of the SITC.

22. As on an earlier occasion, this statement must be qualified by the observation that the partner's potential is assessed through what it actually exports. It is possible that with the introduction of discrimination in its favor, the partner would be found to export some new goods to the home country, displacing the latter's own production.

23. No regression analysis similar to the one represented in Table 9.1 has been tried in this case. The construction of the production–exports index is a much more demanding task than that which is required for the estimate of the imports–exports index, and a mass production of the former is not feasible. The difficulties originate mostly in the scarcity of production data classified in sufficient detail, as well as the need to then match classifications of trade and production.

References

Bhagwati, J N (1993). Regionalism and multilateralism: An overview, in de Melo, J and Panagariya, A (eds.), *New Dimensions in Regional Integration*, Cambridge: Cambridge University Press, pp. 22–51.

Bhagwati, J N and Panagariya, A (1996a). Preferential trading areas and multilateralism: Strangers, friends or foes?, in Bhagwati, J and Panagariya, A (eds.), *The Economics of Preferential Trade Agreements*, Washington, DC: American Enterprise Institute, pp. 1–78.

Bhagwati, J N and Panagariya, A (1996b). The theory of preferential trade agreements: Historical evolution and current trends, *American Economic Review*, 86, 82–87.

Corden, W M (1966). The effective protective rate, the uniform tariff equivalent and the average tariff, *Economic Record*, 42, 200–216.

Grubel, H G and Lloyd, P J (1975). *Intra-Industry Trade: The Theory and Measurement of International Trade in Differentiated Products*, London: Macmillan.

Haberler, G (1936). *The Theory of International Trade*, London: Hodge and Company.

Krueger, A O (1993). Free trade arrangements as a protectionist device: Rules of origin, *NBER Working Paper*, No. 4342.

Lipsey, R G (1960). The theory of customs unions: A general survey, *Economic Journal*, 70, 496–513.

Meade, J E (1955). *The Theory of Customs Unions*, Amsterdam: North-Holland Publishing Company.

Michaely, M (1962a). *Concentration in International Trade*, Amsterdam: North-Holland Publishing Company.

Michaely, M (1962b). Multilateral balancing in international trade, *American Economic Review*, 52, 685–702.

Michaely, M (1977). *Theory of Commercial Policy: Trade and Protection*, Oxford: Philip Allan, and Chicago: University of Chicago Press.

Michaely, M (1980). The economic significance of peace with Egypt, *Economic Quarterly* (in Hebrew), 105, 116–122.

Michaely, M (1996). Trade preferential agreements in Latin America: An *ex-ante* assessment, Washington, DC: *World Bank Policy Research Working Paper*, No. 1583.

Panagariya, A (1995). Rethinking the new regionalism, Washington, DC: The World Bank Conference on Trade Expansion.

Panagariya, A (1996). The free trade area of the Americas: Good for Latin America?, *The World Economy*, 19, 495–515.

Summers, L (1991). Regionalism and the world trading system, in *Policy Implications of Trade and Currency Zones*, Federal Reserve Bank of Kansas City, pp. 295–301.

Viner, J (1950). *The Customs Union Issue*, New York: Carnegie Endowment for International Peace.

Wonnacott, P and Wonnacott, R (1981). Is unilateral tariff reduction preferable to a customs union? The curious case of the missing foreign tariffs, *American Economic Review*, 71, 704–714.

Chapter 10

Ex-Ante Assessment of a Preferential Agreement: An Application to Latin America[1]

Introduction

Outside of Europe, in which a major, continent-wide, preferential trade agreement has been fully implemented, nowhere has the issue of preferential trade agreements been as much a center of trade-policy discussion — and experimentation — as in Latin America. This is true both for contemplation of agreements within Latin America and for potential associations with other major traders — mostly the US. In the present chapter, the measures of *ex-ante* assessment of a preferential agreement, which have been suggested in the previous chapter, will be applied to the concrete case of Latin-American countries. Most of the analysis will refer to potential agreements *within* Latin America; however, some attention will also be paid to the possibility of concluding an agreement with the US. The data used here will be those available in 1995, when the analysis of this chapter was carried out. This analysis has two purposes. One is to make an actual contribution to policy considerations in the Latin-American continent. The other is to demonstrate the potential of the suggested methods of assessment for yielding useful inferences in a concrete case.

The Initial Level of Tariffs

We recall, from the discussion of the last chapter, that one of the obvious criteria for an *ex-ante* assessment of an agreement's effectiveness is the initial level of tariffs (that is, the level on the eve of the contemplated agreement). This applies to the tariffs in both the home and the partner's countries.

174

Tariff levels in Latin America (and also, it might be noted, the levels of NTB's) had been very high indeed for decades. The wave of trade liberalizations in the continent, mostly undertaken in the late 1980s and early 1990s, led to a dramatic decline of these levels, in practically all Latin-American countries. Not only average levels but also the degrees of dispersion are now low. This may be seen from Table 10.1, which shows average levels and the ranges of tariffs at the end of the introduction of liberalization in most Latin-American countries (tariff schedules in all these countries have changed only little since then).

These low schedules of tariffs mean that, by and large, the tariff levels of *both* the home country and its potential partner are low when the contemplated partner is another Latin-American country or a group of countries. It should similarly be noted that the average tariff level is also low (in this case, it has been so for many years) in the US — another potential partner for preferential agreements with Latin-American countries.

Recalling our *a priori* grounds for assessment, this observation leads immediately to an important inference, namely unless indicated otherwise by other criteria, a strong *prima facie* presumption exists that preferential trade agreements among Latin-American countries are not likely to yield positive results or to be relevant — less likely, that is, than in other places or at other times. This inference may be viewed as a bit paradoxical

Table 10.1:   Tariff levels in Latin America.

Country and year	Average level (arithmetic, unweighted)	Range of tariff schedules (minimum–maximum)
Argentina, 1991	15	5–22
Bolivia, 1991	8	5–10
Brazil, 1992	21	0–65
Chile, 1991	11	11
Colombia, 1992	12	5–20
Costa Rica, 1992	15	5–20
Ecuador, 1991	18	2–40
Guatemala, 1992	19	5–20
Jamaica, 1991	20	0–45
Mexico, 1991	4	0–20
Paraguay, 1989	16	3–86
Peru, 1992	15	5–25
Uruguay, 1992	18	12–24
Venezuela, 1991	19	0–50

Sources: Edwards (1993, Table 5.2) and Primo *et al.* (1994, Table 1). These sources have drawn partly on Alam and Rajapatirana (1993).

and counter-intuitive — it certainly differs from what appears to be the conventional wisdom today. It has been stated quite often in recent years that preferential trade agreements in Latin America are contemplated as part of the opening-up process and an extension of liberalization, and hence, by inference, that they are good. By contrast, in the past — mainly in the 1960s — preferential agreements in the continent (such as the original Andean Pact, or the Central-American Common Market) were conceived as an extension of the trade-restrictive, import-substituting regime and as such, by inference, were seen as being harmful — the regime itself being so. Although such statements about intentions and atmosphere are correct, in fact the outcome is quite the opposite; other things being equal, preferential trade agreements in Latin America prior to the process of liberalization were more likely to yield a positive impact than preferential agreements would be following it[2] (but that does not mean, by itself, that past agreements indeed had a positive consequence!).

Shares of Intra-Regional Trade

We recall that, given any size of a country's trade, the higher the share of imports from the potential partner, the more a PTA is likely to be relevant and to lead to less trade diversion and more trade creation. Similarly, a higher share of exports to the partner will be beneficial, contributing more to an improvement of the country's terms of trade following the removal of tariff by the partner. The share of trade with the partner is thus an important consideration in pre-judging the likelihood of a beneficial agreement.

Table 10.2 shows the share of each Latin-American country,[3] as well as the region as a whole and the US, as a provider of imports of each of the other Latin-American countries (Part a) and as a buyer of its exports (Part b). Its results are quite revealing.

Overall, the share of any single Latin-American country in the trade of another is uniformly low. Brazil and, to a lesser extent, Argentina are the only two countries in Latin America with which trade is of some importance to any other Latin-American country. However, even here the highest observed ratios, in Uruguay's and Paraguay's trade with Brazil, are only of the order of 20–25 percent (of these two countries' exports or imports). Other than in trade with Brazil, Bolivia's trade with Argentina is the only case in which a trade flow from one Latin-American country to another exceeds 10 percent of either country's trade; even ratios above

Table 10.2: Shares of intra-regional trade in Latin America. Shares in (a) imports and (b) exports.

(a) *Imports of country in row from country in column, in percentage of the former's aggregate imports*

	Arg.	Bol.	Bra.	Chi.	Col.	Cos.	Ecu.	Sal.	Gua.	Hon.	Jam.	Mex.	Nic.	Pan.	Par.	Per.	Uru.	Ven.	LAC	USA
Arg	—	1.0	12.4	4.1	0.7	0.1	0.6	0.1	0.2	0.0	0.0	2.0	0.0	0.0	1.5	1.7	2.6	1.7	28.7	10.4
Bol.	29.2	—	4.6	3.7	3.4	0.0	0.1	0.0	0.0	0.0	0.0	0.4	0.0	0.2	0.2	6.0	0.2	0.4	48.4	21.9
Bra.	4.7	0.8	—	2.1	0.5	0.2	0.4	0.0	0.1	0.1	0.0	2.4	0.0	0.0	1.6	0.7	1.1	1.4	16.1	20.2
Chi.	2.9	1.3	5.3	—	0.6	0.1	0.6	0.1	0.1	0.0	0.0	0.5	0.0	0.1	0.4	1.6	0.3	0.6	14.5	15.5
Col.	0.5	0.1	0.7	2.3	—	0.9	1.7	0.1	0.2	0.1	0.0	0.8	0.2	0.3	0.0	2.9	0.1	5.9	16.8	38.8
Cos.	0.0	0.0	0.0	0.1	0.2	—	0.2	2.7	3.6	1.2	0.4	0.8	3.6	0.1	0.0	0.0	0.0	0.3	13.2	47.6
Ecu.	0.5	0.0	0.3	3.7	1.1	0.1	—	0.0	0.8	0.0	0.0	0.7	0.0	0.0	0.0	5.8	0.0	0.2	13.2	49.2
Sal.	0.3	0.0	0.0	0.1	0.0	7.6	0.0	—	18.4	3.7	0.0	1.4	4.0	0.0	0.0	0.0	0.1	0.0	35.6	34.8
Gua.	0.0	0.0	0.0	0.1	0.3	6.3	1.1	12.9	—	3.6	0.4	5.2	4.2	0.0	0.0	0.1	0.0	0.0	34.2	37.8
Hon.	0.0	0.0	0.0	0.0	0.2	0.4	0.5	2.7	1.4	—	0.0	0.6	0.7	0.0	0.0	0.0	0.0	0.1	6.6	53.9
Jam.	0.0	0.0	1.2	0.0	0.0	0.0	0.0	0.0	0.0	0.0	—	0.1	0.0	0.0	0.0	0.0	0.0	0.0	1.3	31.7
Mex.	0.7	0.0	0.7	0.5	0.6	0.3	0.2	0.4	0.8	0.2	0.2	—	0.1	0.0	0.1	0.3	0.1	0.4	5.6	69.5
Nic.	0.0	0.0	0.0	0.0	0.5	4.5	0.0	7.2	4.3	3.3	0.0	4.9	—	0.0	0.0	0.0	0.0	0.0	24.7	20.0
Pan.	0.1	0.2	0.0	0.0	1.0	7.8	0.8	1.9	1.9	1.1	0.1	3.8	0.9	—	0.0	0.4	0.0	0.8	20.8	40.6
Par.	6.1	0.3	27.5	6.5	0.1	0.0	0.0	0.0	0.1	0.0	0.0	0.1	0.0	0.1	—	0.5	1.5	1.6	44.4	4.7
Per.	1.1	0.7	3.5	2.3	3.3	0.3	1.4	0.1	0.1	0.1	0.0	2.4	0.0	0.1	0.0	—	0.1	2.7	18.2	19.1
Uru.	10.4	0.2	24.4	1.4	0.5	0.1	0.1	0.0	0.0	0.0	0.0	1.8	0.0	0.0	0.7	0.5	—	0.3	40.4	10.1
Ven.	0.4	0.0	2.2	1.0	2.0	0.5	0.3	0.4	0.5	0.2	0.4	0.9	0.0	0.0	0.0	0.6	0.2	—	9.6	52.0

(*Continued*)

Table 10.2: (Continued)

(b) Exports of country in row to country in column, in percentage of the former's aggregate exports

	Arg.	Bol.	Bra.	Chi.	Col.	Cos.	Ecu.	Sal.	Gua.	Hon.	Jam.	Mex.	Nic.	Pan.	Par.	Per.	Uru.	Ven.	LAC	USA
Arg	—	3.0	19.0	2.8	0.4	0.0	0.3	0.0	0.0	0.0	0.0	2.2	0.0	0.0	0.5	0.6	2.0	0.3	31.1	18.1
Bol.	11.2	—	14.3	6.4	0.7	0.0	0.1	0.0	0.0	0.0	0.0	1.1	0.0	0.0	0.4	2.1	0.3	0.4	37.0	25.9
Bra.	7.6	0.8	—	2.3	0.3	0.0	0.0	0.0	0.0	0.0	0.1	1.0	0.0	0.0	1.0	0.5	1.9	2.4	17.9	23.5
Chi.	7.4	1.3	9.4	—	2.1	0.0	1.6	0.0	0.0	0.0	0.0	1.9	0.0	0.0	0.8	0.9	0.3	2.7	28.4	21.2
Col.	1.8	0.1	3.2	0.9	—	0.1	0.7	0.0	0.1	0.0	0.0	3.3	0.0	0.0	0.0	2.3	0.2	6.9	20.1	35.0
Cos.	0.6	0.0	3.1	0.7	1.6	—	0.5	2.1	3.7	0.3	0.0	3.9	0.5	0.5	0.0	0.4	0.1	5.2	22.9	51.3
Ecu.	3.4	0.0	5.9	2.7	4.1	0.3	—	0.0	0.8	0.0	0.0	1.4	0.0	0.2	0.0	1.5	0.1	1.8	22.0	31.9
Sal.	0.7	0.0	2.0	0.4	0.5	2.9	0.0	—	11.6	1.3	0.0	0.7	1.2	0.0	0.0	0.2	0.0	4.1	26.0	41.1
Gua.	0.9	0.0	1.9	0.5	0.8	2.3	2.4	5.3	—	0.5	0.0	6.6	0.3	0.4	0.0	0.1	0.0	4.5	26.3	42.6
Hon.	0.3	0.0	1.9	0.4	0.8	2.1	0.1	2.1	4.4	—	0.0	5.5	0.9	0.1	0.0	0.2	0.0	5.2	24.0	48.7
Jam.	0.1	0.0	0.9	0.0	0.2	0.3	0.0	0.0	0.1	0.0	—	3.9	0.0	0.0	0.0	0.0	0.0	5.4	10.9	52.4
Mex.	1.0	0.0	2.0	0.1	0.1	0.1	0.0	0.1	0.2	0.0	0.0	—	0.0	0.0	0.0	0.3	0.1	0.4	4.4	64.7
Nic.	0.1	0.0	0.9	0.2	0.6	9.8	2.8	3.8	8.6	1.3	0.0	2.1	—	0.0	0.0	0.2	0.0	1.8	32.2	25.6
Pan.	0.4	0.2	1.4	0.3	2.0	2.8	6.2	0.5	1.3	0.1	0.0	1.8	0.0	—	0.0	0.4	0.0	2.7	28.5	35.8
Par.	12.0	0.3	17.3	2.7	0.1	0.0	0.0	0.0	0.0	0.0	0.0	0.8	0.0	0.0	—	0.0	0.8	0.1	34.0	15.0
Per.	7.3	0.8	5.9	3.0	7.5	0.0	4.8	0.0	0.0	0.0	0.0	3.0	0.0	0.2	0.4	—	0.4	3.5	36.8	25.7
Uru.	17.5	0.1	24.0	1.7	0.1	0.0	0.0	0.0	0.0	0.0	0.0	1.9	0.0	0.0	0.7	0.2	—	2.3	48.5	9.9
Ven.	2.2	0.0	4.5	0.5	2.9	0.0	0.1	0.0	0.0	0.0	0.1	1.5	0.0	0.0	0.1	0.9	0.1	—	12.9	47.8

Source: Calculated from data in Comtrade, UN Statistical Office.

5 percent are infrequent. Mexico, the other major trader in the region, reaches this level (around 5 percent) only in the imports of two Central American countries (Guatemala and Nicaragua).

Even when observing the share of the whole of Latin America in the trade of each individual country in the group, the role of the continent does not look impressive, the trade shares being moderate at best. They are distinctly higher than all the rest — around 40–45 percent, for each country's trade flows — for Bolivia and Paraguay. Perhaps not coincidentally, these are the two landlocked countries in the continent. This raises the probability that the trade flows in question to a large extent involve transit trade, rather than transactions originating from the partner country's producers and consumers.

The low levels in intra-regional trade flows in Latin America are, undoubtedly, primarily a consequence of the small size of trade of most of the countries. This is recorded in Table 10.3. It may be seen that even the trade of the largest countries — Brazil and Mexico — barely reaches 1 percent of world trade. For most countries, the share is below one quarter of 1 percent. It might have been expected that geographical and cultural proximity would make trade among Latin-American countries substantially more important that their share in world trade would indicate. However, this tends to be outweighed by structural attributes of production and trade of these economies, to which we now turn.

Diversity of Economies

An economy may, as a rule, be expected to be highly diversified when it is highly developed, in the sense of having a high level of per capita product, and in particular — a closely related attribute — when it is mostly engaged in manufacturing, rather than in primary production.[4]

Table 10.4 presents the shares of agriculture, mining, manufacturing, as well as the levels of per capita income, for the Latin-American countries and for the US. Most Latin-American economies are quite similar in per capita income, sharing a moderately low level — within the range of $1000–$3000 per year, contrasting with a level of $23,000 for the US (and a roughly similar level for other highly developed economies). The majority of Latin-American economies also display a relatively large role of the primary sectors — agriculture and mining. However, the "minority" consists of Argentina, Brazil, Mexico, Peru, and Uruguay — a group of countries that accounts for most of the continent's income and trade: in these, the

Table 10.3:   Share of trade of Latin-American countries in world trade, 1991.

Country	Imports		Exports	
	Size of imports ($b.)	Percentage of world imports	Size of exports ($b.)	Percentage of world exports
Argentina	8.28	0.25	11.97	0.39
Bolivia	0.99	0.25	0.90	0.03
Brazil	22.98	0.70	31.62	1.03
Chile	7.45	0.23	8.96	0.29
Colombia	4.97	0.15	7.27	0.24
Costa Rica	2.23	0.07	1.63	0.05
Ecuador	2.33	0.07	2.85	0.09
El Salvador	0.88	0.03	0.37	0.01
Guatemala	1.85	0.06	1.20	0.04
Honduras	0.96	0.03	0.62	0.02
Jamaica	1.70	0.05	1.05	0.03
Mexico	38.07	1.15	26.96	0.88
Nicaragua	0.67	0.02	0.27	0.01
Panama	1.69	0.05	0.34	0.01
Paraguay	1.46	0.04	0.74	0.02
Peru	2.81	0.09	3.09	0.10
Uruguay	1.55	0.05	1.57	0.05
Venezuela	10.04	0.30	15.13	0.49
LAC Total	110.93	3.36	116.53	3.53
USA	508.94	15.43	400.98	13.07
World	3297.90	100.0	3068.46	100.0

Source: Calculated from data in Comtrade, UN Statistical Office.

manufacturing sector provides roughly 70 percent of the production of goods versus between 25 and 55 percent for the rest. Not surprisingly, those countries (excluding Peru) also enjoy the region's higher per capita income levels. They also tend to be (here Uruguay is the exception) the region's larger economies, in terms of population and aggregate income levels, as we shall see soon. Judged solely by this criterion, this would be the list of Latin-American countries, which would be considered as promising partners to a PTA. Obviously, the US, by this criterion, is a far better candidate for partnership than any single Latin-American economy.

By the same token it appears that, with the exceptions noted above, enlarging the number of partner countries within the region of Latin America is not going to add much to diversity of the "partner" bloc. That is, a low measure of diversification within one (partner) country is not going to be compensated by variations among (partner) countries, which might have led to structural diversity in the "partner" bloc despite the absence

Table 10.4:   Per capita income and shares of major sectors, 1992.

	Per capita annual GDP ($)	Percentage in aggregate production of goods		
		Agriculture	Mining	Manufacturing
Argentina	6050	22.9	5.8	71.3
Bolivia	680	53.9	18.6	26.5
Brazil	2770	23.5	4.5	72.0
Chile	2730	20.2	36.8	43.0
Colombia	1290	38.0	14.0	48.0
Costa Rica	2000	45.8	0	54.2
Ecuador	630	31.5	21.6	46.9
El Salvador	1170	43.9	0.5	55.5
Guatemala	980	62.2	0.7	37.1
Honduras	580	56.0	4.0	40.0
Jamaica	1340	20.1	24.9	54.9
Mexico	3470	20.6	8.6	70.8
Nicaragua	410	61.3	1.1	37.6
Panama	2440	61.7	0.4	37.9
Paraguay	1340	63.2	1.0	35.8
Peru	950	20.5	5.5	73.9
Uruguay	3340	32.0	0.4	67.6
Venezuela	2900	18.8	31.1	50.2

Source: World Bank data.

of this trait in each of its components. We shall come back soon to other representations of this nature of the economies.

The economic size of a country is, we recall, another indicator of whether it is likely to be diversified, and hence resemble other economies in its structure and be more likely to confer the benefits of trade creation. The single best yardstick for "economic size" is a country's aggregate value of income or production. Table 10.5 presents the GDP of Latin America's economies, along with that of the US.

It is immediately apparent that the size of most Latin-American economies is very small indeed. For only three of them does the country's share in world GDP reach 1 percent or exceed it: Brazil (about 2 percent of world income); Mexico (about 1.4 percent); and Argentina (close to 1 percent). The combined share of all the rest of Latin America reaches only about 1 percent. It thus appears that only a "partner" grouping to a trade agreement, which includes Brazil, Mexico, and Argentina, would have an economic size of some significance, and that any grouping, which does not include at least one of these three, particularly either Brazil or Mexico,

Table 10.5:   Shares of Latin America's economies in world income, 1992.

Country	Aggregate annual GDP ($b.)	Percentage of world GDP GDP
Argentina	200	0.98
Bolivia	5	0.02
Brazil	425	2.05
Chile	37	0.18
Colombia	45	0.21
Costa Rica	6	0.03
Ecuador	12	0.05
El Salvador	6	0.03
Guatemala	10	0.05
Honduras	3	0.01
Jamaica	3	0.01
Mexico	285	1.41
Nicaragua	1	0.01
Panama	6	0.03
Paraguay	6	0.03
Peru	21	0.14
Uruguay	10	0.05
Venezuela	59	0.26
USA	5904	28.50

Source: Calculated from data in *World Bank Atlas*, 1994.

would have a minute economic size, and would have little promise of any trade creation.

In contrast, of course, the US income is a substantial part of the world's income. By this criterion, again, a preferential agreement with the US, or with any grouping which includes the US,[5] would seem to have a high potential for trade creation.

Compatibility of Trade Flows

The index of trade compatibility, the formulation of which was presented at some length in the last chapter, will now be employed to examine the extent to which the existence, or absence, of appropriate matches of intra-regional trade flows may, or may not, indicate a promise for the effectiveness of PTAs within the Latin-American region.

The index of export–import compatibility is presented in Table 10.6 in a matrix form.[6] The countries listed in the vertical column are *exporters*, and they are the potential *partners* to each importing country listed horizontally.

Table 10.6:   Indices of trade compatibility in Latin America, 1990.

Exports	Arg.	Bol.	Bra.	Chi.	Col.	Cos.	Ecu.	Gua.	Hon.	Jam.	Mex.	Nic.	Pan.	Per.	Par.	Sal.	Uru.	Ven.	AVG	USA
Arg.	0.24	0.28	0.28	0.29	0.37	0.36	0.33	0.37	0.36	0.34	0.37	0.31	0.32	0.41	0.26	0.41	0.32	0.36	0.34	0.28
Bol.	0.13	0.03	0.09	0.06	0.05	0.05	0.05	0.06	0.05	0.07	0.10	0.06	0.08	0.09	0.03	0.08	0.07	0.08	0.07	0.08
Bra.	0.38	0.33	0.31	0.38	0.40	0.37	0.43	0.36	0.36	0.37	0.43	0.31	0.39	0.37	0.30	0.39	0.34	0.43	0.37	0.42
Chi.	0.18	0.16	0.16	0.12	0.15	0.14	0.11	0.12	0.12	0.15	0.16	0.11	0.14	0.12	0.09	0.14	0.13	0.18	0.14	0.16
Col.	0.15	0.37	0.37	0.29	0.17	0.24	0.14	0.23	0.27	0.21	0.18	0.31	0.33	0.24	0.22	0.25	0.31	0.16	0.24	0.31
Cos.	0.19	0.19	0.19	0.20	0.18	0.29	0.18	0.21	0.22	0.26	0.24	0.22	0.26	0.18	0.18	0.22	0.19	0.18	0.20	0.26
Ecu.	0.06	0.26	0.26	0.17	0.09	0.12	0.05	0.15	0.17	0.11	0.07	0.22	0.20	0.14	0.14	0.15	0.22	0.05	0.14	0.18
Gua.	0.19	0.19	0.19	0.20	0.16	0.24	0.19	0.23	0.28	0.23	0.22	0.25	0.30	0.20	0.19	0.31	0.22	0.16	0.22	0.21
Hon.	0.09	0.08	0.08	0.08	0.06	0.09	0.06	0.07	0.08	0.11	0.12	0.09	0.10	0.08	0.09	0.08	0.09	0.07	0.08	0.12
Jam.	0.10	0.10	0.09	0.09	0.08	0.10	0.08	0.09	0.10	0.11	0.13	0.12	0.16	0.09	0.11	0.11	0.10	0.11	0.10	0.14
Mex.	0.35	0.53	0.45	0.45	0.35	0.37	0.33	0.41	0.42	0.30	0.35	0.52	0.45	0.34	0.34	0.38	0.50	0.38	0.40	0.52
Nic.	0.09	0.10	0.10	0.10	0.08	0.10	0.09	0.09	0.10	0.11	0.13	0.08	0.10	0.12	0.06	0.12	0.09	0.10	0.10	0.09
Pan.	0.15	0.16	0.14	0.14	0.13	0.16	0.13	0.17	0.20	0.21	0.20	0.16	0.21	0.17	0.13	0.20	0.17	0.15	0.16	0.17
Per.	0.15	0.13	0.14	0.14	0.17	0.18	0.12	0.20	0.20	0.21	0.16	0.12	0.15	0.16	0.15	0.23	0.15	0.16	0.16	0.17
Par.	0.05	0.06	0.05	0.05	0.07	0.06	0.05	0.06	0.08	0.10	0.09	0.06	0.08	0.08	0.02	0.09	0.08	0.09	0.07	0.07
Sal.	0.19	0.16	0.20	0.20	0.18	0.25	0.21	0.24	0.26	0.23	0.23	0.22	0.31	0.18	0.19	0.27	0.21	0.19	0.21	0.22
Uru.	0.16	0.18	0.18	0.18	0.18	0.21	0.18	0.20	0.21	0.23	0.20	0.23	0.27	0.23	0.15	0.23	0.19	0.18	0.20	0.20
Ven.	0.13	0.31	0.23	0.23	0.11	0.14	0.11	0.17	0.18	0.10	0.12	0.26	0.23	0.14	0.14	0.17	0.24	0.11	0.17	0.20
AVG	0.17	0.20	0.19	0.19	0.17	0.19	0.16	0.19	0.20	0.19	0.19	0.20	0.23	0.19	0.15	0.20	0.20	0.17	0.19	0.21
USA	0.53	0.52	0.54	0.56	0.56	0.52	0.50	0.48	0.44	0.50	0.63	0.40	0.43	0.48	0.39	0.46	0.46	0.58	0.49	0.60

A high coefficient would mean that a preferential agreement between an "importing" country and an "exporting" one would have a high likelihood of attracting imports of the former to the "exporting" country. For instance, the column for Argentina will show the compatibility of its imports with the exports of, in turn, Bolivia, Brazil, Chile, and so on. Thus, the column would show the potential for directing Argentina's imports to, in turn, Bolivia, Brazil, Chile, etc.

It is immediately evident that almost all the indices are rather low. The exceptions occur mainly where the exporting country is either Brazil or Mexico or, to a lesser extent, Argentina. Thus, for all the Latin-American countries as importers, a preferential agreement with almost any other Latin-American country is not likely to lead to much trade diversion. The (unweighted) averages for the importing countries are shown as a separate row (they are 0.16 for Argentina, 0.15 for Bolivia, and so on). As can be seen, these averages are remarkably similar for the individual countries — and are all low: they range from a high of 0.23 for Panama to a low of 0.15 for Bolivia and Paraguay. Interestingly enough, the average index of compatibility is within this range (it is 0.21) also for the US, that is, as an importing country, the US would realize little trade diversion in potential preferential agreements with Latin-American countries. Once more Brazil and Mexico (for the latter this is, of course, more than a "potential") are the exceptions. This stands in sharp contrast to the position of the US as an exporter in such agreements, which will be noted shortly.

As exporters, the indices of compatibility of any given Latin-American country with imports of the others naturally vary somewhat. However, for each individual exporting country, the variance is small enough to make the average index a meaningful representation of its position. These averages are shown in the column following that of Venezuela (they are 0.34 for Argentina, 0.07 for Bolivia, and so on). In Table 10.7, the countries are ranked by this average, which is presented along with four other variables: the degree of commodity concentration of exports, measured by the Gini–Hirschman coefficient; the level of per capita income; the size of aggregate income; and the share of manufacturing in the total production of goods.

These variables are clearly inter-related to each other; they all represent factors mentioned earlier as likely to lead to the high effectiveness of a preferential agreement. As has been shown in the earlier chapter, the index of compatibility tends to be higher when the country is large (in terms of aggregate GDP), rich (in terms of high per capita income), has a production pattern in which manufacturing is predominant, and

Table 10.7:   Average indices of trade compatibility and explanatory variables (1990 data).

Country	Average compatibility index	Coefficient of export concentration	Per capita annual income ($)	Aggregate annual income ($b.)	Percentage of manufacturing in production of goods
Mexico	0.41	0.36	3470	295	55.6
Brazil	0.38	0.16	2719	425	49.0
Argentina	0.32	0.20	6050	200	57.1
Colombia	0.25	0.34	1290	45	39.1
Costa Rica	0.22	0.33	2000	6	48.7
Guatemala	0.22	0.32	980	10	n.a.
El Salvador	0.22	0.45	1170	6	26.7[a]
Uruguay	0.20	0.27	3340	10	54.8
Panama	0.17	0.34	2440	6	n.a.
Venezuela	0.17	0.80	2900	59	29.8
Peru	0.16	0.32	950	21	52.3
Chile	0.14	0.44	2730	37	46.7[a]
Ecuador	0.14	0.52	630	12	42.0
Jamaica	0.11	0.66	1340	3	37.0
Nicaragua	0.10	0.37	410	1	36.4
Honduras	0.09	0.46	580	3	42.9
Bolivia	0.07	0.36	680	5	28.3[a]
Paraguay	0.07	0.47	1340	6	34.8
USA	0.52	0.14	23,120	5904	61.1[a]

[a] 1980 data; otherwise, data in this column are for 1994.
Source: Author's estimates from World Bank, World Development Report, various issues.

has diversified exports. At the top of the list stand, as a group apart, Mexico, Brazil and, to a lesser extent, Argentina: Latin America's largest countries, belonging to the region's richest, possessing highly diversified exports (less exceptionally so for Mexico), and manifesting the highest shares of manufacturing production. The indices of all other economies are substantially lower. At the bottom are Nicaragua, Honduras, Bolivia, and Paraguay — among the poorest economies (except for Paraguay), the smallest (in economic size), the least industrialized, and with a relatively highly concentrated structure of exports. The outlier, in its position, seems to be Uruguay: despite its small economic size, the other variables would lead us to expect a higher compatibility of its exports with other trade flows than its index actually shows. By this measure, then, Mexico, Brazil, and Argentina would appear to be the likeliest candidates as partners for an effective preferential agreement (but not necessarily a beneficial one — the promise here is for trade diversion!).

How does the region of Latin America compare, on this score, with other parts of the world? To start with, and of immediate significance for the purpose at hand, Table 10.6 shows also the indices of trade compatibility for the US. These are substantially higher than any of the indices of Latin-American countries, either in their average level (0.48 vs 0.40 and 0.37 even, respectively, for Mexico and Brazil — Latin America's highest), or in relationship to any individual Latin-American country (the US indices range from a low of 0.39 for trade with Paraguay to a high of 0.63 for trade with Mexico). This, of course, is not surprising in view of the size of the US aggregate income and its per capita income levels, and the high degree of dispersion of its export structure. Thus by this yardstick — as by judgments made on the basis of earlier observations — the US, whether alone or through NAFTA, would be a significantly more relevant partner for a preferential trade agreement with any Latin-American country than any other Latin-American country by itself (including Brazil and Mexico) or any combination of countries within Latin America.

It is useful to compare Latin-American countries with members of the most successful — or at least, the most effective — contemporary customs-union organization, namely, the European Economic Union. This latter group is presented in Table 10.8, where the indices of present members of the EU are shown. The US is again added to the list.

It is immediately apparent that these compatibility indices are uniformly higher — usually substantially so — than they are for Latin-American economies. In fact, the lowest (by far) indices in Europe, those of Greece and of Norway, are about as high as those of Argentina, Brazil, and Mexico, the three countries whose indices far exceed all the rest among Latin-American countries. Not surprisingly, in Europe too the determinants of the extent of trade compatibility seem to be the level of development and the degree of dispersion of exports: of the four countries with distinctly lower indices than the rest, two — Greece and Portugal — have substantially lower levels of per capita income than the rest of Europe, whereas the other two — Finland and Norway — have a substantially less diversified structure of exports. Compatibility of US exports with imports of the European countries is on the same level as that found among the European countries themselves, and it is somewhat higher than US compatibility with imports of Latin-American countries — equal to the highest of these, i.e., to the level recorded in US trade with Mexico.

It may be argued that a particularly high degree of compatibility among European trade flows in fact reflects the effect of the long existence of trade preferences practiced in this bloc. For this reason, it is also interesting to

Table 10.8: Indices of trade compatibility in Europe, 1990.

Exports	Imports															
	Blx.	Dnk.	Esp.	Fin.	Fra.	Ger.	Grc.	Ita.	Nld.	Nor.	Prt.	Swe.	UK	USA	AVG	Xcc
Blx.	0.72	0.61	0.56	0.58	0.63	0.62	0.61	0.63	0.59	0.53	0.57	0.57	0.60	0.55	0.59	0.17
Dnk.	0.55	0.61	0.53	0.56	0.54	0.53	0.56	0.51	0.55	0.55	0.48	0.56	0.53	0.45	0.53	0.13
Exp.	0.61	0.62	0.62	0.62	0.65	0.64	0.60	0.60	0.60	0.57	0.61	0.63	0.63	0.61	0.61	0.17
Fin.	0.48	0.53	0.49	0.49	0.48	0.47	0.49	0.46	0.49	0.48	0.46	0.50	0.48	0.44	0.48	0.28
Fra.	0.69	0.67	0.71	0.69	0.74	0.72	0.68	0.69	0.69	0.64	0.69	0.70	0.72	0.62	0.68	0.12
Ger.	0.67	0.68	0.71	0.72	0.73	0.69	0.65	0.67	0.67	0.64	0.68	0.74	0.69	0.62	0.68	0.14
Grc.	0.40	0.36	0.30	0.34	0.35	0.40	0.35	0.36	0.35	0.34	0.33	0.35	0.34	0.33	0.35	0.18
Ita.	0.61	0.64	0.60	0.67	0.67	0.67	0.61	0.56	0.63	0.62	0.63	0.69	0.63	0.58	0.63	0.12
Nld.	0.65	0.66	0.59	0.60	0.66	0.65	0.59	0.63	0.67	0.58	0.55	0.61	0.62	0.54	0.61	0.13
Nor.	0.36	0.39	0.40	0.38	0.39	0.37	0.37	0.38	0.38	0.36	0.37	0.37	0.36	0.38	0.38	0.38
Prt.	0.45	0.46	0.43	0.46	0.47	0.49	0.44	0.43	0.46	0.45	0.43	0.46	0.46	0.46	0.45	0.16
Swe.	0.58	0.61	0.65	0.67	0.63	0.61	0.57	0.59	0.60	0.57	0.61	0.66	0.61	0.59	0.61	0.16
UK	0.65	0.68	0.72	0.71	0.73	0.70	0.66	0.69	0.71	0.65	0.66	0.74	0.76	0.66	0.69	0.12
USA	0.61	0.61	0.68	0.63	0.64	0.64	0.54	0.63	0.65	0.59	0.61	0.64	0.68	0.60	0.63	0.14

Source: Calculated from data in Comtrade, UN Statistical Office.

Table 10.9:   Indices of trade compatibility in Europe, 1962.

Exports	Imports						
	Blx.	Fra.	Ger.	Ita.	Nld.	AVG	Xcc.
Blx.	0.58	0.46	0.50	0.46	0.55	0.49	0.16
Fra.	0.64	0.56	0.57	0.54	0.66	0.60	0.14
Ger.	0.56	0.50	0.40	0.49	0.58	0.54	0.19
Ita.	0.55	0.48	0.49	0.41	0.56	0.52	0.18
Nld.	0.52	0.47	0.53	0.46	0.58	0.50	0.15

Source: Calculated from data in Comtrade, UN Statistical Office.

make a comparison with European Union trade flows when the integration process had just started. Table 10.9 therefore presents the indices of compatibility in trade among the six original members of the Community (Belgium and Luxembourg (combined), France, Germany, Italy, and the Netherlands) in 1962, an early year of the Community's existence.

It appears that indices of compatibility were, indeed, lower in this group in the early 1960s than they were by the early 1990s. To what extent this may be explained by preferential agreements rather than by factors such as much higher income levels or somewhat higher levels of trade diversification is a question which we do not propose to resolve; however, it may be observed that the US indices in trade with these countries also increased, albeit somewhat less. Be that as it may, we see that the indices for 1962 are still much higher than those for present-day Latin-American countries — including Brazil and Mexico (in fact, since lower-income countries such as Greece Portugal, and Spain were not part of the group in 1962, the average level for the Union was higher at that time than in the early 1990s!). Thus, as potential partners for a PTA, the original members of the European Community look much more promising, in terms of effectiveness of the agreement, than any potential bloc of countries within Latin America — though not necessarily partnership combinations of Latin-American countries with the US or with NAFTA.[7]

Finally, a comparison of Latin America may be made with another group of countries that have often been contemplated as members of a potential trade-preferential bloc: these are the members of Asian-Pacific Economic Cooperation (APEC), a group which includes in it two Latin-American countries (Chile and Mexico). The indices of compatibility of trade within this group are presented in Table 10.10.

Table 10.10: Indices of trade compatibility in Asia-Pacific group, 1990.

Exports								Imports										
	Aus.	Can.	Chl.	Chn.	Hkg.	Ind.	Jpn.	Kor.	Mex.	Mys.	Nzl.	Phl.	Png.	Sgp.	Tan.	USA	AVG	Xcc
Australia	0.3	0.28	0.25	0.26	0.24	0.27	0.39	0.32	0.24	0.30	0.26	0.43	0.25	0.25	0.34	0.28	0.29	0.27
Canada	0.5	0.59	0.43	0.40	0.33	0.43	0.51	0.45	0.44	0.42	0.50	0.47	0.39	0.40	0.48	0.59	0.45	0.18
Chile	0.2	0.17	0.12	0.13	0.15	0.14	0.26	0.16	0.16	0.16	0.16	0.16	0.14	0.13	0.19	0.16	0.16	0.44
China	0.4	0.46	0.41	0.42	0.56	0.38	0.47	0.39	0.43	0.34	0.43	0.39	0.32	0.42	0.43	0.50	0.42	0.14
Hong Kong	0.4	0.33	0.27	0.29	0.53	0.20	0.26	0.24	0.31	0.30	0.35	0.23	0.25	0.39	0.28	0.36	0.29	0.20
Indonesia	0.2	0.25	0.29	0.19	0.28	0.21	0.47	0.30	0.20	0.20	0.26	0.30	0.19	0.34	0.25	0.36	0.27	0.31
Japan	0.6	0.62	0.55	0.47	0.43	0.50	0.30	0.47	0.55	0.56	0.55	0.41	0.43	0.59	0.54	0.58	0.53	0.20
Korea	0.4	0.42	0.39	0.38	0.62	0.35	0.36	0.40	0.39	0.47	0.46	0.35	0.35	0.50	0.45	0.50	0.43	0.16
Mexico	0.4	0.48	0.45	0.28	0.29	0.40	0.47	0.42	0.35	0.34	0.46	0.43	0.31	0.44	0.42	0.52	0.40	0.36
Malaysia	0.3	0.34	0.38	0.30	0.40	0.28	0.48	0.43	0.31	0.42	0.37	0.37	0.24	0.54	0.41	0.45	0.37	0.24
New Zealand	0.3	0.27	0.22	0.20	0.25	0.21	0.36	0.28	0.29	0.23	0.25	0.24	0.24	0.24	0.29	0.28	0.26	0.23
Philippines	0.3	0.27	0.20	0.22	0.35	0.18	0.31	0.24	0.23	0.24	0.24	0.37	0.21	0.26	0.29	0.34	0.26	0.33
Papua New Guinea	0.1	0.11	0.09	0.11	0.08	0.09	0.15	0.11	0.08	0.14	0.10	0.09	0.09	0.10	0.09	0.10	0.10	0.51
Singapore	0.5	0.45	0.41	0.36	0.50	0.35	0.38	0.45	0.46	0.50	0.46	0.34	0.40	0.65	0.50	0.49	0.44	0.25
Taiwan	0.5	0.44	0.39	0.38	0.62	0.34	0.33	0.38	0.45	0.43	0.46	0.34	0.35	0.51	0.42	0.50	0.43	0.14
Thailand	0.4	0.34	0.28	0.27	0.52	0.22	0.36	0.29	0.35	0.31	0.32	0.27	0.33	0.39	0.32	0.43	0.33	0.16
USA	0.7	0.68	0.54	0.49	0.46	0.54	0.50	0.58	0.63	0.59	0.61	0.53	0.52	0.56	0.65	0.60	0.57	0.14

Source: Estimated from data in Comtrade, UN Statistical Office.

As may be seen from a comparison of Tables 10.10 and 10.6, trade compatibility in this group is much higher than within Latin America, although the differences are not as stark as in the comparison with European countries. As was the case with regard to Latin-American countries — by now, this should certainly not be a surprise — compatibility is highest in trade relationships with the US; in this sense, the position of the US within the Asian-Pacific group is very similar to its position *vis-à-vis* the Latin-American economies. As in the other group of economies, compatibility appears to be determined by economic size, level of development, and export diversification. Next to the US comes Japan — a country of a roughly similar economic size and level of development as the US, but with a somewhat less diversified structure of exports. Interestingly, Japan's trade is not more but somewhat less compatible than that of the US in relation to practically all of its Asian neighbors (Singapore is a slight exception); this supports the hypothesis that the aforementioned factors (size, richness, diversity of exports, and the share of manufacturing) rather than geographical proximity are the important determinants of compatibility of trade flows among countries. In the same vein, it may be seen that Mexico's indices of compatibility are roughly the same in the present group as in trade with its neighbors in Latin America, or, similarly, that Chile's exports — due to their very high level of concentration — are as incompatible in relation to Asian countries as in trade with the country's Latin-American neighbors. In sum, overlooking the US and Canada as potential partners, it appears that a preferential group of Asian-Pacific countries, while not promising to be as effective as a grouping of European economies, would still be more relevant than any contemplated grouping within Latin America. This is undoubtedly due to Latin-American economies (with the important exceptions of Brazil and Mexico) being much smaller, poorer, and less diversified economically than those in the Asian-Pacific group.[8]

Conclusions

This chapter's analysis uses several criteria suggested in the preceding chapter to assess *ex-ante* the chances for effective preferential trade agreements among Latin-American countries and between them and North America, particularly the US.

The inferences from these yardsticks are practically uniform: the evidence strongly suggests that the likelihood of agreements within Latin

America being effective is rather low. To start with, the intense liberalization of recent years has paradoxically lowered the likelihood of a beneficial agreement: with a low starting level of tariffs (and nontariff barriers) on trade flows between Latin-American countries, a preferential agreement is more likely to have an adverse rather than a beneficial impact (though this impact would be small in any case). Other criteria point in the same direction: small shares of Latin-American countries in world trade and in trade with each other; small shares of these countries in world income; a low level of economic development of most of these economies; and, associated with it, the absence of economic diversification in the majority of countries.

Some of these factors are reflected in the level of a composite index devised for the purpose at hand, namely, the index of compatibility of trade flows, which describes the match between a country's imports and its partner's exports. This index is generally higher the higher the partner country's level of economic development, its economic size, and the degree of diversity of its exports. The index of trade compatibility yields the same indication as those of the other criteria: that is, it suggests, by and large, a small likelihood of successful preferential agreements within Latin America. As a rule, such agreements would be far less meaningful than they are in today's Europe, or even than could have been predicted when the European Economic Community was formed. Perhaps less expected is the indication that such agreements within Latin America are also, as a rule, less promising than potential agreements between countries in the Asian-Pacific region — another part of the world in which a discussion of intra-regional preferences is also popular.

On the other hand, the US is, by the above criteria, a promising partner for preferential agreements with the large majority of Latin America's countries. Going beyond the scope of the present analysis, it should be pointed out that the target of "locking in" the (hitherto multilateral) process of trade liberalization through a commitment undertaken in a bilateral or multilateral preferential agreement would also be served much better by an agreement with the US than by any intra-regional agreement in Latin America.

Given that an intra-Latin-American agreement must be commonly of little significance, those that would still be of some relevance are agreements that involve Brazil, Mexico or, to a lesser extent, Argentina. Since Mexico is a NAFTA member, an agreement with Mexico would most probably mean an agreement with (or perhaps access to) NAFTA — where the major impact would be due to the involvement of the US. This leaves virtually only Brazil as a potential Latin-American partner for at least a marginally significant preferential agreement. Within the present context of existing regional agreement, this would mean an accession to MERCOSUR — a relationship that would be only slightly more meaningful than an agreement which involves just Brazil. Judging by the indicators of this study, Bolivia is the distinct case in which a preferential agreement with Brazil, or an accession to MERCOSUR, might be fruitful.

Notes

1. The analysis will generally refer also to the Caribbean countries, and "Latin America" will stand as shorthand for "Latin America and the Caribbean." In abbreviation, though, we shall use "LAC."

2. This inference is restricted to the trade aspect: past agreements pertained also to determination of comparative advantage, a pattern of specialization, and allocation of investment — a highly damaging component, which, fortunately, will not form a part of any agreement contemplated at present. It should also be noted that the past levels of common external tariffs — an element abstracted from in the present analysis — were much higher than any levels that may follow preferential agreements, which are contemplated today.

3. The countries in the table are: Argentina (Arg.), Bolivia (Bol.), Brazil (Bra.), Chile (Chi.), Colombia (Col.), Costa Rica (Cos.), Ecuador (Ecu.), Salvador (Sal.), Guatemala (Gua.), Honduras (Hon.), Jamaica (Jam.), Mexico (Mex.), Nicaragua (Nic.), Panama (Pan.), Paraguay (Par.), Peru (Per.), Uruguay (Uru.), and Venezuela (Ven.).

4. In fact, part of the diversification, which is normally an element of development, is the increased size and proliferation of a variety of services. We ignore these in the present context since most of the services are predominantly nontradable, whereas the economic relationships that are relevant for the purpose at hand are those which concern only tradable activities.

5. The share of NAFTA countries (the US, Canada, and Mexico) in world GDP in 1992 was close to one-third.

6. The index has been constructed for 1990 because it is the latest year for which data were available for *all* countries when the analysis was carried out. However, indices have also been constructed for 1988 and 1989, as well as for the averages of 1988–1990, and only minor differences appear in comparing them with the indices for 1990.

7. By way of a footnote, we may digress for a moment on a somewhat different issue. The *diagonal* in the matrices of the index of trade compatibility represents the degree of similarity between the structures of each country's own exports and imports. Thus, this is an index of the importance, for each country, of *intra-industry* trade: an index of unity would represent the case in which all of the country's trade is intra-industry (by the way "industries" are defined in the classification scheme used). A comparison of Latin-America with Europe will show that intra-industry trade is very small indeed in the former. In the smaller economies, such as Bolivia or Paraguay, it is practically nonexistent. It is highest in the largest two economies — Brazil and Mexico — but even there it is much smaller than in Europe. Portugal, with the lowest proportion of intra-industry trade among European countries, still conducts more of it (in proportion of aggregate trade) than Mexico, the economy with most intra-industry trade in Latin America. In Europe, as may be seen from a comparison of Tables 10.8 and 10.9, intra-industry trade increased in importance over time. In the major European economies most trade now is intra-industry trade; it is somewhat less so in the US. As with the index of compatibility, the level of intra-industry trade appears to be a function of the economic size of the country, its richness, and the diversity of its trade flows. For discussions relating intra-industry trade to, *inter alia*, PTAs see Balassa and Bauwens (1988) and Syrquin (1992).

8. Intra-industry trade follows the patterns of trade compatibility: overall, it is higher in the Asian-Pacific group than in Latin America, but substantially lower than the norm in Europe. Aside from the US and Canada, the index of intra-industry trade reaches European levels only in Singapore — an economy with an exceptionally high proportion of essentially transit trade. The real surprise, in this sense, is the very low level of intra-industry trade in Japan, only slightly less surprising is the low level of such trade in Australia. In both economies, protection of importables is high; this, presumably, leads to the absence or low levels of many imports whose existence would otherwise have meant a higher level of intra-industry trade.

References

Alam, A and Rajapatirana, S (1993). Trade policy reform in Latin America and the Caribbean in the 1980s. World Bank Policy Research Working Paper No. 1104, Washington, DC.

Balassa, B and Bauwens, L (1988). *Changing Trade Patterns in Manufactured Goods.* Amsterdam: North-Holland Publishing Company.

Edwards, S (1993). *Latin America and the Caribbean: A Decade After the Debt Crisis.* Washington, DC: The World Bank.

Primo, B C A, Safadi, R and Yeats, A (1994). Regional integration in the Americas: "Déja Vu All Over Again"? The World Bank, Washington, DC (mimeo).

Syrquin, M (1992). Industrialization, integration and trade in Latin America, The World Bank, Washington, DC (mimeo).

Chapter 11

Assessing the Bias in Trade Expansion Following a Preferential Agreement

Introduction

The conclusion of a preferential trade agreement is expected to lead to the expansion of trade among the partners to the agreement. Whether this will also raise welfare levels in these economies is a separate issue, the answer to which must depend on the pattern of any trade expansion and the nature of distortions relieved or created by the preferential agreement. However, first, an assessment should be made of the degree to which a trade expansion has indeed taken place, that is, the extent to which the preferential agreement has been at all relevant. This is the central issue of the present chapter. While the analysis of the last chapter was meant to suggest measures for an *ex-ante* prediction, we now move to an *ex-post* discussion of developments. That is, the relevance of the trade agreement will not be assessed by some attributes of the economies involved, but by the analysis of changes, which have actually taken place following the introduction of an agreement.

In principle, trying to identify *ex-post* the impact of a trade agreement (or of any other "disturbance") can be done by two alternative approaches. One is the formulation of a full-fledged model and its estimation. Whether this is feasible or not, for the issue at hand, this is *not* the route followed here. The other approach, adopted in the present study, is the construction of a variety of measurements, which are intended to separate out the impact of the change under observation, that is, to try to abstract it from the effects of other simultaneous changes that presumably also affect the trade flows. In essence, these assume "neutrality," that is, they assume that in the absence of the preferential agreement, the trade flows under consideration would remain a constant proportion of magnitudes, which are presumed to determine trade flows (that is, of world trade, or of trade of some particularly relevant segment of the world, and so on).[1] Suggesting such a variety of indices is the purpose of this paper.

The use of several measures, rather than a single one, is based on the realization that *no* single measure can serve as "the" index — one which, on analytical grounds, will provide the "true" *cardinal* assessment of the level of the phenomenon under consideration (that is, the extent of a bias in trade expansion). Moreover, no *combination* of the alternative estimates, through one formulation or another, can yield such a "true" index. However, using several alternatives and finding *uniformity* (or close to it) in the directions indicated by each will provide a strong *ordinal* inference about changes (that is, whether a bias, in one direction or another, may indeed be judged to have taken place). Moreover, if alternative measures indicate *strong* changes, it is justified to conclude that the biased pattern of change must have been significant.

The development of these indices will be presented in the following section, whereas the following one will illustrate the use of the suggested measurements in one concrete, recent case — the Andean Pact, which is a preferential trade agreement among five countries in Latin America.

Indices of Trade Performance

The Intensity Ratio

This ratio, which was discussed in Chapter 9 in the context of an *ex-ante* assessment, has long been used as an elementary, popular measure of the bias in one country's trade with another, that is, the extent to which this trade flow exceeds, or falls short of, what can be explained just by the sizes of aggregate trade of the two partners.[2] The formulation of this ratio was presented in the last chapter and will not be repeated here. This index is applied here, though, in a different way: Our present concern is the bias revealed in the pattern of trade *expansion*, and for that, the observation required is the *change* in intensity ratios over a given period. That is, to take once again the flow of exports from home country j to partner country k,

$$B_{0,1}^x = \frac{IR_{jk,1}^x}{IR_{jk,0}^x},$$

where $B_{0,1}^x$ is the index of biased change of j's exports to k between periods 0 and 1; $IR_{jk,0}^x$ the intensity ratio of j's exports to k in period 0; and $IR_{jk,1}^x$ the intensity ratio of j's exports to k in period 1.

An index of unity would indicate a "neutral" expansion; an index above unity — a positive bias — and an index below unity — a negative bias (that is, a relative contraction of the trade flow under consideration).

The Commodity-Adjusted Intensity Ratio

The rationale of this concept and the formulation of the index have also been presented in Chapter 9. Its application in the present context should be obvious. It is conceivable that (say) a relative expansion of home country j's exports to partner k is due not to any bias toward that partner but to a changing *commodity composition* of the home country's exports: over the period under consideration, this composition might have changed to include more (or less) of what the partner country particularly requires. To abstract from the impact of such change, in order to try to better identify the impact of the policy change (the conclusion of a preferential agreement), the adjusted concept of the intensity ratio should be employed. For our present purpose, again, the *change* of the index over the relevant period is the observation required; a comparison of the "adjusted" ratio with its "simple" version will show to what extent a change in the intensity ratio is the product of a changing commodity structure of the trade flows of the two countries, rather than a change due to a country-directed bias. When the two intensity ratios — the "adjusted" and the "simple" — are equal to each other (or roughly so), a change of the intensity in the two countries' trade with each other does *not* result from changes in their specific trade structures. When the "adjusted" ratio is lower than the "simple" ratio, changes in an apparent preference of the two countries to increase their trade with each other are due, to one extent or another, to changes in their trade structures (the "extent" being indicated by the size of the gap between the two ratios). When the "adjusted" rate is higher, on the other hand, than the "simple" one, changes in trade structures are revealed to *lower* the apparent degree of trade preference, that is, without the structural changes, the increase in the tendency of the two partners to trade with each other will appear stronger. An implied assumption of these formulations, both in the definition of a given index and of its change over time, is that commodity structures of the trade flows, and of changes in them over time, are autonomous, *independent* of the geographic structures and of their changes. This is obviously an assumption, which is not fully defensible — a deficiency which must be borne in mind when the use of commodity-adjusted indices is made.

It should be noted that the "adjustment" carried out by using the proposed index is only partial. Thus, for instance, in the formulation presented earlier, it is only the change in the *partner-country's* structure of *imports*, not the home country's structure of exports, which is abstracted from. To take care of changes in both structures simultaneously, a much more complicated formulation would be required, and it probably would lose most of its operational value. The index discussed next offers another channel for addressing this issue.

Compatibility Indices

These indices, which again were presented in Chapter 9, are, strictly speaking, *not* measurements meant to gauge the bias in trade expansion: on the contrary, they may be used to *abstract* from other changes, so that the "net" geographical bias may be better identified.

A *change* in a compatibility index over an observed period would indicate the extent to which changes in the commodity structures of trade of the two partners should, by themselves, lead to a larger or smaller role of each partner in the trade of the other. This measure, it should be noted, provides only an *ordinal* indication: it *cannot* be inferred that, for instance, a doubling of the compatibility index between the trade flows of two partners will lead to a doubling of the (relative) size of this trade, or any other such quantitative relationship. Moreover, and more importantly in the context of our discussion, one *cannot* feed a (change of) compatibility index into another measure of trade expansion (for instance, divide the size of change of a trade flow by a change in a compatibility index) to get a "net" size of the geographical bias in trade expansion. The use of a compatibility index may serve, in this context, a more modest purpose: its observation will give a rough impression of the degree to which changes in trade structures may have been significant in leading to an observed bias in the geographical pattern of trade.

The Partner's Share in Trade Expansion

Suppose the aggregate trade of the home country increases over a given period, and so does its trade with its partner. The simplest way of examining whether the trade expansion over the period has been biased toward, or away from, the specified trade partner is to observe the *average* share of the partner in the home country's aggregate trade: an increase in this average will, almost by definition, indicate a positive bias of trade expansion in this direction (*regardless* of its causes, that is, whether it is indeed a "net" geographical bias or is a development explained by factors such as changes in commodity structures or similar factors). However, while such comparison of averages certainly yields a useful inference, this information is still limited. Specifically, the same change in averages may be yielded by a small or a weak impact of the trade-expansion bias, depending on the initial share of trade with the partner and the extent of expansion of the aggregate trade of the home country.

To complement the impression yielded by the comparison of averages and add more useful information, observation of the *marginal* share is suggested: it shows how important the partner has been in *trade expansion* of the home country. Taking, again, the flow of exports from the home country to its partner, the partner's "marginal" share is defined as:

$$SM_{jk}^x = \frac{X_{j \cdot k1} - X_{jk,0}}{X_{j \cdot 1} - X_{j \cdot 0}} = \frac{(\Delta X_{j \cdot k})}{(\Delta X_{j \cdot})},$$

where SM_{jk}^x is the marginal share of (partner) country k in export expansion of (home) country j; X_{jk} the exports of (home) country j to (partner) country k; $X_{j \cdot}$ the aggregate export of country j; and subscripts 0, 1 indicate sizes for periods 0, 1.

This share shows, as such, the role of partner k in j's export expansion (similarly, SM_{jk}^m would indicate k's marginal share in j's import expansion). However, for the purpose of indicating a *bias* in the pattern of trade expansion, a comparison of this marginal share with the *average*, at the initial position, is required. Thus, we should look at the ratio:[3]

$$E_{jk}^x = \frac{\Delta X_{jk,0-1}}{\Delta X_{j \cdot,0-1}} \Big/ \frac{X_{jk,0}}{X_{j \cdot,0}} \,,$$

which can also be written as

$$\frac{\Delta X_{jk,0-1}}{X_{jk,0}} \Big/ \frac{\Delta X_{j \cdot,0-1}}{X_{j \cdot,0}} \,.$$

The latter formulation suggests an elasticity and may indeed be referred to as the "elasticity" of expansion of the home country's trade with its partner — explicitly noting, though, that this "elasticity" does *not* convey any behavioral relationship. A unit elasticity indicates the absence of bias in the pattern of trade expansion; an elasticity above unity — a positive bias toward trade with the partner — and a below-unity elasticity — a negative bias.

A deficiency of this index, which must be noted, is that it is *not* applicable to a situation in which the home country's trade with the partner expands, whereas its aggregate trade falls, or the other way around. With changes in the two trade flows having opposite signs, the ratio under consideration would not make sense.

Decomposition of Trade Expansion

A still different method of identifying the bias in trade expansion is to *decompose* a change in the trade flow between the two partners: to identify the "neutral" elements of this change and abstract from them, leaving just the element, which will indicate a bias. For simplicity, we shall talk throughout about trade expansion, although the procedure analyzed will serve as well for trade contraction (in its total or in any of its elements).[4]

Trade expansion between the two partners may, first, be due to an increased size of the *aggregate* trade (say, exports) of the home country. An assumption of neutrality would call for a trade expansion between the two partners in the same proportion as the expansion of the home country's aggregate trade. This change would, thus, be a "neutral" element of trade expansion between the two partners. Similarly, the trade flow analyzed might have increased due to an increased size of trade (imports) of the *partner*: when the latter is a larger trader, its trade with the home country should increase, under "neutrality," in the same proportion as its aggregate trade. This would be, then, a second element of "neutral" expansion. Subtracting these two elements from the actual expansion of the trade flow will then leave, as a residual, the biased component of the trade expansion, that is, the element that *cannot* be explained by "neutral" responses to developments in either partner country. In symbolic terms, using the same designations as before:

(a) $\Delta X_{jk} = X_{jk,1} - X_{jk,0}$.

This is the actual trade expansion, which is decomposed into, first:

(b) $N_j^x = (X_{j\cdot,1} - X_{j\cdot,0}) \left(\dfrac{X_{jk}}{X_{j\cdot}}\right)^0$

This is the trade expansion due to an increase in home country j's aggregate exports, with a constant share of partner k, Second:

(c) $N_k^x = (M_{k\cdot,1} - M_{k\cdot,0}) \left(\dfrac{M_{kj}}{M_{k\cdot}}\right)^0$.

This is the trade expansion due to the increase in the partner's aggregate imports, with a constant share of the home country. And, finally:

(d) $B_{jk}^x = (a) - (b) - (c)$.

This is the biased component of the expansion of exports from j to k. Formulating this element as a ratio (of the initial position), the index $\bar{B}_{jk}^x$ derived is

$$\bar{B}_{jk}^x = \frac{B_{jk}^x}{X_{jk,0}}.$$

Similarly, the three elements — (b), (c), and (d) — may be presented as shares of (a) (summing up to unity). These ratios thus express the importance of each of the "neutral" elements, as well as of the bias, in "explaining" an observed change in the flow of trade between the two partners over a given period. A slightly different formulation of $\bar{B}_{jk}^x$ would add elements (b) and (c) to the denominator, that is, it would show the ratio of the biased element of trade expansion to what the trade flow would have been without this bias.

The Impact of Universal Liberalization

We want, finally, briefly to extend the discussion into an analytic area in which we suggest no method of estimation; nor, in fact, do we have a concrete answer even on principles or directions.

The issue is as follows. Very often — in the last two decades, this applies probably to a majority of the episodes — a preferential trade agreement among a group of countries is concluded simultaneously with the introduction of *universal*, nondiscriminating trade-liberalization policies in (most or all) individual countries of which the group is formed. Is it conceivable that an observed (favorable) bias in trade expansion among the group's members is due not to the preferential agreement, but rather to the universal trade-liberalization policies?

A universal, multilateral trade liberalization of a given country might be biased in favor (or against) any specific partner if the latter possesses some attributes which other trade partners do not. For instance, if a specific partner exports in large proportions goods, which were subject to particularly high protection prior to liberalization, the home country's import expansion would be expected to be biased in favor of this partner following the liberalization. By and large, one cannot expect on this score a bias toward or against partners to a preferential agreement: there is no reason why these partners should, as a rule, possess such attributes more frequently than other countries. There is one attribute, though, which may be an exception, namely, geographical *proximity*: partners to a preferential agreement are very often — although not inevitably — geographically close to each other. An analysis of the impact of proximity on trade expansion following liberalization will be provided in the next chapter. It will be concluded there that proximity would indeed lead to a bias (in the sense of a differential proportional impact on trade flows), but the bias could run either way. A general inference, which can be mentioned, is that the bias would tend to be in favor of the near-by partner, the more liberalization tended to introduce new goods into the trade flow, whereas a distant partner would be favored the more the liberalization policy induces the expansion of trade in goods that are already traded prior to it. Without possessing some specific knowledge, no rule may hence be derived. Thus, while the possibility that some bias exists due to a general liberalization policy must be acknowledged, this will not generally be of much use in the analysis of a bias found in trade expansion following the introduction of any concrete preferential agreement.

Biased Trade Expansion in the Andean-Pact Trade

Nature of the Andean Preferential Agreements

The Andean Pact or Andean Group (GRAN — Grupo Andino) incorporates five countries: Bolivia, Colombia, Ecuador, Peru, and Venezuela. It was established as early as in the late 1960s.[5] At that time, it was supposed to serve largely as a mechanism for joint decisions by its members on industrial allocation of investment, within a regime of insulation from the rest of the world. It was, however, almost completely inoperative and for some twenty years existed in nothing but name.

Early in the last decade, however, the Pact was re-activated. In 1991, the *Agreement of Cartagena* specified a complete full-fledged customs union among the five countries — though Peru postponed its effective membership (notwithstanding the fact that the Pact's headquarters are located in Lima). In 1992 (though this became a formal commitment only in late 1994) a common external tariff was agreed upon, specifying five tariff levels within the range of 0–20 percent. The large majority of tariff items appears to be subject to tariff rates within the range of 10–20 percent. A major outlier is the tariff on automobiles, which was fixed at the level of 40 percent (later lowered to 35 percent).

In effect, though, the "common" external tariff is far from being common. Aside from the (self) exclusion of Peru, "exceptions" have been applied to the tariff schedules of all other four members. Some of these are presumed to be "permanent." Thus, Ecuador is entitled to establish tariff rates for 990 tariff items, which deviate from the common tariff, up or down, by 5 percent (or less), whereas Bolivia is allowed to maintain (again, "permanently") its pre-agreement tariff schedule of just 5 and 10 percent. In addition, on a "temporary" basis, Colombia, Ecuador, and Venezuela have been allowed to establish different (unbound) tariff levels for several hundred tariff items (different in each case). Similarly, each member country is free to apply its own tariff schedule on imports from countries with which it concludes a (bilateral) preferential agreement. Thus, the Andean Pact despite having on paper a "common" external tariff is, in fact, not a customs union but, at best, an imperfect free trade area.

NTBs are presumably not a subject matter for a preferential agreement within the Andean Group, since they are supposed not to exist (with very minor exceptions). Where the practice is different, however, from this presumption, Andean trade partners may not fare better than others.

With Peru being formally a bystander,[6] and Bolivia too not sharing the common external tariff, the other three Andean members have formed a group within a group. These three — Colombia, Ecuador, and Venezuela — have established the Andean Community (CAN — Comunidad Andina de Naciones), with separate secretariat, head-quarters, meetings, etc. The Andean Community may be said to be an agreement exceeding a free trade area, though still falling short of a full fledged customs union.

It should be noted that at about the same time as the introduction of preferential agreements, all five members of the Andean Pact (like most other Latin-American countries) implemented a radical reform of their trade-policy regimes, shifting from extreme restrictiveness to a pervasive openness. Most members — Colombia, Ecuador, Peru, and Venezuela — introduced this change in the late 1980s or early 1990s, whereas Bolivia followed this course as early as in the mid-1980s. Once this change was made, not much further progress was recorded, that is, no significant further trade liberalization has taken place since 1992 or 1993 — just as in the case of the preferential agreement.

Assessment of Trade Expansion

The expansion of trade among the Andean-Pact members will now be analyzed through the use of most of the measures suggested in the preceding section.

Intensity ratios. All five Andean-Pact members being quite small economies, their bilateral trade flows can naturally be expected to be small too. Their geographic proximity, on the other hand, should tend to partly offset the impact of size and lead to a bias in favor of trading with each other. This, indeed, is revealed by the level of intensity ratios of the mutual trade flows.

Table 11.1 indicates that even in 1980, prior to any (effective) preferential agreements, intensity ratios in intra-bloc import flows were quite high — as a rule, considerably above unity. The major exception

Table 11.1:   Trade intensity ratios: 1980, 1989, 1997.

From	Imports					Average of five
	Bolivia	Colombia	Ecuador	Peru	Venezuela	
1980						
Bolivia	—	2.6	1.2	17.5	0.4	5.5
Colombia	2.1	—	12.7	5.1	7.1	6.7
Ecuador	0.9	12.3	—	3.3	2.5	4.8
Peru	20.7	11.1	19.0	—	2.6	13.3
Venezuela	0.1	3.8	0.9	1.1	—	1.5
Average of five	5.9	7.4	8.5	6.7	3.2	6.3
Rest of LAC	7.9	2.3	1.6	3.2	2.0	3.4
1989						
Bolivia	—	4.2	0.3	35.1	0.7	10.1
Colombia	2.1	—	11.4	17.0	6.8	9.3
Ecuador	0.8	44.5	—	59.2	0.3	17.9
Peru	26.3	23.6	16.1	—	6.6	18.1
Venezuela	0.6	8.5	1.9	3.7	—	3.7
Average of five	7.5	12.0	7.4	28.8	3.6	11.8
Rest of LAC	12.9	4.5	5.6	6.3	2.9	6.5
1997						
Bolivia	—	22.3	2.4	73.2	0.3	24.5
Colombia	9.0	—	44.4	30.0	27.5	27.7
Ecuador	3.8	23.4	—	26.2	3.0	14.1
Peru	39.9	8.1	10.4	—	7.2	16.4
Venezuela	2.6	22.0	14.2	14.0	—	13.2
Average of five	13.8	19.0	17.9	35.8	9.5	19.2
Rest of LAC	7.5	2.3	3.1	3.7	3.2	4.0

Source: Calculated from World Bank data.

to that were the flows of imports from Venezuela to the other four Andean partners. Over the 1980s, as the data for 1989 show, the level of intensity ratios increased even further — it almost doubled, on average. However, this increase did not exceed, in proportion, the increased level of intensity ratios in the imports of Andean-Pact members from the rest of Latin America. During the eight years from 1989 to 1997, roughly the period following the implementation of the preferential agreement, the level of intensity ratios increased much more dramatically — in contrast, this time, with the members' imports from the rest of Latin America, where intensity ratios actually declined, on average. This time, even Venezuela was not an exception. The average level of intensity ratios in intra-bloc trade approached 20 — an extremely high level. This tends to provide an indication that following the implementation of preferential agreements, trade expansion was indeed biased toward intra-bloc trade.

The commodity-adjusted intensity ratios. Table 11.2 shows this index, again for the *imports* of each of the five Andean countries (with exports of its partner used for weights). The estimates are shown for the years 1990 and 1997, with a comparison of the two thus reflecting changes following the

Table 11.2:   Trade-intensity ratios: "Commodity-Adjusted" vs "Simple."

Partner Country	\multicolumn{10}{c}{Importing country}									
	a	s	a	s	a	s	a	s	a	s	a	s
	Bolivia		Colombia		Ecuador		Peru		Venezuela		Average	
1990												
Bolivia	—		6.7	4.1	1.5	0.4	34.8	61.6	5.0	1.6	12.0	16.9
Colombia	7.7	3.1	—		10.1	16.0	23.8	19.2	14.2	11.2	14.0	12.4
Ecuador	1.5	1.6	13.3	10.1	—		62.6	65.5	2.1	0.8	10.9	19.5
Peru	31.5	33.3	17.4	18.3	14.4	16.6	—		7.6	9.0	17.7	19.3
Venezuela	0.6	0.6	19.5	10.8	1.3	3.3	3.3	4.0	—		6.2	4.7
Average	10.3	9.7	14.2	10.8	6.8	9.1	31.1	37.6	7.2	0.7	13.9	14.6
1997												
Bolivia	—		12.7	23.8	3.9	2.5	56.0	78.2	0.4	0.4	18.3	26.2
Colombia	11.1	10.2	—		43.5	51.8	23.2	35.0	92.8	32.0	42.7	32.3
Ecuador	6.5	4.3	24.6	27.1	—		24.1	30.3	8.0	3.5	15.8	16.3
Peru	36.6	42.5	8.4	8.6	11.3	11.0	—		7.2	7.6	15.9	17.4
Venezuela	2.2	3.0	22.4	25.6	10.5	16.5	11.7	16.3	—		11.7	15.3
Average	14.1	15.6	17.0	21.3	17.3	20.5	28.8	40.0	27.1	10.9	20.9	21.7

a = "adjusted" ratio and s = "simple" ratio.
Source: Calculated from World Bank data.

implementation of trade preferences. The table shows the "adjusted" ratios along with the levels of the "simple" ratios (the use of 1990 here rather than 1989 as in Table 11.1 was due to some technicalities).

We can see that the two alternative intensity ratios appear to be of roughly the same order of magnitude in most trade relations within the Andean Group. Moreover, this seems to be the case in 1997 as well as in 1990: the "adjusted" intensity ratios mostly increased, from 1990 to 1997, to about the same extent as did the "simple" ratios. The major exception appears to be the flow of Venezuela's imports from Colombia: here, the "adjusted" ratio increased over the 1990s much more than the "simple" ratio — in 1997 reaching an extremely high value of about 93. That is, Venezuela's preference for importing from Colombia increased substantially (the "simple" ratio went up from 11 to 32) *despite* a change in Colombia's commodity structure of exports that, by itself, should have *lowered* (in relative terms) Venezuela's imports from Colombia.

The share in trade expansion. Table 11.3 provides the data required for estimating the measure of bias in trade expansion through the observation of "marginal" shares, and the estimate itself. It analyzes two periods: the

Table 11.3:　Shares of the Andean Group in import expansion.

	Imports in initial year (in m. $)		Expansion over period (in m. $)		Ratios (in percent)		
	From world (1)	From Andean Group (2)	From world (3)	From Andean Group (4)	(2)/(1) (5)	(4)/(3) (6)	(6)/(5) (Multiple) (7)
1980–1989							
Bolivia	654.6	29.8	−34.7	−8.1	4.6 (−)23.3		(−)5.1
Colombia	4662.6	378.9	347.9	4.5	8.1	1.3	0.2
Ecuador	2215.3	166.0	−355.6	−73.1	7.5 (−)20.6		(−)2.7
Peru	2573.3	99.0	−564.7	134.2	3.9		
Venezuela	10,700.0	264.6	−3670.4	−112.9	2.5	(−)3.1	(−)1.2
Total group	20,805.8	938.9	−4277.5	−55.4	4.5	(−)1.3	(−)0.3
1989–1997							
Bolivia	619.9	21.7	1245.6	143.7	3.5	11.5	3.3
Colombia	5010.5	383.4	10,389.5	1843.1	7.7	17.7	2.3
Ecuador	1859.7	92.9	2650.9	750.1	5.0	28.3	5.7
Peru	2008.6	233.8	6549.3	1337.9	11.6	20.4	1.8
Venezuela	7029.6	151.7	6170.4	878.5	2.2	14.2	6.5
Total group	16,528.3	883.5	27,005.7	4953.3	5.3	18.3	3.5

Source: Calculated from World Bank data.

changes from 1980 to 1989, and from 1989 to 1997 — the latter being, again, the period following the introduction of trade preferences.

Columns 1 and 2 show, respectively, the country's aggregate trade (imports) and its trade with its Andean Group partners, in an initial year, whereas columns 3 and 4 record the *changes* in these two respective flows over a given period. Column 5, yielded by dividing 2 by 1, thus shows the "average" share of intra-Group trade in total, in the initial position. Column 6, on the other hand, yielded by dividing 4 by 3, represents the "marginal" share, that is, the share of the expansion of intra-Group trade in each country's aggregate trade expansion. Column 7, finally, dividing 6 by 5, shows a multiple which, since it is yielded by the division of a marginal by an average value, we have termed the "elasticity" of intra-Group trade expansion (without assigning, at this stage, any causal relationship).

The exercise is conducted, again, separately for the 1980s (the change from 1980 to 1989) and the 1990s (from 1989 to 1997). In line with our earlier observation, trends over these two periods appear to be radically different. In the first period (1980 to 1989), trade *contraction* was recorded in three countries — *Bolivia, Ecuador,* and (slightly) *Venezuela,* and it was *larger,* in relative terms, for intra-Group trade of these countries than for aggregate trade. In these three economies, thus, intra-Group trade fell in relative terms.[7] In *Colombia,* expansion occurred both in the aggregate and in the intra-Group trade flows, but it was smaller for the latter than for the former, that is, the "elasticity" of the intra-Group trade expansion was below unity. Only in *Peru* is a trend seen favoring intra-Group trade, which expanded while the aggregate trade flow declined.[8]

The changes during the 1990s, from 1989 to 1997, stand in sharp contrast. All trade flows of the five countries expanded — both the aggregates and the flows of intra-Group trade. At the margin, intra-Group trade contributed 18.3 percent of the aggregate expansion of the Group's trade, in comparison with an initial share (in 1989) of merely 5.3 percent. The "elasticity" of intra-Group trade expansion was thus 3.5 — very high indeed. This elasticity was above unity in each individual country. It was highest in *Venezuela* and in *Ecuador*: in the latter, intra-Group trade provided as much as 28 percent of the expansion of aggregate trade (in comparison with a share of just 5 percent in the initial year, 1989).

Thus, by this measure too, trade expansion in the Andean countries was heavily biased toward intra-bloc trade following the implementation of the Andean Pact.

The decomposition of trade expansion. We apply, finally, the measure of decomposition to estimate the bias in trade expansion. We recall that this measure decomposes a given size of trade expansion between two partners into three elements. Two — the expansions due to changing sizes of aggregate trade of either the home country or its partner — represent the "neutral" elements of trade expansion between the two, whereas the third, a residual, represents the element of (positive or negative) biased expansion.

To economize on space, the derivation of the three elements in the case on hand, which is quite straightforward, is not shown here. Table 11.4, on the other hand, puts the element of biased expansion identified in this way in perspective. It is shown, first, as a fraction of the aggregate change in the trade flow (as on earlier occasions, just imports), and, second, as a multiple of the size of trade (that is, imports) in the initial position (1980 for the change from 1980 to 1990, and 1990 for the change from it to 1997). Observation of these estimates yields, indeed, interesting inferences.

First, not much of any pattern is shown for the period of the 1980s (1980 to 1990): the estimates yield conflicting evidence for the trade flows of the different member countries.[9] For changes over the 1990s, on the other hand, the pattern is clear and striking. The large majority of the biased changes in the bilateral trade flows (16 out of 20) are *positive*, and for the aggregate of each country's trade with the other four partners the (five) biased changes are all positive. As a fraction of the aggregate change in each trade flow, the biased changes are mostly large — often close to 100 percent (that is, explaining fully the change in the trade flow). When the aggregates (five altogether) of each country's trade with its other four partners are observed, their (unweighted) average amounts to over 60 percent, that is, the "biased" expansion in intra-Group trade, over this period, accounts for the major part of the overall expansion of this trade. The mild exception to this pattern is provided by *Peru*, in which some of the biased changes in trade were negative. The overall biased change (that is, in combined trade with all other four partners) was positive, but significantly lower than for the other four (around 38 percent of total expansion of intra-Group trade for *Peru* vs an average of 66 percent for the rest).

The outcome for the 1990s appears even more dramatic when the biased change is presented as a multiple of the size of trade in the initial year. This multiple is very high — often within the range of 5–10. Beyond the (20) bilateral trade flows the multiple in question for the (five) aggregates of each country's trade with its four partners range from −2.0 to 5.9, with

Table 11.4:   Decomposition of changes in trade flows.

| | The "Biased" change in imports | | | |
| | Percentage of change in imports | | Multiple of starting-year imports | |
Exporter	1980–1990	1990–1997	1980–1990	1990–1997
Imports of Bolivia				
Colombia	81.1	78.8	0.32	6.37
Ecuador	28.0	77.3	0.03	5.83
Peru	(−)156.5	49.3	−0.20	1.67
Venezuela	98.7	80.6	5.25	7.14
All four	−1023.8	63.0	−0.04	4.02
Imports of Colombia				
Bolivia	(−)231.5	85.7	−0.35	10.51
Ecuador	(−)147.9	76.6	−0.61	5.72
Peru	−443.4	201.7	−0.16	−1.17
Venezuela	69.4	56.0	0.44	2.23
All four	21.8	52.7	0.05	2.41
Imports of Ecuador				
Bolivia	(−)77.2	86.3	−0.67	9.44
Colombia	●	79.5	0.10	5.81
Peru	(−)68.4	−45.2	−0.43	−0.47
Venezuela	148.0	82.5	0.61	7.06
All four	(−)31.2	75.4	−0.09	5.88
Imports of Peru				
Bolivia	96.4	6.7	0.63	0.16
Colombia	99.0	55.5	2.39	2.80
Ecuador	99.8	−206.2	10.90	−1.51
Venezuela	97.7	75.2	0.77	6.81
All four	99.1	37.8	2.40	1.99
Imports of Venezuela				
Bolivia	●	(−)259.4	0.23	−1.62
Colombia	●	79.5	0.19	3.85
Ecuador	(−)49.1	89.2	−0.44	8.20
Peru	●	6.3	0.41	0.07
All four	●	74.0	0.16	3.97

Source: Calculated from World Bank data.
− indicates a minus sign for numerator ("biased" change) and a positive denominator.
(−) indicates both numerator and denominator (total change) with a minus sign.
● (inapplicable) indicates a positive "biased" change and a negative total change.

an average of 3.7 and a weighted average of 3.0. That is, just the "biased" element in the expansion of intra-Group trade amounted to three times the absolute level of this trade in the initial position (1990). Such a change, over just seven years, must be considered a strong indication indeed of a heavily biased expansion of intra-Group trade among the Andean countries.

Conclusion

We have used four of the measures proposed in the earlier section to estimate the extent of a bias toward (or away from) intra-bloc trade in trade expansion of the Andean countries following the implementation of the Andean Pact. As we noted earlier, no single measure provides "the" index whose value would give the quantitative level of the phenomenon under consideration, nor would a combination of the measures provide such a single index. In case of conflicting indications, it would be difficult to reach a definite inference. As it happens, in the case at hand not only do all measures point in the same direction, that is, toward a positive bias in trade expansion toward intra-bloc trade, they also indicate, sometimes dramatically, that the bias is very strong. This unanimity of inferences, and their strength, must suggest a very high probability that the outcome is not accidental but that a causal relationship exists, that is, that the introduction of a preferential trade agreement led to a substantial proportional increase of intra-bloc trade in the Andean region. This, of course, does not necessarily imply that the Pact also yielded an increase of *welfare* in the countries involved; but this would be a separate issue.

Notes

1. "Gravity models," which are sometimes used for the purpose at hand, are basically similar to the approach used here: they do not incorporate *behavior*, but estimate the impact of a given change through a deviation of the outcome from a given pattern. The earliest application of a "gravity model" to the assessment of a PTA is probably provided in Aitken (1973). For a recent and elaborate use, see Saloga and Winters (1999).
2. A survey of early uses of this index for the purpose at hand is provided in Drysdale and Garrant (1982). A recent application may be found in, for instance, Yeats (1998).
3. Note that this ratio is *not* the same as the ratio of averages at the two points of observation, with which we started our discussion. The latter ratio is

$$\frac{X_{jk,1}}{X_{j\cdot 1}} \bigg/ \frac{X_{jk,0}}{X_{j,0}} \quad \text{or} \quad \frac{X_{jk,1}}{X_{jk,0}} \bigg/ \frac{X_{j\cdot,1}}{X_{j\cdot,0}}.$$

4. Essentially, this is a "gravity-model" decomposition.
5. Chile was originally a sixth member of the Pact. It withdrew its membership in the 1980s.

6. Peru has recently joined the free trade area component of the Andean Pact (*not* the common external tariff). Prior to that, Peru's trade with the other four Andean countries was governed by separate, bilateral free trade agreements of Peru with its partners. These led to vastly different proportions of actually free trade between Peru and its neighbors. Thus, in 1994, the proportion of free trade items in Peru's *imports* ranged from 100 percent for imports from Bolivia to 8 percent for imports from Ecuador. For Peru's *exports*, the proportions varied between, again, 100 percent in Bolivia's imports from Peru and 57 percent for Ecuador's imports.

7. In changes with these signs, the "marginal" analysis does not contribute much.

8. Once more, in changes with these signs, the "elasticity" has no clear meaning.

9. Even much of this evidence is not meaningful: when the "biased" change is positive and the aggregate change is negative, or the other way around, the ratio of the former to the latter does not yield an obvious interpretation.

References

Aitken, N D (1973). The effect of the EEC and EFTA on European trade: A temporal cross-section analysis. *American Economic Review*, 63, 881–892.

Drysdale, P and Garnant, R (1982). Trade intensities and the analysis of bilateral trade flows in a many-country world: A survey. *Hitotsubachi Journal of Economics*, 2, 62–84.

Sologa, I and Winters, L A (1999). Regionalism in the nineties: What effect on trade? The World Bank, Washington, DC (mimeo).

Yeats, A J (1998). Does Mercosur's trade performance raise concerns about the effects of regional trade arrangements? *World Bank Economic Review*, 12, 1–28.

Chapter 12

Proximity, Partnership to Trade Preferences, and the Impact of Liberalization

This chapter and the following chapter will address two issues involved in the role of proximity of economies. First, whether a preferential trade agreement (PTA) looks more promising when concluded between neighboring countries than between distant partners. Second, when an overall (nondiscriminating) trade liberalization is implemented, should it be expected that the trade flows between a home country and its neighbor will be affected differently from trade flows with distant economies?

The present chapter, while presenting the components of the first issue, will discuss primarily the second. Whereas the following chapter will focus on the role of geographic proximity, which may be assigned to the impact of distance.

Proximity and the Choice of Partners

The Issue

Is a neighboring country a more promising candidate than a distant one for a PTA? Consequently, does a "regional" PTA stand a better chance of success than an agreement between noncontiguous countries? This is certainly not a novel topic. In recent years it has been widely discussed, most often under the rubric of "natural trade partners." Among the supporters of this presumption in recent controversies, Krugman and Summers[1] may be the most prominent; while Bhagwati and Panagariya stand out as representatives of the nay-sayers.[2]

Some confusion exists as to the nature and definition of the issue, and it may be best to start by clarifying these. The question posed may be broken down into three separate elements, namely:

(i) What is the impact of the size of trade with a partner on the promise of a PTA with that partner?
(ii) What, in turn, is the significance of geographic proximity and low transport costs for the size of trade with a (potential) partner?
(iii) Finally, given the size of trade, is there a separate additional impact, which may be assigned to geographic proximity *per se*?

The second element mentioned — geographic proximity and the size of trade — will be addressed in the following chapter. Here we shall review the other two elements. However, we should note, beforehand, that this part of the presentation — surveying, in fact, on-going analyses — will follow these in focusing on trade diversion, that is, trade creation and trade expansion are taken for granted, and only the implications of proximity for trade diversion are explored. We shall return to this point later in this section.

The Impact of Size of Trade with the Partner

First, to minimize confusion, it should be clear that "size" of trade refers to relative size. This is understood as relative to the home country's aggregate trade (more specifically, the ratio of the country's imports from the partner to its aggregate imports) and not as relative to the home country's aggregate economic activity. So far as the latter ratio is concerned, it has long been established — in Meade's analysis and, even more so, in Lipsey's,[3] and not disputed since — that the higher this ratio, the smaller the capacity for replacing the home country's own production by imports from the partner, that is, the smaller the trade creation, the welfare-enhancing element of a PTA.

The Meade–Lipsey analysis, repeated recently under the "natural trade partners" mantle, asserts a positive relationship between the ratio of a partner in the home country's trade and the welfare-enhancement potential of a PTA: a large size of trade in this sense (meaning, by definition, a small proportion of trade with the rest of the world, ROW) leaves less room for trade diversion, hence a weaker potential for welfare contraction.[4] In the extreme case, in which all the home country's imports originate in the partner, no trade diversion at all will be possible. In a limited sense, a PTA with such a partner (with the complete elimination of tariffs) would be equivalent to moving the home country to a complete free-trade regime.[5]

This tenet of conventional wisdom has recently been disputed by Bhagwati and Panagariya. They conclude that "the volume of trade criterion is conceptually inappropriate and must be summarily rejected".[6] This conclusion, however, is not warranted: the analysis of Bhagwati and Panagariya raises valid points, but these do not address the specific issue at hand.[7] The conventional-wisdom proposition must still stand: *Ceteris paribus* (including, under this proviso, a given ratio of the home country's aggregate imports to its domestic activity), the higher the share of imports from the potential partner in the home country's aggregate imports, the more promising is a PTA.

Significance of Distance Per Se

We now reach the third element mentioned in our breakdown of the issue of proximity and the share of trade, namely beyond the potential impact of distance on the size of trade — that is, at any given trade size — should the distance between economies be of any concern for assessing the promise of a PTA? Put slightly differently: given the size of trade with a partner, is it of any interest, for the purpose at hand, to know whether this size is due to some (high or low) level of transport costs rather than to a variety of other factors?

To answer these questions in the affirmative, a reason must exist to presume that if trade with a specific country is due to low (or high) transport costs, that country could potentially displace trade of the home country with others more or less easily than otherwise, or that any displacement would tend to have a smaller or a higher welfare loss. We do have one demonstration — valid, I believe — that proximity *per se* should be a consideration against preferential treatment. This is provided by Bhagwati and Panagariya (1996, pp. 40–43) in their contribution discussed above. They take two trade partners whose "inherent" supply conditions for a given good are similar, but one is closer to the home country than the other. At any given import price, the marginal cost (to the home country) would be *higher* in trade with the nearby country: its sale of the import good would be larger than that of the distant country, implying a lower elasticity of supply. The home country would thus be better off if some of its imports could be diverted toward the distant country. Thus, a policy that discriminates against the nearby country and in favor of the distant one, taking advantage of the differential effects of the home country's tariffs on its terms of trade, would be welfare enhancing.

It should be noted, though, that the meaning of *ceteris paribus* is somewhat different here from the one used in the context in which the issue has been discussed thus far: to abstract from the criterion of size of trade, and separate out the impact of proximity *per se*, we have postulated equal sizes of imports (from alternative potential partners) rather than equal "inherent" production costs. With equal import sizes, the marginal costs of imports from the two alternative sources will also be equal. However, this observation does not negate the Bhagwati–Panagariya conclusion that, whatever other criteria (including that of size of trade) tell us, a low level of transport costs *per se* is a consideration against a PTA with the contemplated partner. Whether this element of assessment is of much quantitative significance may be doubted — and it is difficult to conceive a way of actually calibrating it. Two points, however, should be observed. First, this analysis is applicable to any case in which one trading partner is lower cost than another, whether the excess cost is due to transport costs or any other "inherent" reasons. This will hold as long as the cost differential is constant per unit; otherwise, the conclusion will either be reinforced or will tend to be offset. Second — probably of much significance — the analysis is applicable to a large home country, which faces rising supply curves of its partners' exports. For a small price-taking home country, this analysis will be of no consequence. In the latter instance, it seems obvious that a lower-cost country (whether due to low transport or other costs) is likely to become a better potential partner for a PTA; the loss per unit of trade diversion (the terms-of-trade loss) toward such partner is likely to be smaller than otherwise. It is also more likely, the lower the partner's cost, that this partner will be the cheapest source of imports to start with, so that no trade diversion will be involved.

Expanding somewhat the scope of discussion of the transport-cost issue, a question may be raised concerning the relationship of proximity to the *structure* of trade with a partner (rather than to its size). In the most obvious way, trade with a distant partner will tend to have a heavier representation of goods whose transport costs are low (relative to value). This by itself, though, will have little bearing on the issue of the promise of a PTA. Of more interest is another structural feature related to transport costs — that of its commodity concentration. The higher the transport costs in trade with a given partner — just as the higher the level of man-made barriers to trade — the smaller will be the range of goods imported from the partner (or exported to it): the higher the barrier, the more will goods in which the partner (where imports are concerned) has a relatively low "inherent" comparative advantage drop out of the actual import list.[8] This shortening of the list, making (actual and potential) imports from the partner more concentrated among fewer goods, is relevant to the assessment of a PTA; however, the information indicated by it is fully revealed by observing the trade structure. Whether goods are not imported due to high "inherent" production costs to the partner or to high transport costs is immaterial to the assessment of the promise of any concrete PTA. Proximity or transport cost *per se* should thus not form a separate element in such assessment.

Proximity and Trade Creation

As noted earlier, the discussion of the "natural trade partners," which we have followed thus far, has been focused solely on the trade diversion element of a PTA: in essence, the question addressed has been whether an agreement with a proximate country tends to minimize the loss from trade diversion. The trade-creation and trade-expansion elements (for brevity, we shall refer to both as "trade creation") have remained in the background. Without their existence, an agreement would certainly not be worth undertaking, and the discussion would be a futile exercise; however, the relationship of proximity to trade creation, which may conceivably be of greater significance than its impact on trade diversion, has commonly been ignored.

To start with, we should note that the analyses of trade creation and trade diversion, in this context, are not symmetrical. For trade diversion, the (relative) size of trade with the partner seems to be the crucial element, and proximity seems to be of significance primarily due to its expected relationship to this size. For trade creation, on the other hand, the size of trade with the partner is not at all a relevant factor: instead, it is prices in the partner country, in relation to prices in other countries, which should matter. We have seen, though, that at least in one form, through the expected impact on the extent of worsening of the home country's terms of trade, this is also an element in the analysis of trade diversion.[9]

Here, the reasoning is straightforward and the outcome unambiguous. The lower the price charged by the partner, the larger should be the scope for trade creation, and the larger, hence, the benefit from it.[10] Transport costs are lower — by definition — in trade with a proximate country. Hence, *ceteris paribus* (understanding by this proviso not given sizes of trade, but equal "inherent" costs, or FOB prices), the foreign price facing the home country, will be lower when the foreign source is a proximate rather than a distant country.[11] The benefit from trade creation will definitely be expected to be positively related to proximity of the contemplated partner to a PTA.[12]

Proximity and Trade Expansion Following Liberalization

The Issue

This section will address another facet of the relationship of proximity of countries to commercial policies. This time we assume that a policy of universal, nondiscriminatory (among trade partners) trade liberalization (complete or partial) is implemented by the home country. We pose the question: should this policy measure be expected to have a different quantitative impact — in the sense of proportional changes — on trade with proximate countries than on trade with those that are far away?

This issue has not, apparently, been raised before, and it is of some importance. Take, for instance, an issue which has been discussed earlier, in the context of an ex-post assessment of the liberalization policies introduced in Latin America in the late 1980s and early 1990s.[13] The majority of the countries involved have followed two parallel tracks, almost simultaneously: a radical, universal, nondiscriminating trade liberalization, and the conclusion of PTAs (or the actual implementation of an arrangement that previously existed in name only). These are MERCOSUR — for Argentina, Brazil, Paraguay, and Uruguay — and the Andean Pact involving Bolivia, Colombia, Ecuador, Peru, and Venezuela. Quantitative analyses of trade within each of these groups show a dramatic increase (proportionately, of course) in intra-bloc trade flows. In interpreting these changes, is it legitimate to assign such increases, as a working hypothesis, to the impact of trade preferences? Or alternatively, can the outcome be predicted from the expectation that trade flows between neighboring countries should expand more than others following the general trade-liberalization policies? These two alternative interpretations indicate quite different implications for the expected outcome of the conclusion of a PTA.

A Tentative Analysis

The issue at hand will be addressed here in a very rudimentary fashion, specifically, by using a partial-equilibrium analysis and by an intuitive extension of its inferences.

Start with Fig. 12.1. We assume two potential providers (to the home country) of a given import good. The two partners are inherently equal, that is, their FOB supply curves are identical.[14] However, one of the partners, N, is nearby, with low transport costs in trade with the home country, whereas trade with the other partner, F, is subject to higher transport costs. For simplicity (this is irrelevant to the outcome), assume that transport costs with N, the nearby partner, are zero, and that they are constant per unit of the imported good in trade with F, the far-away partner. S_N is thus the supply curve (to the home country) of both N and F without transport costs,[15] and it is indeed the supply curve of N to the home country. S_F, on the other hand, is partner F's supply curve: it lies at a given distance, equal to the level of transport costs (in trade with F), above S_N.

The home country's demand curve is not shown. Suffice it to know that prior to liberalization, given some (geographically uniform) tariff imposed by the home country on imports of the good in question, the equilibrium price (net of duty) received by the exporter (whether N or F) is P^0. At

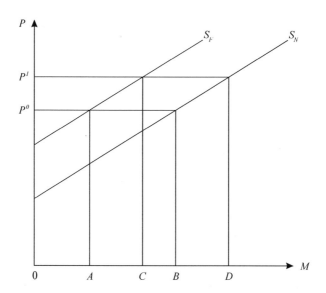

Figure 12.1:   Expansion of imports from two partners.

this price, the amount imported from N is OB, whereas imports from F — smaller, of course — are OA (OB and OA together being the equilibrium quantity). Suppose, now, that the duty is removed (or just lowered — this is immaterial), and the new exporter's price becomes P^1.[16] At this new price, imports from N will expand from OB to OD, and imports from F — from OA to OC. The absolute expansions (BD or AC) are equal in both trade flows. However, given the difference in initial flows, the proportional expansion is higher for the imports from F than it is for imports from N. That is, import expansion will be proportionately higher in trade with the distant partner.[17]

Figure 12.2 describes a different initial position and a different outcome — with the same basic assumptions. Here, at the initial price P^0 (under the existence of a tariff), the good in question is imported solely from the nearby partner N. With the removal of the tariff, the exporter's price becomes P^1. At this higher price, imports are still bought only from N, with the size of these imports increasing by AC. In this case, all import expansion occurs in trade with N. The comparison of proportional expansion of imports of a given good from the two partners becomes meaningless in this case. It obtains meaning only when imports of the specific good are contemplated in the context of overall imports: these do expand in trade

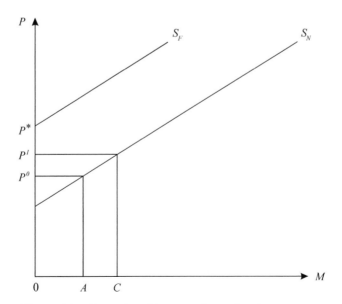

Figure 12.2: Expansion of imports: alternative circumstances.

with nearby partner N, whereas no expansion takes place in trade with far-away partner F. In this instance, thus, a bias toward expansion of trade with the nearby partner is evident — in contrast to the case analyzed earlier.

Still another possibility — not shown explicitly in the diagram — is where the initial position is as shown in Fig. 12.2 (at price P^0); however, at the post-liberalization price P^1 some imports appear also in trade with partner F (that is, P^1 will be somewhere above P^*). In this case, the proportional expansion of imports from F must be infinite; however, this is almost meaningless. The real consideration here, too, involves the impact on overall imports. In absolute amounts, the expansion of imports from F of the specific good in question is smaller than the expansion of imports from N. We also know that if in each market the same assumptions are made as in this analysis, initial overall imports from F will be smaller than imports from N. Hence, with no further information, we will not know what the differential impacts on the expansion of this specific good imply for the proportional changes of overall imports from the two alternative partners.

The outcome of this analysis is that "anything could happen"; that is, we are not able, on the basis of *a priori* analysis, to provide a definite proposition on the likelihood of a uniform, nondiscriminatory liberalization provoking an expansion of imports, which would be (in proportional terms, of course) biased either toward or away from nearby partners. What may be stated by way of generalization is that:

(i) The absolute expansion of trade will always be larger (equal to, in the limiting case) in trade with the neighboring country than with the distant country.

(ii) The proportional trade expansion — the size, which is relevant in the present context — will tend to be biased in favor of the neighboring country the more the tariff reduction (elimination) introduces new goods into the trade flow, whereas the distant country will be favored the more the price change induces the expansion of trade flows of goods that are already traded prior to the policy change.

It should be noted that the analysis here is symmetrical for the two directions of price changes — that is, it may be applied equally to cases in which the tariff is increased (or newly imposed). There is no general answer to the question of whether increased restrictiveness of the home country's trade — imposition or intensification of its barriers on trade — will be a greater constraint (in proportional terms) on the country's trade with its neighbors or with distant trade partners.

Notes

1. See Krugman (1991) and Summers (1991).
2. Several papers, but primarily Bhagwati and Panagariya (1996).
3. Meade (1955) and Lipsey (1960).
4. Needless to say, a large size of exports to the partner would be beneficial, in having a substantial impact on the home country's gain from a rise of its export price. Note, though, an asymmetry: unlike the case of imports, the gain on the export side is related positively to the ratio at hand.
5. "In a limited sense" — because a difference does exist. While a PTA would not result in any displacement of present (pre-PTA) imports from the ROW — there are none — it might still lead to the displacement of potential imports that would have been forthcoming had tariffs on imports from the ROW also been removed.
6. See Bhagwati and Panagariya (1996, p. 40).
7. Bhagwati and Panagariya offer three grounds for rejection of the conventional proposition. First, they contend, with regard to the expected impact of a PTA it is not the "actual" but the "potential" trade diversion, which counts, and the latter is a function not just of the size of imports (from the partner), but also of the "cross elasticity of (the home country's) demand for the partner's goods with respect to the price of its own goods, relative to that with respect to the price of the outside country's goods." (p. 35). The second argument suggests that a large initial size of trade from the partner may in itself not reflect free-market forces but be the product of existing preferences (i.e., those in place prior to the contemplated PTA). The third argument asserts that the loss from trade diversion is greater than meets the eye: what we (notionally) observe is the distortion of the present trade system; however, potential future changes in patterns of comparative advantage (whatever their direction) will increase the loss from trade diversion.

   The second of these three arguments is misplaced. It does seem likely that a future PTA is contemplated more often with a partner to which some privileged treatment has already been accorded. However, if this preference has indeed led to welfare loss, this will be a sunk cost, immaterial to the issue of whether further preferences are likely to lead to a gain or to a loss. The first and the third arguments, on the other hand, do seem valid, but their relevance in the present context is not indicated. These two arguments propose additional considerations as to why a PTA is more likely to lead to a loss through trade diversion rather than to a gain. However, unless a bias is demonstrated, tying these additional sources of loss to the size of trade — and no such bias is suggested in the Bhagwati–Panagariya analysis — these arguments do not address the issue of size, which is the present subject matter.

8. See the analysis in Chap. 6.

9. Summers (1991, p. 298) notes that PTAs among countries, which already maintain "disproportionately strong trading relationships... are likely to be trade creating rather than trade diverting." This may reflect a proposition about the strength of trade creation, not just about the weakness of trade diversion. However, if so, it would assign the impact on trade creation to the (relative) size of trade flows — a relationship, we note, for which no *a priori* justification can be pointed out.

10. This can easily be demonstrated rigorously, through either a general-equilibrium or a partial-equilibrium analysis; but such a demonstration would seem to be redundant.

11. As noted earlier, the lower the partner's price, the higher also is the probability that even prior to a PTA this partner was the source of supply of the home country's imports, so that this price was the "world" price.

12. As will be recalled from our earlier discussion, this does not necessarily translate into a similar proposition concerning *neighboring* countries.

13. See the analysis of trade expansion among the Andean Pact members in Chap. 11.

14. Without such an assumption, any differential impacts would be assigned (at least partly) to factors other than distance.

15. S_N represents an assumption of a rising supply curve. This is necessary in the present context: with infinitely elastic supply curves, all imports would come from a single source — the cheapest — so that an analysis of proportional trade expansion could not be undertaken. However, see the analysis further on for a different meaning of "proportional expansion."

16. The distance between P^1 and P^0 will normally be lower than t — the rate of tariff duty (or the part of it which is removed).

17. Another way of inferring the same outcome originates in the realization that at any given *home* price, the elasticity of supply of exports should be higher in the distant country: any change in this price will imply a larger proportional change in that country of the net (of transport costs) exporter's price.

References

Bhagwati, J and Panagariya, A P (1996). Preferential trading areas and multilateralism — strangers, friends, or foes? In *The Economics of Preferential Trade Agreements*, Bhagwati J and Panagariya A (eds.), pp. 1–78. Washington, DC: American Enterprise Institute.

Krugman, P (1991). The move towards free trade zones. In *Policy Implications of Trade and Currency Zones*, pp. 7–41. Federal Reserve Bank of Kansas City.

Lipsey, R G (1960). The theory of customs unions: A general survey. *Economic Journal*, 70, 496–513.

Meade, J E (1955). *The Theory of Customs Unions*. Amsterdam: North-Holland Publishing Company.

Summers, L H (1991). Regionalism and the world trade system. In *Policy Implications of Trade and Currency Zones*, pp. 295–301. Federal Reserve Bank of Kansas City.

Chapter 13

Proximity: The Role of Distance

General Considerations

Having dealt in the earlier chapter with the role of the size of trade in contemplating trade-preferential policies, it is now time to look more closely at the relationship between geographical proximity and the size of trade. The general issue is, thus as follows: does proximity — and if so, to what extent — lead countries to tend to trade more with each other; and, in that sense, to make them "natural" partners to a preferential trade agreement (PTA)? It should be noted that this issue is not relevant for the assessment of a specific concrete PTA: for this purpose it is enough to know the size of trade, disregarding the factors that might have contributed to it (but see a proviso in Chap. 7). Even as a proxy, distance cannot, in pragmatic terms, represent shares of trade: trade data are more readily available and are subject to clearer interpretation, than data on (effective) distances (a concept which is obviously more intricate than a number of miles measured on the map). The issue of proximity is thus relevant not for the evaluation of a specific contemplated PTA but for generalizations; primarily, for the question whether in general regional PTAs (i.e., groupings of geographically proximate countries) stand a better chance of "success" (in the very limited sense of leading to trade expansion among partners) than agreements among distant countries.

There can be no doubt about the principle. Geographic proximity must involve (or, by some definition of "proximity," would even logically imply) low transport costs. It should thus necessarily lead, *ceteris paribus*, to a larger size (and share) of trade among proximate partners. As a general proposition, this should not require any empirical verification. As an issue worthy of investigation, the question may be broken down into two: (a) is the impact of transport costs of *much* quantitative significance. And

(b) is the *ceteris paribus* framework of analysis legitimate, that is, are there no other attributes (beside transport costs), which are related to distance and which might be expected to affect the size (and structure) of trade between countries, one way or another?

Most of the present chapter will address the former of these two components. The latter will be mentioned explicitly on occasion and will sometimes be implied in investigations of costs and distance. Here we shall only briefly mention what these "other" considerations are. Most of them have often been referred to in the literature; but some have not been paid much attention to.

Geographic proximity may indeed often be related to attributes (beyond transportation costs), which may either facilitate or hamper trade among nations. These are mostly quite well known. The foremost attributes leading to closer commercial ties are ethnic, cultural, and linguistic affinities, which are frequently found among neighboring countries, often related to a shared history. Notable examples today are Chinese ethnic origin, language, and culture in Southeast Asia; Spanish language and culture, as well as a much shared history, in South and Central America; or Arabic language and culture, as well as shared religion, in much of the Middle East and North Africa. Recent changes in political divisions and definitions offer now another obvious region may now be added: countries of the former Soviet Union, sharing a widespread use of the Russian language and legacies of the Soviet regime.

An exceptional importance may be attached to the extreme degree of geographical proximity of countries, that is, to the case where the neighbors share a common border. This element may certainly be expected to have (as indeed we shall see) a particularly strong impact on trade between the neighboring countries.

A negative element tends to work against the intensity of trade relationships among neighbors: it is not universally prevalent, but is crucial where it exists. One should recall that wars, hostilities, and historic fears of the other are much more common between neighbors than between distant countries. Notable examples today would be the Indian subcontinent, the Middle East, or the Caucasian region. That this element tends to hinder trade, is only too obvious.

Another element working against trade among neighbors, which has not been paid much attention to in the literature, is of a purely economic nature: this is the structure of economic activity and of trade flows.[1] This element is of only limited importance when the neighboring economies are highly developed, largely industrialized and highly diversified. But among less-developed economies, specializing in a narrow range of goods, which are based on the availability of natural resources, the pattern of specialization often tends to be similar among neighboring countries. This is due to the similarity, within regions, of climatic conditions, soil properties, availability of minerals, and the like. Thus, a whole region, rather than a single country within it, will specialize in oil, bananas, or coffee. Needless to say, trade among such similar economics would tend to be small even if transport costs are of little consequence.

The remaining sections of this chapter will be organized as follows. First, we shall try to infer the potential impact of proximity (or its inverse, remoteness) by looking at the level of transport costs. Then, in the following section, we shall survey existing findings that refer directly to the impact of distance — regardless of what constitute the components, which lead distance to have such impact. Finally, in the last section, we shall contrast the outcome of these two channels of investigation.

The Level of Transport Costs

Actual data of transportation costs in international trade are not easy to come by. Quotations of shipping costs of individual goods are plentiful, but not comprehensive, consistent and reliable estimates.

One such set of estimates will be quoted here. It comes from an old study — (Moneta, 1958) dating to the early 1950's — and confined to the trade of a single country — Germany. Yet, it is instructive. The most salient findings of this study are presented in Table 13.1.

Table 13.1:   Freight costs of German imports, by area, 1951.

Area of origin	Freight costs (in percentage of F.O.B.)
Africa	10
Europe	12
Latin America	11
North America	21
Far East	7
Middle East	35
Oceania	6
Total	14.3

Source: Moneta (1959, Table 4, p. 47).

Two observations stand out clearly. One, that on average freight costs are low — less than 15 percent is of the F.O.B. price. Moneta also presents a table, which shows that the "adjustment factor" used for moving from F.O.B. to C.I.F. Valuation for balance-of-payments purposes, in a dozen, mostly European countries, is on average some 10 percent — with very slight variations. The other observation is that variations of this "freight factor" by geographical origin of imports have practically no relationship to distance. If anything, it is a *negative* relationship: the freight factor for imports from the relatively close Middle East area — 35 percent — is roughly five times the levels found for imports from the far-away Oceania (6 percent) or the Far East (7 percent).

This presumed "negative relationship" of freight costs and distance should obviously not be taken seriously. It only serves to demonstrate that the area of origin of imports — which is a proxy for distance — must be dominated, as a determinant of costs, by other considerations. Chief of these must be the *structure* of trade. Indeed, Monete's estimates (1959, Table 4, p. 47) show a very large variance of freight costs by goods. At the top, one finds freight costs of 64 percent for crude petroleum, and 53 percent for coal. The levels for ores, fertilizers, and petroleum products are within the range of 30–40 percent. At the bottom, on the other hand, the freight factors for textile fabrics or for machinery are as low as 1 percent. Put slightly different: roughly a half of the aggregate cost of freight of the country's imports originates from just three goods, which jointly amount to about 15 percent of aggregate imports.

It is obvious that this wide range of the levels of freight costs by goods leads to the predominance of the *structure* of imports in determining freight costs by countries, or areas, of origin of imports. The most glaring demonstration of this predominance is the Middle East, where its relative proximity to Germany is far outweighed by the fact that petroleum and its products were (and still are) the major component of this area's exports. Another illustration may be provided by the fact that the freight factor of imports from the US falls from 22 to 14 percent by the exclusion of a single good — coal.

A much more recent study (Hummels, 2001) yields estimates, which, though not strictly comparable with those of Moneta, appear to be even lower. Thus, transport factors for aggregate imports by countries range from as low as 3.6 percent (for the US) to 13.3 percent (for Paraguay). The variation over goods remains substantial: for the US imports, the average freight factor for the category of crude fertilizers is 27 percent and is as low as 1 percent for transport equipment.

Hummels (2001) also conducts an interesting exercise in estimating the cost of *time* involved in the shipment of goods. He comes out with an estimate of an average cost of 0.8 percent of the value of the good for each day spent in the process of moving the good. Thus, for instance, shipping over a distance, which requires travel time of three weeks, would double the shipping costs involved in a distance, which requires a travel of only four days. Given the initial level found typically, this would mean adding some 5–10 percent to the F.O.B. price of a typical good. This would still be a minor cost, in most instances. However, it may outweigh the cost of shipment in the narrow sense and would bear a relationship to the role of distance, to which we shall return shortly.

What has happened to the "freight factor" over time? The absence of comprehensive, comparable estimates does not enable a reliable answer to this question. One must, thus, rely rather on conjectures.

Two major components should lead to expected changes. One is the change in cost of transportation for any given good. It is generally believed that this cost has gone down, over the last two generations, in absolute (real) terms: ships have become bigger and more efficient; the use of containers for general cargo has lowered costs, etc. The question is, however, whether costs have fallen in *relative* terms, that is, as a proportion of the (F.O.B.) price of the good. This becomes, then, an issue of relative changes in productivity — in international movement of goods vs the processes of production and within-borders movement and other transaction costs. To this issue not even a guess would be ventured here.

The other component, as should seem obvious from our earlier observation, would be a change in the commodity structure of trade.[2] While again, no comprehensive studies of the changing structure are readily available, it would appear intuitively clear that a massive transformation has taken place in the last two generations, from trade in natural-resource-based goods to sophisticated manufactured goods, and that the latter have a significantly higher ratio of value to volume, hence a lower ratio of transport cost to value. The only exception may be trade in petroleum and its products, which are today a major component of international trade, probably exceeding its share two generations ago. It should be noted, though, that trade in petroleum has expanded to a very large extent at the expense of trade in coal — a commodity whose "freight factor" appears in the aforementioned Moneta estimates to be quite close to that of petroleum, and much higher than the freight cost of petroleum products.

Another component of change, strongly related (both ways) to changes in commodity structure, derives from the pattern of *modes* of transportation. Specifically, shipment by air, barely present at the middle of the 20th century, has become significant. This is obviously a more expensive mode, and it, partly at least, tends to offset the changes in commodity structure of trade. As a broad generalization, it should be expected that the higher the ratio of value to volume, the more will transportation by air be considered as an alternative to other modes (ships, trains, or trucks). This should then partly qualify the expectation based on the nature of traded goods.[3]

This variety of observations indicates that shipping costs today are low — for most countries, probably in the range of 5–15 percent of the F.O.B. value of aggregate imports. Other transaction costs of trade must be added, though, and these may be significant. To this category belong costs of activities such as getting permits, inspection, consular authorization, or other "paper work."[4] That such costs are important is highly relevant to the issue of the relationship of costs to distance, to which we now turn.

Even if transportation costs are generally low, a relevant question for our purposes should be: how do these costs *vary* with the distance over which goods are shipped, in other words: what is the relationship of the *marginal* cost of transportation to the average cost? Here, even more than before, we must rely on conjectures.

Much of the cost of shipment is a *fixed* component, i.e., costs that do not depend on the distance traveled. The "office" part of costs, which has just been mentioned, is clearly of that nature. So are the physical activities of packing, loading and unloading (including waiting time at the ports). The *variable* component of the costs is thus only a fraction of the total. It would consist to a large extent of the cost of *time* in ocean shipping, though not in airfreight. In the latter, the extra cost of fuel may be of much significance. Altogether, it may be guessed that the variable component is low, for reasonable distances, in comparison with the fixed costs. Redding and Venables (2006, p. 149), citing studies by Hummels and by Limao and Venables, observe that "these studies typically have elasticities of transport costs with respect to distance of between 0.2 and 0.3, meaning that a doubling of the distance over which goods are shipped increases freight costs by around 20 percent. The impact of distance on transportation costs would thus seem to be quite weak."

Direct Estimates of the Impact of Distance

The impact of distance on the size of trade among nations has been a popular topic of empirical studies since the early 1960s. Almost exclusively, these were econometric studies utilizing the "gravity model," or "gravity equation."[5] In such formulation, the size of trade is determined primarily by two variables: the level of income of each of the partners and the distance between their markets. Other variables that presumably affect the size of mutual trade — mostly common language, common religion, specific history (such as colonial ties), or shared borders — are entered into the estimates as "dummies" (that is, as a variable that either exists or it does not).

"Distance" is defined, in most of these studies, as (roughly speaking) the number of miles measured on the globe from a single center of activity in one country to a similar center in its partner. Needless to say, such "distance" bears only a partial relationship to "distance" in its economic sense, namely, a variable representing the cost of conducting transactions (mainly, presumably, transportation costs) between the two partners to the transaction. For any given geographic distance, transportation costs would vary greatly according to whether the cheapest mode of transportation is by land, sea, or air, and this, in turn, obviously depends on the product in which the transaction is carried out, the nature of the terrain, the availability and quality of infrastructure, and the like. While large-scale studies may not be feasible without recourse to this "distance on the map," the inadequacy of this definition should be borne in mind.

Studies of this nature have been carried out, in increasing frequency, for the last two generations (since the early 1960s). In most of them, the impact of distance on the size of trade is presented in the form of elasticity (of trade on distance). The level of this elasticity appears to be surprisingly high in the vast majority of these studies. A recent study (Disdier and Head, 2008), which reviews and analyzes findings in over 100 published studies, containing almost 1500 estimates, finds that almost all the estimated elasticities fall within the range of about (minus) 0.5 and 1.5. The median of the findings is 0.87, and the mean −0.91 (with a standard deviation of 0.39), that is, the typical findings yield approximately a unit elasticity of trade to distance. Thus, for instance, doubling the distance between two observed centers would lower the trade between them to a half, and quadrupling the distance would shrink the size of trade to just one quarter. The estimated elasticity seems to vary slightly over time showing some tendency of the impact of distance to actually increase in more recent years, and not to radically differ by the precise methods followed in the studies.[6]

Normally, as mentioned, the impact of distance would be separated from the impact of other variables, which may be related to distance — such as shared ethnic origin, language, religion, or borders — by assigning zero or unitary values to the absence or existence of such variables. This, presumably, would lead to estimating the impact of distance on trade just as a function of the relationship of distance to the size of transportation costs.

A very recent study (Helpman *et al.*, 2008), while still a variant of a gravity analysis, takes a different route from that of earlier studies and comes to somewhat different conclusions. Developing a model based on a firm-level activity, the authors conclude, beside other inferences, that the coefficients estimated in prior gravity-model studies were biased upwards.[7] The extent of the bias is estimated to be substantial — roughly one-third of the conventionally estimated coefficients: whereas the typical elasticity of trade to distance is around unity; the Helpman *et al.* estimation would yield an elasticity of only $(-)0.6$ to 0.7. Still, as will be noted shortly, this is a rather high level of the elasticity.[8]

The Impact of Transport Costs and of Distance: Can the Two be Reconciled?

The data and estimates mentioned on the previous two sections show high levels of persistence and consistency; but, alas, they run in opposite directions.

Transport costs appear convincingly to be *low*. A "transport factor" of an order of 10 percent would appear to be typical, either for the aggregate trade of an "average" country or for most goods for "average" distances. Moreover, the *marginal* transport factor — i.e., its increase with distance — must be substantially lower than its average level. But even overlooking this discrepancy between marginal and average, the impact of distance should be weak. Take, for instance, a quadrupling of distance, hence, a quadrupling of the transport factor from the typical 10 to 40 percent. This would mean a price change in the importing country from 1.1 to 1.4 times the F.O.B. price of the exporter. Unless demand elasticities of substitution are extremely high, both among goods and among alternative suppliers, this would still leave the majority of the import flow intact.

The estimated elasticities of trade volume on *distance*, on the other hand, are of an entirely different order of magnitude. They are, we recall, of a typical value of unity. Conduct the same exercise as before: a quadrupling of distance would shrink, with unit elasticity, the volume of trade to just one quarter of its level at the lower distance. This is obviously a different matter altogether from the prior inference for the impact of varying transport costs.[9]

This glaring conflict of the two sets of estimates and predictions has been noted often in the literature. The obvious — indeed, inevitable — inference is that "distance," while partly reflecting transport costs, is a representation of a variety of other factors, which have bearing on the size of bilateral trade flows. Most of these have been mentioned in the opening section of the present chapter. Another element, which has recently drawn attention (such as in Anderson and van Wincoop, 2004) is the more elusive concept of "information costs."

This inference — almost a logical necessity — would have to face at least one major challenge, namely: these "other" variables — at least those that are most obvious — are present in the econometric estimates of the gravity-model family, normally appearing as "dummies" with a zero–one value. Hence, presumably, their impacts are accounted for *separately*, isolating the impact of distance as such (that is, letting "distance" represent only transport costs). Hence, it must be concluded that either (or both) (a) the estimation of the impact of "other" variables is deficient and, specifically, suffers from a downward bias; and (b) that there may be still different variables that have an impact on trade, which are related to distance and which are not accounted for.

As to the first possibility of a downward bias in the estimates of impacts of shared borders, shared language, or shared history, no alternative methods of estimation will, needless to say, be suggested here. It may only be pointed out that, despite the essential stability of the major findings of the gravity equations, the history of the gravity model does suggest a potential for future changes. These may originate from varying econometric techniques, varying measurements of the variables, or theoretical elaborations of the nature of the models. The possibility that further developments might yield substantially different findings may thus not be excluded.

The inference that "distance" incorporates still other variables, which are not represented by those incorporated specifically and explicitly in the model, tends to become now the conventional wisdom. Such factors may be cultural ties (which are not embedded in "language"); ease of communication; shared social structures; similar commercial practices; similar legal systems and practices; and possibly a few other attributes of this nature. This inference suggests, thus, that (1) these attributes have an overwhelming impact on the size of bilateral trade between nations; and (2) that they are closely related to distance — the further apart are the trading partners geographically, the less frequent are such similarities and shared attributes. This interpretation must also mean that the attributes concerned (which, again, are missing in the models and their estimations) have a much stronger impact on trade flows than that of (measurable) transportation costs of trade.

Some other considerations may be suggested as (partial, of course) explanations of the radical difference between inferences drawn from estimated "distance" elasticities and observed levels of transportation costs. One is inaccuracies in distance estimates. The most obvious source of such deficiencies is the very determination of "distance" (roughly, we recall, a distance on the globe between two centers of activity). A given "distance" of this nature may have entirely different significance for transportation costs depending on whether it is predominantly distance covered by sea or by land, the nature of the terrain, and the like, or (for large countries) on whether the actual origin of the trade flow may not be far removed from the "center." These distortions must involve gross inaccuracies; but whether such inappropriate measurement of distance should lead to a bias in the estimate, one way or another, is not at all obvious.

Another potentially important consideration should be the role and impact of the trade in oil and its products. Oil is a major component of international trade. For this trade flow, available estimates indicate particularly high transport costs — several multiples of the average costs for other components of trade; likewise, it seems likely that in transportation of oil, the ratio of marginal (to distance) costs to their average level is higher than in most other goods. At the same time, the transport costs of oil are (apparently) not represented in the conventional quotations of C.I.F. to F.O.B. prices (even the definition of this ratio may not be straightforward in the case of oil). Moreover, the reaction to price differentials should be particularly strong for trade in oil. This is as uniform a product as might be found (variations in quality are also well defined). It has a uniform world price (or a number of comparable prices), and its origin of supply and destination of delivery may easily change (sometimes, as the lore is, destinations are changed in mid-trip). That is, elasticities of substitution between alternative sources of supply may be uniquely high in this case. Hence, a relatively small difference in distance may be important in determining directions of trade flows, that is, the elasticity of trade flows to distance should be particularly high for trade in oil (an impact that would not be expected, we recall, by just observing C.I.F./F.O.B. price ratios).

A still different consideration would be the role of *Europe*. Much of the international trade is conducted within Europe, between European partners. Trade relationships among the major European traders have been particularly strong, developing with occasional interruptions, over centuries.[10] And, obviously, distances among centers of activity in most (Western) European countries tend to be relatively very short. It is thus possible that much of the estimated high elasticity of trade flows to distance originates from this cluster of neighboring major traders, and that the impact of distance would appear to be significantly different had Western Europe been excluded. Such exclusion would not be warranted if one wishes to estimate trade–distance relationships as they actually exist in today's world; but it would be required for the investigation of trade relationships, or potentials, in other parts of the world.

Thus, it might be a task for further empirical studies to isolate the impact of both trade in oil and trade within Western Europe, and see whether much of the chasm between the inferences drawn from observed levels of freight costs and estimated distance elasticities of trade might be bridged in this way.

The recognition that "distance" is a representation not only of transportation costs but also of other unobserved attributes — which presumably may far outweigh the impact of transport costs — is of utmost practical importance. Suppose, to make the distinction sharply, that close proximity of countries tends to make them sharing those "other" attributes. But, once moving beyond the immediate circle of proximate countries, the "basket" of attributes is not shared by the potential trading partners, *whatever* the distance. That is, if one could measure it, the impact of this basket on reducing the level of trade would be very substantial in making what one may call a "first step" — moving from very close countries to those in a further circle; but would be negligible for further movements to still outward circles. When moving beyond the "first circle," the impact of distance should thus be just that of the change in transportation costs, and the elasticity of trade to distance would be just that — relating trade responsiveness to transportation costs, which should be far below the conventionally estimated elasticity of distance. General use of the latter for predicting the impact of changing distance on the size of trade would then grossly over estimate the real impact — a classical case of "misplaced concreteness."[11]

In the next chapter, the impact of proximity will be investigated in a different manner: it will be done through classification of countries into regional groupings, observing the differences between intra-regional trade and the trade of the region's members with the outside world.

Notes

1. The impact on the tendency of countries to trade with each other of levels of development and of the nature of trade — the shares of resource-based ("Heckscher–Ohlin") vs scale and monopolistic-competition ("Lynder") goods — has been explored extensively. But the relationship between proximity and trade structure, and through it its impact on the size of trade, has not been part of this literature. For a representative sample, see Helpman (1987), Bergstrand (1990), Hummels and Levinsohn (1995), and Evenett and Heller (2004).

2. Baier and Bergstrand (2001) provide estimates of C.I.F.–F.O.B. price ratios, for 16 OECD countries, for two points of time: 1958–1960 and 1986–1988. These are derived by dividing each country's recorded value (at C.I.F. prices) of aggregate imports by the aggregate value (at F.O.B. prices) of the recorded exports of the rest of the world to this country. They find that this indicator of freight costs *declined* over time. The average ratio for the earlier period was 8.2 percent, and for the latter — 4.3 percent. The range of the estimates was, for the earlier period, from 1.4 percent (for Switzerland) to 20.1 percent (for Japan), with a median of 7.0 percent. For the latter period, the range was from 1.0 percent (again for Switzerland) to just 6.9 percent (for Italy–Japan's was 6.8 percent), with a median of 4.5 percent. It should be noted, though, as the authors themselves do, that these changes in aggregate freight costs combine the impact of changes in freight costs of individual goods and in the commodity structure of trade, with no possibility of distinguishing between the two.

3. When *time* is taken into consideration, though, transport by air would appear to be less expensive — may be much so — than its recorded rate would suggest. Based on Hummels (2001) estimates, a recent study (Redding and Venables, 2006) observes: "The share of US imports going by air freight rose from zero to 30 percent between 1950 and 1998, and containerization approximately doubled the speed of ocean shipment. Together these give a reduction in shipping time of twenty-six days,

equivalent to a shipping cost reduction worth 12–13 percent of the value of goods traded" (p. 150).

4. A recent study (Anderson and Wincoop, 2004) provides an estimate of an aggregate of 44 percent (of the original price) for overcoming border-related barriers involved in trade between two different political entities. These include "... an 8 percent policy barrier; a 7 percent language barrier; a 14 percent currency barrier... a 6 percent information barrier; and a 3 percent security barrier for rich countries..." (p. 693). Presumably, these costs components are mostly over and above the elements mentioned in the text.

5. The cornerstones of the vast structure of literature of the gravity model are the contributions of Tinbergen (1962) and Linneman (1966). Significant further additions to the theory and its application, which might be noted, include Anderson (1979), Bergstrand (1985), and Anderson and van Wincoop (2004). Two other, more recent studies are referred to in the text.

6. The survey notes that the estimated impact of distance on trade is stronger for trade among less-developed than among developed economies and presumes that this is due to the lower quality of transportation infrastructure in poorer economies. My own hunch would assign this difference in impacts primarily to the presumption that the commodity structures of these alternative trade flows would greatly differ from each other.

7. One of the important advantages of this model over preceding variants is that it *does not* involve a built-up inference of balanced bilateral trade flows: the conventional gravity-model analysis should, by construction, predict the same level of exports (impacts) from country i to country j as that of exports (imports) from j to i. Needless to say, this is a glaring flaw of the model.

8. Helpman *et al.* argues that the bias pointed out exists also for the coefficients, which relate trade volume to *other* variables than distance. Indeed, the coefficients of these variables (such as a common border, or a common language) appear, in these new estimations, to have no (acceptable) significance at all. This is explained by the argument that the impact of these variables is to "... reduce the fixed costs of trade: they have a great influence on a firm's choice of export location, but not on the export volume once the exporting decision has been made" (p. 404).

9. The same contrast may be illustrated by pointing out varying estimates in a given study. In a paper by Limão and Venables (2001), the elasticity between trade volume and distance is estimated at −1.37; whereas the estimated elasticity of trade to the ratio of C.I.F. to F.O.B. prices — presumably, a good approximation of the level of the "transport costs factor" — is as low as −0.21 (Table 5, p. 465).

10. In terms of the preceding discussion, the prevalence and impact of the "unobserved" attributes are particularly present among European countries.

11. In the aforementioned recent study by Helpman *et al.* (2008, p. 474), the authors do indeed restrict their use of the estimated distance elasticity to changes of 10, or at most 20 percent.

References

Anderson, J E (1979). A theoretical foundation for the gravity equation. *American Economic Review*, 69, 106–116.

Anderson, J E and van Wincoop, E (2004). Trade Costs. *Journal of Economic Literature*, 42, 691–751.

Baier, S L and Bergstrand, J H (2001). The growth of world trade, tariffs, transport costs, and income similarity. *Journal of International Economics*, 52, 1–27.

Bergstrand, J H (1985). The gravity equation in international trade: Some microeconomic foundations and empirical evidence. *Review of Economics and Statistics*, 67, 474–481.

Bergstrand, J H (1990). The Heckscher–Ohlin–Samuelson model, the Lynder hypothesis and the determinants of bilateral intra-industry trade. *Economic Journal*, 100, 1216–1229.

Disdier, A-C and Head, K (2008). The puzzling persistence of the distance effect on bilateral trade. *Review of Economics and Statistics*, 90, 37–48.

Evenett, S J and Heller, W (2004). On the success of the gravity equation. *Journal of Political Economy*, 110, 281–316.

Helpman, E (1987). Imperfect competition and international trade: Evidence from fourteen industrial countries. *Journal of Japanese and International Economics*, 1, 62–81.

Helpman, E, Melitz, M and Rubinstein, Y (2008). Estimating trade flows, trading partners and trading volumes. *Quarterly Journal of Economics*, 123, 441–488.

Hummels, D and Levinsohn, J (1995). Monopolistic competition and international trade: Reconsidering the evidence. *Quarterly Journal of Economics*, 110, 799–836.

Hummels, D (2001). Toward a geography of trade costs. Unpublished Manuscript, Pardue University.

Limão, N and Venables, A J (2001). Infrastructure, geographical disadvantage, transport costs and trade. *World Bank Economic Review*, 15, 451–479.

Linneman, H (1966). *An Econometric Study of International Trade Flows.* Amsterdam: North-Holland Publishing Co.

Moneta, C (1959). The estimation of transportation costs in international trade. *Journal of Political Economy*, 67, 41–58.

Redding, S and Venables, A J (2006). The economics of isolation and distance, Chapter 5. In *WTO at the Margins*, Grynberg, R (ed.), pp. 145–163. Cambridge: Cambridge University Press.

Tinbergen, J (1962). *Shaping the World Economy: Suggestions for an International Economic Policy.* New York: The Twentieth Century Fund.

Chapter 14

Trade Relationships Within Regional Groupings

Regional Groupings

Whatever the precise level and origins of the impact of distance, it is clear from the preceding analysis that it is substantial rather than minor, that is, that, *ceteris paribus*, the closer (geographically) are two potential trading partners to each other, the stronger will be their tendencies to trade with each other. Hence, if one of the pre-conditions for the creation of a preferential agreement for a given set of countries is that trade within this set should be potentially substantial, a set of geographically proximate countries should — again, *ceteris paribus* — be a more promising candidate for such co-operation than a set of countries, which are far apart from each other. This, in essence, is the "natural trade partners" argument.

In the following analysis, the existence, or the extent, of such trend for extensive trade among geographically proximate countries will first be investigated through the observation of several such sets of proximate countries, or "regions." Following this, we shall look at more specific attributes of countries within each region, to see to what extent such attributes tend to strengthen (or weaken) the tendency of countries to trade with their potential partners in the region.

In principle, the definition and selection of "regions" are intended to be as inclusive as possible, that is, to cover as many groupings as one could identify in the present-day world. A few words of explanation and caution are, however, in order. First, as would be obvious, some arbitrariness in the selection of countries to be included in or excluded from a "region," or in defining a border between adjacent regions, is inevitable. Second, some countries (normally, for obvious reasons, smaller countries) are excluded for absence or deficiency of data. Third — and this point should particularly be emphasized — the "regions" take in countries as a *tabula rasa*.

That is, the definition of a "region" disregards completely the possibility (which often materializes) that some preferential agreement (or more than one) already exists within the region, or among one or more countries within the region and other countries outside it. Fourth, Western Europe is excluded here altogether: to include it on the *tabula rasa* basis would be such a flagrant contradiction of reality that the findings of such observation would be of little consequence. For similar reasons, the US and Canada are also excluded.[1] Nine "regions" are thus defined and investigated. Their compositions are presented in Table 14.1.

Table 14.1:   Regional grouping of countries.

South America	Central America	Eastern Europe	North Africa
Argentina	Costa Rica	Belarus	Algeria
Bolivia	Guatemala	Czech Republic	Egypt
Brazil	Honduras	Estonia	Morocco
Chile	Mexico[a]	Hungary	Sudan[b]
Colombia	Nicaragua	Latvia	Tunisia
Ecuador		Lithuania	
Paraguay		Moldova	
Peru		Poland	
Uruguay		Romania	
Venezuela		Russia	
		Slovakia	
		Ukraine	

Southern Africa	East Africa	West Africa	South Asia
Malawi	Burundi	Burkina Faso	Bangladesh
Mozambique	Ethiopia	Cameroon	India
Namibia	Kenya	Cote d'Ivoire	Pakistan
South Africa	Sudan[b]	Gabon	Sri Lanka
Swaziland	Tanzania	Ghana	
Zambia	Uganda	Mauritania	
Zimbabwe		Niger	
		Nigeria	
		Senegal	
		Togo	

South-East Asia and Oceania

Australia	Malaysia	Singapore
China	New Zealand	Thailand
Indonesia	Philippines	Vietnam

[a]Mexico is included in the group termed "Central America" although it is formally part of North America.
[b]Sudan is classified within both North Africa and East Africa.

Of these groupings, the one which probably least qualifies as a "region" would be that of South-East Asia and Oceania. Measuring distances on the map, some of its members are not really "proximate." Nevertheless, in view of the fact that distances to other potential trade partners are normally much longer and that most of these countries share the Pacific Ocean — which would make them more of "neighbors" than the distance on the map would suggest — we decided to classify this grouping as well a "region."

Intra-Regional Trade: Intensity Ratios[2]

The basic index used here to indicate the tendency of countries to trade with each other is the "intensity ratio" of trade — a long-used, simple and conventional measure. It indicates the extent to which one country's trade with a partner exceeds, or falls short of, the size of trade that would be "explained," or "justified," by the partner's share in world trade. This index has been discussed at some length in Chap. 9 and used frequently in other chapters of this book. However, to facilitate reading, it will be restated here briefly:

$$I_{jk}^m = \frac{M_{jk}}{M_{j\cdot}} \bigg/ \frac{X_{\cdot k}}{X_w},$$

where I_{jk}^m is the intensity ratio of country j's ("home country") imports from (partner) country k; M_{jk} the country j's imports from country j; $M_{j\cdot}$ the aggregate imports of country k; $X_{\cdot k}$ the aggregate exports of country k; and X_w the aggregate world exports.

Similarly, the intensity ratio of j's exports to k is as follows, with the appropriate changes:

$$I_{jk}^X = \frac{X_{jk}}{X_{j\cdot}} \bigg/ \frac{M_{\cdot k}}{M_w}.$$

An intensity ratio of unity thus describes "neutrality." A level above unity indicates a trade of the home country with a partner beyond what the partner's share in world trade would "justify," whereas its opposite is indicated when the ratio is below unity.

The intensity ratios for *imports trade* between countries in each region are presented in Table 14.2. It should be read as follows. The countries listed at the top row are the "home countries," whereas the countries listed on the left-hand column are the partners, the intensity of trade with

Table 14.2: Intensity ratios in imports, by regions and countries.

Eastern Europe

$k \backslash j$	Belarus	Czech Rep.	Estonia	Hungary	Latvia	Lithuania	Moldova	Poland	Romania	Russia	Slovakia	Ukraine	Average
Belarus	—	0.1	23.3	0.4	51.5	9.0	317.3	0.9	0.9	4.1	0.6	4.9	37.5
Czech Rep.	4.2	—	17.7	4.4	14.1	7.1	105.5	4.2	7.9	0.5	41.7	3.9	19.2
Estonia	0.5	0.1	—	0.2	67.2	14.9	9.6	0.1	0.1	0.1	0.1	0.7	8.5
Hungary	2.1	2.7	24.1	—	8.4	3.7	112.5	2.2	11.6	0.5	10.4	4.3	16.6
Latvia	3.2	0	42.9	0	—	17.7	14.3	0.2	0	0.1	0.1	0.5	7.2
Lithuania	6.7	0.1	66.4	0.1	117.0	—	39.6	0.6	0.2	0.3	0.1	1.6	21.2
Moldova	2.6	0	0.3	0	0.6	0.2	—	0	0.9	0.3	0.1	0.5	0.5
Poland	18.2	6.3	42.9	5.0	51.5	35.3	219.7	—	9.2	1.4	12.2	9.0	37.3
Romania	0.3	0.4	1.7	2.3	0.5	0.3	806.0	0.5	—	0.1	1.5	0.8	74.0
Russia	426.0	5.5	160.3	8.6	91.3	106.5	1055.1	8.4	25.0	—	28.7	105.7	183.7
Slovakia	1.6	7.0	4.6	3.1	7.9	1.7	56.2	1.9	3.8	0.3	—	2.2	8.2
Ukraine	20.8	1.1	24.1	1.4	29.0	7.0	2143.4	1.4	9.9	3.8	4.3	—	204.2
Average	44.2	2.1	35.0	2.3	35.2	17.7	414.7	1.8	6.2	0.7	9.0	11.8	51.5

West Africa

$k \backslash j$	Burkina Faso	Cameroon	Cote d'Ivoire	Gabon	Ghana	Mauritania	Niger	Nigeria	Senegal	Togo	Average
Burkina Faso	—	0	0.1	0	0	0	1281.7	0	0.1	683.2	218.4
Cameroon	13.3	—	4.8	96.3	0.1	0.1	30.6	0	32.7	39.6	24.2
Cote d'Ivoire	3920.8	46.2	—	61.1	39.9	0	3063.4	0.3	230.5	1275.9	959.8
Gabon	0	10.9	0.5	—	0.1	0.2	0.4	0.3	4.7	2.2	2.3
Ghana	948.3	1.2	3.5	1.5	—	0.6	555.9	0.5	34.1	368.6	212.7
Mauritania	0	40.3	15.2	0.4	36.8	—	62.0	0.3	1.2	123.8	31.1
Niger	17.1	0	0.1	0.1	0.3	0	—	0	0	3.0	2.3
Nigeria	335.1	422.1	265.8	4.6	44.9	3.9	2437.1	—	767.6	237.7	502.1
Senegal	404.7	21.8	8.2	16.9	4.4	94.4	225.0	0.8	—	185.5	107.0
Togo	252.8	2.1	0.4	6.6	0	2.3	612.1	5.8	6.8	—	98.8
Average	654.7	60.5	33.2	21.0	14.1	11.3	918.8	0.9	119.7	324.4	215.9

(*Continued*)

Table 14.2: (Continued)

East Africa

$k \backslash j$	Burundi	Ethiopia	Kenya	Sudan	Tanzania	Uganda	Average
Burundi	—	0	0	0	0.1	0.6	0.1
Ethiopia	31.1	—	1.1	0.3	4.4	1.3	6.4
Kenya	32288.1	102.8	—	29.6	549.8	3366.4	6056.1
Sudan	0	52.7	1.7	—	0	1.4	9.3
Tanzania	18312.6	10.4	18.0	0	—	133.1	3079.0
Uganda	12460.8	11.0	8.6	19.5	32.3	—	2088.7
Average	10515.4	29.4	4.9	8.2	97.8	583.8	1873.2

North Africa

$k \backslash j$	Algeria	Egypt	Morocco	Sudan	Tunisia	Average
Algeria	—	43.6	7.9	0	5.2	14.2
Egypt	2.4	—	4.7	166.1	4.4	44.4
Morocco	0.5	0.7	—	0.1	4.4	0.3
Sudan	0	5.7	0	—	0.1	1.5
Tunisia	1.6	0.6	4.1	0.3	—	1.7
Average	1.1	12.7	4.1	41.6	3.5	12.6

Southern Africa

$k \backslash j$	Malawi	Mozambique	Namibia	South Africa	Swaziland	Zambia	Zimbabwe	Average
Malawi	—	67.2	0	0.3	0	19.8	18.3	17.6
Mozambique	2543.0	—	0	0.1	25.3	5.8	102.1	446.1
Namibia	1.8	47.3	—	0	1.0	14.5	2.8	11.2
South Africa	5943.4	1874.5	3023.1	—	3544.8	2519.9	2383.5	3214.6
Swaziland	103.4	33.2	10.5	0	—	13.6	18.3	29.8
Zambia	726.5	1.9	1.9	0.7	0.1	—	152.9	147.3
Zimbabwe	891.4	27.6	1.9	1.9	0.2	315.6	—	210.6
Average	1701.6	341.8	510.6	0.5	595.2	481.5	446.3	582.5

(Continued)

Table 14.2: (Continued)

South America

k\j	Argentina	Bolivia	Brazil	Chile	Colombia	Ecuador	Paraguay	Peru	Uruguay	Venezuela	Average
Argentina	—	611.1	7.9	52.0	10.0	40.4	1129.6	47.3	658.4	4.5	284.6
Bolivia	1.5	—	1.0	0.7	5.5	4.5	17.5	10.6	1.0	3.0	5.0
Brazil	84.7	1006.2	—	34.2	42.1	73.1	1466.9	59.0	644.2	18.7	381.0
Chile	4.5	230.3	2.0	—	10.6	53.0	65.2	39.7	55.6	3.6	51.6
Colombia	0.5	126.6	0.2	3.7	—	159.4	4.8	65.8	2.5	23.6	43.0
Ecuador	0.6	20.0	0.1	1.7	11.8	—	0.9	56.4	1.4	1.8	10.5
Paraguay	4.2	39.6	0.4	1.2	1.9	4.1	—	7.2	15.4	1.2	8.3
Peru	0.4	262.4	0.5	8.7	7.6	29.6	2.0	—	8.6	2.0	35.8
Uruguay	2.5	7.9	0.7	0.9	0.6	2.7	107.3	2.5	—	0.4	14.0
Venezuela	0.4	20.8	0.3	2.2	32.7	80.5	14.6	58.5	1.7	—	23.5
Average	11.0	258.3	1.5	11.8	13.6	49.7	312.1	38.6	154.3	6.5	85.7

Central America

k\j	Costa Rica	Guatemala	Honduras	Mexico	Nicaragua	Average
Costa Rica	—	120.0	342.7	0.2	1081.7	386.1
Guatemala	28.7	—	647.1	0.1	868.6	361.1
Honduras	6.5	44.7	—	0	294.5	66.4
Mexico	75.6	239.2	413.4	—	928.1	414.1
Nicaragua	9.2	13.0	112.2	0	—	33.6
Average	30.0	104.2	353.9	0.1	793.2	256.3

South Asia

k\j	Bangladesh	India	Pakistan	Sri Lanka	Average
Bangladesh	—	0.1	1.6	1.6	1.1
India	116.9	—	16.6	275.2	136.2
Pakistan	13.0	0.1	—	21.9	11.7
Sri Lanka	0.9	0.4	1.7	—	1.0
Average	43.6	0.2	6.6	99.6	37.5

(Continued)

Table 14.2: (*Continued*)

South-East Asia and Oceania

$k \backslash j$	Australia	China	Indonesia	Malaysia	New Zealand	Philippines	Singapore	Thailand	Vietnam	Average
Australia	—	0.3	6.9	1.2	91.9	2.9	0.5	1.6	4.5	13.7
China	13.4	—	12.8	6.8	43.6	13.3	4.1	7.8	47.5	18.6
Indonesia	2.3	0.2	—	2.7	4.9	4.7	2.4	2.2	6.9	3.3
Malaysia	4.1	0.5	5.2	—	10.6	9.7	6.3	5.3	12.6	6.8
New Zealand	3.7	0	0.7	0.2	—	1.4	0.1	0.2	1.1	0.9
Philippines	0.5	0.2	0.7	1.8	1.5	—	1.1	1.5	1.9	1.2
Singapore	4.3	0.4	15.0	7.5	6.0	16.5	—	4.0	37.3	11.4
Thailand	2.7	0.3	8.6	3.8	8.4	7.8	1.7	—	19.2	6.6
Vietnam	1.8	0.1	1.3	0.4	1.4	2.2	0.4	0.4	—	1.0
Average	4.1	0.2	6.4	3.1	21.0	7.3	2.1	2.9	16.4	7.0

each of which is recorded in the column below the "home country." Thus, for instance, looking at the region of South America, the column below Argentina indicates that the intensity ratio of Argentina's imports from Bolivia is 1.5, the intensity of Argentina's imports from Brazil is 84.7, and so on.

Table 14.2, to repeat, presents intensity ratio of imports, and all the rest of the analysis in this chapter will draw inferences from these estimates of the intensity of import trade flows. A parallel investigation might have been carried out concerning the intensity of *export* trade. Indeed, the intensity ratios in exports have been estimated, and this set of estimates is presented in Table 14.10 to this chapter. It appears, however, from cursory observation that the indications provided by the export flow are similar enough to those suggested by the import trade to make the parallel investigation of exports, and its presentation (which must make the text cumbersome), unwarranted. This proximity of the two sets of estimates is, of course, not surprising: one is, in principle, a mirror image of the other.

Looking at Table 14.2, the most striking observation is that the intensity ratios are indeed extremely high, that is, that as a rule, countries in each region do show a very strong preference to import from other partners in the region. Even the lowest regional averages of intensity ratios, in the region of South-East Asia and Oceania (which indeed is the one least qualified as a "region") and the region of North Africa, are as high as, respectively, around 7 and 12, that is, even here countries tend (on average) to import from regional partners roughly 10 times the size that would be indicated by "neutrality." The intensity ratios are particularly high in all three regions of Sub-Sahara Africa, with regional averages ranging from 216 in West Africa to as high as 1873 in East Africa. Individual countries in the latter region reach the incredibly high level of 12,460 — the intensity ratio of Burundi's imports from Uganda; 18,312 — the ratio of Burundi's imports from Tanzania; or even 32,288, for Burundi's imports from Kenya. However, even excluding Burundi altogether, viewing is as a curiosity, intensity ratios in East Africa would appear to be generally very high.

This finding, of very high intra-regional intensity ratios, would tend to support the expectations yielded by the observations of the previous chapter. They would not necessarily, we recall, demonstrate the impact of *distance.* There could be no doubt that short distances must be involved in the tendency for intra-regional trade; however, this cannot be separated from the impact of other potential shared attributes within each region. Two such attributes will be observed shortly.

Table 14.3:   Intra-regional and aggregate exports.

Region	Exports ($b.)		(1)/(2) (%) (3)
	Intra-regional (1)	Region's aggregate (2)	
South America	42.9	240.5	17.8
Central America	3.4	198.5	1.7
Eastern Europe	108.8	508.3	21.4
North Africa	1.5	63.1	2.4
Southern Africa	6.9	50.0	13.9
East Africa	1.1	8.2	12.9
West Africa	3.4	40.4	8.3
South Asia	4.5	107.0	4.2
South-East Asia and Oceania	310.0	1,508.6	20.5

Note: Parallel data on *imports* yield very similar results.

It is interesting to note that despite the strong — sometimes very strong — preferences for intra-regional trade, the share of this trade in the region's aggregate trade with the world is quite minor, in each of the regions, as could be seen from the data presented in Table 14.3. This is obviously due to the fact that most of the countries in most of the regions are small; so that, despite of their preference to trade with each other, the regional partners are normally not predominant as providers of each country's imports. Hence, even though a region's members would mostly qualify as "natural trade partners" by *intensity* of intra-regional trade, the aggregate *size* of such trade would mostly *not* make preferential agreements within such regions promising.

Before turning to some further investigations of the inferences suggested by the estimates of intensity ratios, it may be interesting to look at a somewhat different indicator of preferences in trade, namely the *frequency* of trading with other regional partners. In their aforementioned recent study, Helpman *et al.* (2008) derive, in their model, the occurrence of *any* trade between potential partners as an outcome of distance; and assign particular weight to the incidence of such absences, separately from the impact of distance on the amount of trade when a trade flow does exist. Table 14.4 presents, following this line, the frequency of absence of *any* trade between potential partners within regional groupings and outside them. Columns 1 and 2 record the number of observations for *all* countries in each region with which, respectively, the "home country" does *not* (column 1) or does (column 2) have *any* trade.

Table 14.4: Existence or absence of trade partners.

Region	Number of countries *within* the region with which there is		Number of countries *outside* the region with which there is		Percentage	
	No trade (1)	Some trade (2)	No trade (3)	Some trade (4)	(1)/(2) (5)	(3)/(4) (6)
South America	0	90	130	850	0	15.3
Central America	0	20	63	462	0	13.6
Eastern Europe	0	110	78	1000	0	7.8
North Africa	0	20	48	412	0	10.2
Southern Africa	4	38	164	557	10.5	29.4
East Africa	3	27	131	523	11.1	25.1
West Africa	5	85	231	807	5.9	28.6
South Asia	0	12	39	449	0	8.7
South-East Asia and Oceania	0	72	28	854	0	3.3
Aggregate	12	474	912	5964	2.5	15.3

Note: Parallel data on *imports* yield very similar results.

The universe of countries in this instance is all countries in the region. Similarly, this is done in columns 3 and 4 for the trade relationships of all countries within the region with all the world's countries outside the region. It appears that, indeed, absence of *any* trade between potential partners is much less frequent for a country's partners within its region than with countries outside it. In the majority of the observed regions, the box for absent intra-regional partners is empty: *all* the region's members are actual trade partners, whereas absence of any trade is frequent when partners outside the region are involved. The *a priori* expectation is thus borne out.[3]

Contiguous Countries: The Role of Shared Borders

The impact of having a common border between countries on the size of their mutual trade has been widely discussed in the literature. In gravity-model analyses, it is most often estimated through the introduction of a "dummy" variable; and the findings yielded by this procedure indicate that contiguity, as such, leads to roughly doubling the size of trade. Here, it will be examined by relying on the data presented in Table 14.2 of the intensity ratios in trade. We shall ask: is there a substantial difference in the level of intensity ratios in trade between contiguous countries and other trade

Table 14.5: Impact of contiguity on the size of trade regional averages.

| | Intensity ratios | | | |
Region	Noncontiguous countries (1)	Contiguous countries (2)	(2)/(1) (%) (3)	Percentage of trade with contiguous countries in aggregate intra-regional trade (4)
South America	16.7	178.8	10.7	78.2
Central America	233.1	291.7	1.3	45.8
Eastern Europe	29.0	86.6	3.8	78.3
North Africa	4.7	31.9	6.8	46.9
Southern Africa	531.7	597.7	1.1	73.6
East Africa	1545.1	2283.0	1.5	94.1
West Africa	127.8	528.8	4.1	35.7
South Asia	4.6	136.2	29.6	74.6
South-East Asia and Oceania	—	—	—	—
(Unweighted) Average	311.6	516.8	6.7	65.9

flows? That is, are contiguous countries particularly inclined to trade with each other?

This is addressed by means of Table 14.5. It appears, from columns 1 through 3, that intensity ratios are indeed much higher in trade between contiguous vs noncontiguous countries — on average, something like 3–7 times as high for the former than for the latter. The same phenomenon is represented in a somewhat different fashion by column 4. These data show that, in each separate region, trade between contiguous partners represents a major share — on average, about two-thirds — of aggregate *intra*-regional trade. That is, again, that much of the revealed inclination of members of the region to trade with other members is explained by the existence of contiguity, or shared borders, among the members.

Two qualifications should be added. First, while the data on hand definitely suggest an overall inference, differences among regions should be interpreted with caution. Much of such differences must be due to the geographic location of the region's central economy, whose role will be discussed extensively later in this chapter. Thus, take the first two regions in the table — South America and Central America. In the former, the effect of contiguity appears to be particularly strong, whereas in the latter it is almost nonexistent. However, this contrast must be at least partly related to the fact that in the region of South America the central country, Brazil, borders with most of the region's members, whereas in the region of Central America the predominant member, Mexico, borders with only one (Guatemala) of the other four members. The second qualification will be mentioned here only briefly, since it will be discussed again, shortly. It derives from the issue of whether trade with one's immediate neighbor is genuinely a trade with this partner, or just a use of the partner's territory for what is essentially a transit trade.

Similar to the attribute of contiguity, the extreme situation of a country being completely landlocked has been often addressed in the empirical literature — again, normally, through the representation of this attribute by a dummy variable. Here, we shall observe, in each region, the position of landlocked countries in distinction from others. Since completely, landlocked countries are not abundant, generalizations on this score must be strongly hedged. In our list of countries, 13 are defined as "landlocked."[4] These are Bolivia and Paraguay in South America; Belarus, the Czech Republic, Hungary, and Slovakia in Eastern Europe; Malawi, Swaziland, Zambia, and Zimbabwe in Southern Africa; Burundi and Uganda in East Africa; and Niger in West Africa. The import intensity ratios of these countries,[5] and their contrast with averages for other countries, are presented in Table 14.6.

A priori, one would expect a high, on average, intensity ratio of imports of a landlocked country in its intra-regional trade. By definition, it cannot have any imports transported on the high seas, like most other countries. Thus, except for normally limited airborne imports, the country must constrain its imports to those flowing from the countries with which it borders. Hence, high intensity ratios for imports originating in these countries are derived, and, consequently, a high average intensity ratio for the country should follow.

The (rather limited) evidence presented in Table 14.6 tends to lend support to such expectation. It appears to be borne out in the various regions of Africa, as well as in South America. The evidence is dubious in the region of East Europe: the high average intensity ratio for landlocked countries originates from a single country — Moldova. This exception must be due to, first, the predominant role of trade with Russia, as will be noted soon, and to the fact that at least three of the (four) landlocked countries in this region, which have particularly low average intensity ratios — the Czech Republic, Hungary and Slovakia — have common borders with, or easy access to, countries *outside* this region.

Table 14.6:   Average intensity ratios of landlocked vs other countries.

Region and country	Average intensity ratio
South America	
Bolivia	275.7
Paraguay	345.0
Average, landlocked	310.4
Average, other	21.2
Eastern Europe	
Belarus	44.2
Czech Rep.	2.1
Hungary	2.3
Moldova	443.6
Slovakia	9.1
Average, landlocked	100.3
Average, other	16.7
Southern Africa	
Malawi	1701.6
Swaziland	595.2
Zambia	481.2
Zimbabwe	446.3
Average, landlocked	806.2
Average, other	234.3
East Africa	
Burundi	12, 618.5
Uganda	700.5
Average, landlocked	6659.5
Average, other	42.1
West Africa	
Burkina Faso	654.7
Niger	918.8
Average, landlocked	781.8
Average, other	73.1

Note: There are no landlocked countries in Central America, North Africa, South Asia, and South-East Asia and Oceania.

Before leaving the discussion of this attribute, a comment is in order; as noted before, this is relevant also for the consideration of the role of contiguity. A landlocked country must make its trade (again, except for airborne trade) only through an adjacent other country, and this direction of trade would normally be recorded. However, such trade (imports or exports) may genuinely be intended to be conducted with still another partner, using the adjacent country only as a conduit; in other words, the trade with the adjacent country is, in such case, merely a transit trade. For most purposes of analysis, trade of this nature should be identified, separated out, and attributed to trade with that "other," third country, as the true source of imports or destination of exports. This is obviously not feasible for any geographically comprehensive study. However, the bias (over recording) involved in observing trade with bordering countries, and trade direction of landlocked countries, should be borne in mind.

"Center" and "Periphery": Hub and Spokes

In most of the regional groupings, a central country may easily be identified; one which plays a central role in trade relationships within the group. This will be referred to here as "center" whereas the other members of the regional grouping will form the "periphery." The center — periphery relationships appear to be a focal attribute of intra-regional trade relationships and will be investigated here at some length.

The "center" countries are unequivocally identified. They are, in order, Brazil in South America; Mexico in Central America; Russia in Eastern Europe; South Africa in Southern Africa; Nigeria in West Africa; India in South Asia; and China in South-East Asia and Oceania. In two regions — North Africa and East Africa — no such dominant country stands out.

The center countries are clearly the largest — in terms of income and trade — in their respective regions. Naturally, they may be expected to have a heavy weight also in intra-regional trade. The interesting phenomenon, though, is that the role of each center country in intra-regional trade relationships is *larger* — usually much so — than its size (as trader) would "explain," or "warrant." This is clearly demonstrated simply by comparing intensity ratios — which already take care of the size of the trade partner — of the center and of the peripheral countries.

This is done in Table 14.7, which consists of two parts. Part *a* presents the position of a country as a *source of imports* of its partners. Thus, for instance, the figure of 381.0 for the "center" country in South America is an average of intensity ratios of Argentina, Bolivia, etc. in their imports from Brazil. Part *b*, on the other hand, reflects the opposite: the position of the given country as a buyer of its partners' exports. To take the same countries, again, as an example: Brazil's intensity ratio, of 1.6, recorded in column 5 of Part *b*, indicates the intensity of the flow of Brazil's imports from the rest of the region (a ratio of unity would indicate that Brazil's share as a buyer from its partners just reflects Brazil's share in world imports).

Table 14.7: Intensity ratios — center and periphery.

Region	Whole region (1)	a			b		
		Center country (2)	Periphery countries (average) (3)	(2)/(3) (4)	Center country (5)	Periphery countries (average) (6)	(5)/(6) (7)
South America	84.7	381.0	47.6	8.0	1.6	87.7	0.02
Central America	256.3	414.1	216.8	1.9	0.1	320.3	0
Eastern Europe	51.5	183.7	39.5	4.7	1.0	56.1	0.02
North Africa	12.6	—	—	—	—	—	—
Southern Africa	582.5	3214.8	143.8	22.4	0.5	679.5	0
East Africa	2247.9	—	—	—	—	—	—
West Africa	180.4	522.4	142.5	3.7	0.9	239.5	0
South Asia[a]	37.5	136.2	4.6	29.6	0.2	49.9	0
South-East Asia and Oceania	7.0	18.6	5.6	3.3	0.3	8.3	0.04
(Unweighted) Average, without North Africa and East Africa	133.3	695.8	85.8	6.3	0.7	205.9	0.01

[a]For the South Asia region, "peripheral" and "noncontiguous" countries are identical.

Start with Part *a* of the table. It seems obvious from it that the "center" country is predominant in intra-regional trade — much beyond what its role as a large trader would call for. This is most glaring for the regions of Southern Africa and of South Asia. In these, the average intensity ratio of the center in its trade with the periphery is some twenty to three times higher than the average intensity ratio in trade among the peripheral partners. At its lowest, in Central America (with Mexico as the "center"), the intensity ratio is about twice as high in the center-periphery trade than in intra-peripheral trade. Even excluding the extreme cases of Southern Africa and of South Asia, the (unweighted) average of intensity ratio in the center-periphery trade is about four times the level of the (average) intensity ratio in intra-peripheral trade.

These high intensity ratios in the center's trade with the periphery find a representation also in the figures of Table 14.8, which show the share of center-periphery trade in total intra-regional trade (these reflect, of course, not just the high intensity ratios but also the generally heavy weight of the center as a trader). In the extreme case of Southern Africa, center-periphery trade accounts for over 90 percent of aggregate intra-regional trade, and in other regions, this share appears commonly to be roughly one half.

Looking at the reverse angle, in Part *b* of Table 14.7, it appears that the center country predominates only as a seller of its partners' imports, but *not* as a buyer of their exports. Indeed, quite the reverse is true. The intensity ratios of the center countries as *buyers* in the intra-regional trade are mostly, and on average, below unity, and are only a small fraction of the intensity ratios of the peripheral countries as buyers from each other. Thus, the center-periphery relationship is not bilateral or symmetrical. That is,

Table 14.8:   Shares in aggregate intra-regional exports.

Region	Center (1)	Periphery (2)
South America	40.0	60.0
Central America	94.6	5.4
Eastern Europe	35.7	64.3
North Africa	—	—
Southern Africa	79.9	20.1
East Africa	—	—
West Africa	59.7	40.3
South Asia	74.6	25.4
South-East Asia	47.6	52.4
(Unweighted) Average	61.7	38.3

whereas the peripheral countries rely on the center as a major source of their imports — much beyond its size as an exporter would "explain" — the center does *not* similarly rely on its peripheral partners as a source of its own imports. To the contrary, the periphery appears on this score to be much more minor to the center than the former's size would "justify."

What is it, then, that makes the center much more attractive to its regional partners, as a provider of their imports, than they are to each other (or to the center?). Once more, sheer size is abstracted from. The reasons must be found in some attributes that the center's economy might possess, which are not shared (by and large) with the peripheral economies. One would suspect that the center should be (again, in comparison with the periphery) an industrialized country, more highly developed, a producer and exporter of a wide range of goods, thus with a stronger potential of providing its partners with the imports which they demand than is the case with the other, peripheral countries.[6]

We shall try to verify these hypotheses in the following manner. First, to examine whether the center country does indeed (in comparison with its periphery) provide potentially a wide range of exports to its peripheral countries, we shall use an index of the degree of its export diversification, or, its converse, the degree of its commodity concentration. The Gini–Hirschman coefficient will serve for this purpose. Second — and closely related to the first measure — we shall investigate the extent to which the commodity structure of the center's exports suits the demand structure of its partner, as it is represented by the commodity structure of the partner's imports — again, comparing the center-periphery relationships with those between each pair of peripheral countries.[7]

Both the Gini–Hirschman coefficient of concentration and the compatibility index have been discussed earlier, in Chap. 9. However, as before, to minimize the need for cross references, the formulations of the two indices will be presented again here.

(i) Index of commodity concentration:

$$C_{jx} = \sqrt{\sum_1 \left(\frac{X_{ij}}{X_{.j}}\right)^2},$$

where C_{jx} is the index of commodity structure of exports of country j; X_{ij} the exports of commodity i by country j; and $X_{.j}$ the aggregate exports of country j.

(ii) Index of export–import compatibility:

$$Sx_j\, m_k = 1 - \sum_i |x_{ij} - m_{ik}|,$$

where $Sx_j m_k$ is the index of compatibility of country j's ("home country") exports with country k's imports; | | indicates absolute values (that is, regardless of sign); x_{ij} the share of commodity i in country j's aggregate exports; and m_{ik} the share of commodity i in country k's aggregate imports.

The estimates are presented in Table 14.9. Looking, first, at the index of commodity concentration, it does appear that the expectation is borne out. Mostly, exports are much less concentrated (or more diversified) in the center country than in the periphery. The opposite is the case in (strongly) West Africa and (weakly) Eastern Europe, whereas the center and the periphery appear to be about equal in Central America. In all three regions, the center countries (Nigeria, Russia, and Mexico, respectively) export heavily oil and its products (in Nigeria, almost exclusively), a phenomenon that leads to their relatively high levels of commodity concentration of exports. And, indeed, these are the three regions in which the role of the center as a provider of intra-regional imports does not stand out as clearly as it is in the other (relevant) regions.

Inferences drawn from the observation of compatibility of trade flows are, not surprisingly, rather similar to those suggested by those relating to the level of commodity concentration. First, in the majority of cases, the export structure of the center is indeed much more compatible with the import structure of the average peripheral member than the compatibility found in the relationships among peripheral countries. This is true for the regions of South America, Central America, Southern Africa, and South Asia. Moreover, in all of these regions, this inference holds not just for the *average* of the peripheral countries, but practically for each individual country within the region: the single exception to this (out of 22 observations altogether) is found in the case of Argentina, whose index of compatibility (0.756) exceeds that of Brazil (0.531).

In one region, South-East Asia and Oceania, the degree of export–import compatibility is practically the same for the center-periphery relationship as for the intra-peripheral trade. This is true for the average of the periphery; and, similarly, in 3 out of 8 intra-peripheral estimates compatibility is (somewhat) higher than in the center's (China) trade

Table 14.9: Indices of export concentration and of trade compatibility, by region and country.

		Indices of trade compatibility	
Region and country	Coefficient of export concentration (1)	Country's exports with region's imports (2)	Country's imports with region's exports (3)
South America			
Argentina	0.208	0.756	0.232
Bolivia	0.346	0.216	0.268
Brazil	0.167	0.531	0.396
Chile	0.387	0.198	0.477
Colombia	0.263	0.419	0.289
Ecuador	0.541	0.165	0.302
Paraguay	0.422	0.143	0.266
Peru	0.307	0.208	0.437
Uruguay	0.274	0.242	0.479
Venezuela	0.845	0.161	0.353
Center (Brazil)	0.167	0.531	0.396
Average periphery	0.399	0.279	0.345
Central America			
Costa Rica	0.260	0.368	0.421
Guatemala	0.204	0.458	0.406
Honduras	0.306	0.227	0.220
Mexico	0.254	0.518	0.419
Nicaragua	0.307	0.165	0.156
Center (Mexico)	0.254	0.518	0.419
Average periphery	0.269	0.305	0.301
Eastern Europe			
Belarus	0.280	0.484	0.548
Czech Republic	0.208	0.684	0.668
Estonia	0.225	0.479	0.728
Hungary	0.246	0.610	0.626
Latvia	0.214	0.412	0.696
Lithuania	0.261	0.454	0.634
Moldova	0.345	0.214	0.538
Poland	0.182	0.617	0.678
Romania	0.246	0.460	0.668
Russia	0.365	0.316	0.611
Slovakia	0.258	0.604	0.709
Ukraine	0.204	0.432	0.528
Center (Russia)	0.345	0.316	0.611
Average periphery	0.242	0.482	0.637

(*Continued*)

Table 14.9:   (*Continued*)

| Region and country | Coefficient of export concentration (1) | Indices of trade compatibility | |
		Country's exports with region's imports (2)	Country's imports with region's exports (3)
North Africa			
Algeria	0.651	0.123	0.255
Egypt	0.368	0.315	0.221
Morocco	0.341	0.221	0.319
Sudan	0.790	0.083	0.212
Tunisia	0.372	0.323	0.272
Southern Africa			
Malawi	0.500	0.114	0.251
Mozambique	0.620	0.145	0.207
Namibia	0.345	0.227	0.237
South Africa	0.206	0.456	0.202
Swaziland	0.498	0.175	0.255
Zambia	0.474	0.176	0.196
Zimbabwe	0.301	0.242	0.244
Center (South Africa)	0.206	0.456	0.202
Average periphery	0.456	0.180	0.232
East Africa			
Burundi	0.745	0.074	0.293
Ethiopia	0.484	0.053	0.285
Kenya	0.320	0.325	0.197
Sudan	0.790	0.162	0.220
Tanzania	0.276	0.138	0.282
Uganda	0.308	0.236	0.265
West Africa			
Burkina Faso	0.722	0.144	0.244
Cameroon	0.461	0.198	0.372
Cote d'Ivoire	0.366	0.311	0.404
Gabon	0.755	0.157	0.226
Ghana	0.651	0.145	0.208
Mauritania	0.684	0.026	0.182
Niger	0.555	0.103	0.253
Nigeria	0.964	0.118	0.273
Senegal	0.328	0.340	0.324
Togo	0.330	0.175	0.262
Center (Nigeria)	0.964	0.118	0.273
Average periphery	0.539	0.178	0.275

(*Continued*)

Table 14.9:   (*Continued*)

Region and country	Coefficient of export concentration (1)	Indices of trade compatibility	
		Country's exports with region's imports (2)	Country's imports with region's exports (3)
South Asia			
Bangladesh	0.767	0.086	0.477
India	0.209	0.496	0.152
Pakistan	0.349	0.202	0.413
Sri Lanka	0.527	0.188	0.459
Center (India)	0.209	0.496	0.152
Average periphery	0.554	0.159	0.450
South-East Asia and Oceania			
Australia	0.200	0.367	0.576
China	0.223	0.513	0.689
Indonesia	0.178	0.469	0.451
Malaysia	0.293	0.631	0.712
New Zealand	0.215	0.316	0.522
Philippines	0.485	0.478	0.665
Singapore	0.543	0.610	0.626
Thailand	0.189	0.664	0.616
Vietnam	0.310	0.293	0.469
Center (China)	0.223	0.513	0.689
Average periphery	0.302	0.479	0.580

with the periphery. In this instance, thus, no distinction of the center is pointed out. In West Africa, all compatibility indices are low. They are particularly low for the center (Nigeria): its index of compatibility is below both the average of the intra-peripheral indices and of 7 of the 9 of the latter. This is obviously due to Nigeria's exceedingly high level of commodity concentration of exports, which consist overwhelmingly of oil. Eastern Europe is, in a sense, the more interesting exception, in which the center's (Russia) degree of compatibility of trade structures is below the average of that of the intra-peripheral relationships and of practically all (10 out of 11) of the latter. The predominance of Russia in the intra-regional trade of Eastern Europe thus appears *not* to originate from the range of goods that Russia offers and its potential relevance to the import structure of its regional partners. It is likely that this central role is rather a consequence of the historic geographical structure of trade flows among the (by now independent) republics of the Soviet Union and other members of the centrally planned bloc of countries.

It should be noted that — again, not surprisingly — in all of these three regions (West Africa, Eastern Europe, and South-East Asia and Oceania) in which export–import commodity structures are not more compatible for the center-periphery than for intra-peripheral trade (in two of these, it is the opposite), the center's predominant role, as revealed by intensity ratios, is indeed weaker (mostly considerably so) than it is in the other (relevant) regions, in which the center's trade with the periphery is revealed to have a uniquely compatible commodity structure.

All of the inferences suggested thus far are based on the compatibility of a country's commodity structure of *exports* with that of its partner's *imports*, that is, on the estimates presented in column 2 of Table 14.8. Nothing similar appears from the observation of the reverse comparison, namely, of the country's import structure with that of its partners' exports (column 3). Here, no general distinction may be found between center-periphery and intra-peripheral relationships. This must be due to the fact that imports are, by and large, much more diversified in most countries than are exports, and that, consequently, the levels of diversification do not differ among countries nearly as much as they are in exports. This finding agrees fully with the observation made earlier that the center's predominance in trade with its peripheral regional partners is revealed in its role as provider of imports for the partners, but *not*, conversely, as a buyer of the partners' exports.

Conclusions

This chapter has investigated the role of geographic proximity through the observation of nine regional groupings which, among them, include 67 countries[8] (that is an average of 7–8 countries in each group). Using the basic index of the "intensity ratio," it has been seen that intra-group trade is indeed universally much heavier than trade of the group's members with the world outside it. This would agree with the earlier-noted observation that distance matters much in its impact on the size of trade among potential partners. It is similarly seen that within each regional grouping, practically *all* countries trade with each other, whereas in transactions with the rest of the world, trade flows with other individual countries are often missing altogether.

As might be expected, the existence of common borders, within each region, has a substantial impact on the size of mutual trade of the neighboring countries: trade among contiguous countries is much more intensive than trade among noncontiguous partners. An extreme variant of this relationship is that intensity of intra-regional trade is considerably higher for landlocked countries than for others. A qualification should be borne in mind; however: trade among contiguous countries may be a *transit* trade, intended to be shipped beyond the borders of the immediate neighbor.

Considerable attention is paid in the present investigation to the role of a central country within each region. In seven of the (nine) regional groupings defined here, one country clearly stands up as the "center" of the region. This is, naturally, the largest trading nation within the region. As such, its trade flows with each of its regional partners should obviously be expected to be, most often, larger than bilateral trade flows among other countries in the region — the "periphery." However, this tells only part of the story: in all the seven regions in which this is relevant, trade flows of the center are more important — often by a large multiple — than the sheer size of the center country would explain. Intra-regional trade flows outside the center — that is, among the region's peripheral members — thus form normally only a minor fraction of the region's aggregate intra-regional trade. This relationship is *unilateral*, not symmetrical. That is, whereas the center country is dominant as a provider of imports of its neighbors, it does *not* stand out as a buyer of its' partners' exports.

A priori reasoning would assign the heavy role of the center (as an exporter) to the hypothesis that this large country is more industrialized than its regional partners, that its production structure is more diversified, and hence, that it displays a broader range of potential exports to offer to its partners. Consequently, its export structure should tend to accommodate the import needs of its regional partners. This hypothesis is tested by using two indices, which are partly related to each other. First, the degree of commodity concentration is observed. It is found that indeed, in most regions — though not all — the commodity structure of the center's exports shows a substantially higher level of diversification than that found among the region's peripheral members. The other index used describes the degree of compatibility of one country's commodity structure of exports with the import structure of a potential partner. Again, it is found that most often, this degree of compatibility is significantly higher for the exports of the center with each peripheral country than for the mutual exports of peripheral countries. It would appear that the commodity structure of trade does, indeed, in most regions, provide an explanation of the major role played by the center country.

This "hub and spokes" pattern of intra-regional trade flows suggests, in turn, that by and large, no regional economic association would make much sense unless, as a necessary condition, the center country in the region is part and parcel of it.

Notes

1. Two potential other regional groupings will not be included here. One is the group of countries surrounding the Persian Gulf (Saudi Arabia, Iran, Iraq, and the smaller states and emirates). This is a case which most clearly demonstrates an attribute mentioned in the previous chapter: the availability of similar natural resources in proximate countries — in this instance, the availability of oil — and its predominant role in the exports of each country (with no exception) in this area. Needless to say, trade among these countries could not amount to much, and the group does not appear as a promising channel of investigation. The other potential grouping would be the former Soviet Republics of Central Asia: the widespread absence of reliable data precludes the examination of this area. (It would seem, *prima facie*, that in this area too similarity of availability of natural resources would not be conducive to mutual trade.) Absence of appropriate data for Nepal and Burma makes the regional grouping of "South Asia" rather small, with four countries altogether. Despite this very limited number of observations, it should be worthwhile to include this grouping as a "region."

2. All the estimates in the present chapter use 2004 data, taken from the United Nations Commodity Trade Statistics Database.

3. It should be noted, though, that in general the number of actual trade partners appears to be primarily a function of the size of the "home" country: the larger (not necessarily largest) countries (in terms of size of trade) maintain at least some trade with practically any other country in the world.

4. A "landlocked" country is conventionally defined as one with no access to open waters, and we shall follow here this definition. However, so far as the economic consequences of this attribute are concerned, the distinction is not entirely clear cut. How should one view a country like Uganda (classified here as "landlocked"), which could conduct trade across the Victoria Lake? Or a country like Hungary (again, classified

as "landlocked"), which has access to the Black Sea through the use of the Danube River?

5. To clarify, the intensity ratios of a country presented here is an average of this country's intensity ratios of its imports from its partners (and not the other way around). Thus, for instance, the ratio presented for Burundi (10,515.4) is an average of this country's intensity ratios of its imports from Ethiopia, Kenya, Sudan, Tanzania, and Uganda.

6. A more extensive discussion of these attributes will be found in Chap. 12.

7. The estimation of the index of compatibility deserves some explanations. In investigating the compatibility of the center with its peripheral trading partners, a basket (i.e., aggregate) commodity structure is constructed for all peripheral countries combined. For estimating the center-periphery index, this is fine. However, the *same* aggregate commodity structure is used here for estimating compatibility between each peripheral country and the rest of the periphery. Strictly speaking, this is inappropriate: ideally, the "rest of the periphery" should *exclude* the peripheral member with which compatibility is estimated, and the aggregate commodity structure should exclude the exports of this individual country. The aggregate structure should thus be *different* in each estimate of compatibility between export structures of any given periphery member and the rest of the periphery. Such construction would be elaborate and resource-intensive, and is not undertaken here. The distortion involved in using a single basket for all periphery members could not, however, be of much significance, given that in all regions no single peripheral country is dominant. Similarly, no overall bias may be seen in using the short-cut procedure.

8. Sudan is counted here twice.

References

Helpman, E, Melitz, M and Rubinstein, Y (2008). Estimating trade flows, trade partners and trading volumes. *Quarterly Journal of Economics*, 123, 441–488.

Annex

Table 14.10: Intensity ratios in exports by regions and countries.

Eastern Europe

$k\backslash^j$	Belarus	Czech Rep.	Estonia	Hungary	Latvia	Lithuania	Moldova	Poland	Romania	Russia	Slovakia	Ukraine	Average
Belarus	—	0.2	2.8	0.1	12.6	11.4	797.9	0.8	0.1	7.3	0.4	5.2	30.8
Czech Rep.	2.1	—	4.8	3.5	2.5	1.8	9.5	4.4	1.9	0.9	40.8	2.8	6.8
Estonia	3.6	0.2	—	0.2	46.3	18.0	5.6	0.4	0.1	0.9	0.2	2.6	7.1
Hungary	6.4	3.8	43.7	—	1.8	2.0	73.4	2.6	10.4	1.2	15.5	7.7	15.3
Latvia	12.9	0.2	87.6	0.2	—	36.5	11.3	0.6	0.1	0.8	0.6	3.5	15.4
Lithuania	14.1	0.4	46.0	0.3	52.7	—	12.2	1.7	0.1	1.7	0.7	4.4	12.1
Moldova	2.9	0	0.5	0.1	1.3	0.6	—	0.1	2.4	0.1	0.2	6.2	1.3
Poland	28.8	7.0	11.4	4.2	20.1	17.3	33.2	—	3.6	3.2	16.4	9.2	14.0
Romania	3.1	1.1	0.5	4.6	0.3	0.5	501.7	1.0	—	0.8	3.5	6.9	47.2
Russia	255.2	1.9	68.0	2.4	39.5	33.3	1793.0	3.9	1.4	—	3.6	54.6	205.2
Slovakia	1.9	10.9	1.0	2.8	1.6	0.5	8.6	1.8	0.9	1.1	—	3.7	3.2
Ukraine	21.3	0.9	20.3	1.6	9.9	8.2	328.4	2.8	0.9	5.9	3.2	—	36.7
Average	32.0	2.4	26.1	1.8	17.1	11.8	279.5	1.8	2.0	2.2	7.7	9.7	32.9

South America

$k\backslash^j$	Argentina	Bolivia	Brazil	Chile	Colombia	Ecuador	Paraguay	Peru	Uruguay	Venezuela	Average
Argentina	—	229.6	6.9	4.1	1.2	5.0	331.0	3.1	228.6	0.1	90.0
Bolivia	2.1	—	0.5	1.3	2.0	1.1	72.9	11.1	3.2	0	10.0
Brazil	39.2	1244.4	—	12.9	4.6	11.1	1015.9	30.2	495.5	0.8	317.1
Chile	27.8	89.3	2.4	—	6.4	18.4	96.0	53.7	62.4	0.3	29.6
Colombia	2.0	208.8	1.0	2.8	—	42.0	5.0	22.1	13.6	5.7	33.7
Ecuador	1.4	9.4	0.5	3.0	33.3	—	23.0	17.5	1.4	1.6	10.1
Paraguay	3.5	30.7	0.8	0.3	0.1	0.2	—	0	60.0	0	10.6
Peru	3.6	240.5	0.6	4.8	17.9	89.6	64.4	—	25.1	0.6	49.7
Uruguay	5.0	2.6	0.6	0.6	0.2	0.2	1467.0	0.8	—	0	164.0
Venezuela	3.1	426.2	1.4	2.5	53.4	17.6	29.9	16.6	33.2	—	64.9
Average	9.7	275.7	1.6	3.6	13.2	20.6	345.0	17.2	102.5	1.0	79.0

(*Continued*)

Table 14.10: *(Continued)*

Central America

$k\backslash j$	Costa Rica	Guatemala	Honduras	Mexico	Nicaragua	Average
Costa Rica	—	70.2	43.5	0.1	298.7	103.1
Guatemala	51.0	—	165.2	0.1	190.5	101.7
Honduras	34.7	134.7	—	0.1	333.2	125.7
Mexico	33.4	51.7	84.9	—	235.6	101.4
Nicaragua	41.1	67.6	103.3	0	—	53.0
Average	40.0	81.1	99.2	0.1	264.5	97.0

North Africa

$k\backslash j$	Algeria	Egypt	Morocco	Sudan	Tunisia	Average
Algeria	—	8.1	2.0	0.5	7.9	4.6
Egypt	6.8	—	1.2	46.5	2.2	14.1
Morocco	3.4	3.7	—	0.7	5.4	3.3
Sudan	0	8.7	0	—	0.2	2.2
Tunisia	2.5	1.7	3.0	4.6	—	3.0
Average	3.2	5.6	1.6	13.1	3.9	5.5

East Africa

$k\backslash j$	Burundi	Ethiopia	Kenya	Sudan	Tanzania	Uganda	Average
Burundi	—	0	28.6	0	32.9	157.8	43.9
Ethiopia	1.2	—	18.9	0	7.7	5.1	6.6
Kenya	0	5.8	—	1.8	365.0	669.8	208.5
Sudan	0	69.6	39.3	—	1.1	197.5	61.5
Tanzania	301.4	5.6	155.2	0	—	105.9	113.6
Uganda	1005.7	1.0	341.7	0	51.1	—	279.9
Average	261.7	16.4	116.7	0.4	91.6	227.2	119.0

(Continued)

Table 14.10: (Continued)

West Africa

$k \backslash j$	Burkina Faso	Cameroon	Cote d'Ivoire	Gabon	Ghana	Mauritania	Niger	Nigeria	Senegal	Togo	Average
Burkina Faso	—	0	55.1	0.1	0.5	0	123.8	0	54.4	1981.8	246.8
Cameroon	0	—	16.1	16.4	1.7	4.4	0.1	7.8	26.1	6.6	8.8
Cote d'Ivoire	270.0	2.7	—	15.5	3.3	0	549.6	8.9	95.4	100.1	116.2
Gabon	19.8	56.2	8.0	—	0.7	1.4	4.7	0.1	13.7	24.8	14.3
Ghana	4296.0	1.4	46.4	0.3	—	24.0	823.0	11.3	10.2	1799.7	779.1
Mauritania	0.1	0	1.2	5.4	0.1	—	51.6	0	76.0	21.1	17.3
Niger	203.7	0.3	11.5	0.1	0.8	0	—	0	8.4	508.8	81.6
Nigeria	59.4	36.9	142.4	9.3	15.4	103.9	3136.7	—	10.5	286.2	422.3
Senegal	15.0	19.7	29.0	5.0	10.7	17.7	14.1	6.3	—	573.9	76.8
Togo	4.4	7.8	29.8	3.1	0	3.0	56.8	0.1	44.5	—	16.7
Average	540.9	13.9	37.8	6.1	3.7	17.2	529.4	3.9	37.7	589.6	197.8

Southern Africa

$k \backslash j$	Malawi	Mozambique	Namibia	South Africa	Swaziland	Zambia	Zimbabwe	Average
Malawi	—	143.8	0.2	1.1	18.3	126.3	101.1	65.1
Mozambique	298.0	—	13.5	3.7	209.9	3.9	41.5	95.0
Namibia	0.1	0.5	—	0	0	11.3	30.2	7.0
South Africa	1414.4	612.1	912.9	—	3550.4	1008.5	1196.5	1449.1
Swaziland	7.1	16.2	0.6	0	—	1.3	0.4	4.3
Zambia	136.7	3.0	13.8	3.4	36.6	—	152.0	57.5
Zimbabwe	182.7	97.0	5.4	4.3	25.6	233.7	—	91.5
Average	329.8	145.4	157.7	2.1	640.1	230.8	253.6	251.4

(Continued)

Table 14.10: (*Continued*)

South Asia

k\j	Bangladesh	India	Pakistan	Sri Lanka	Average
Bangladesh	—	1.8	7.2	2.7	3.9
India	9.6	—	5.8	78.1	31.2
Pakistan	4.1	0.6	—	7.9	4.2
Sri Lanka	0.9	1.5	4.9	—	2.4
Average	4.9	1.3	6.0	29.6	10.4

South-East Asia and Oceania

k\j	Australia	China	Indonesia	Malaysia	New Zealand	Philippines	Singapore	Thailand	Vietnam	Average
Australia	—	1.9	5.7	2.3	84.3	2.3	1.7	2.4	20.1	15.1
China	8.7	—	19.2	10.8	31.6	28.3	8.6	11.9	35.0	19.3
Indonesia	1.8	1.2	—	2.1	5.6	1.8	4.9	3.2	4.8	3.2
Malaysia	1.5	1.6	9.7	—	7.1	10.1	7.1	5.2	6.7	6.1
New Zealand	8.4	0.2	0.6	0.3	—	0.2	0.2	0.3	0.5	1.3
Philippines	0.7	1.1	4.0	1.3	6.8	—	1.0	1.8	5.3	2.8
Singapore	2.3	2.9	19.2	12.8	5.0	12.8	—	6.9	15.9	9.7
Thailand	1.7	1.3	6.3	4.1	5.0	5.2	2.0	—	5.5	3.9
Vietnam	0.4	0.9	1.9	0.8	1.9	3.3	0.8	1.9	—	1.5
Average	3.2	1.4	8.3	4.4	18.4	8.0	3.3	4.2	11.7	7.0

Bibliography

Aitken, ND (1973). The effect of the EEC and EFTA on European trade: A temporal cross-section analysis. *American Economic Review*, 63, 881–892.

Alam, A (1992). Country trade profiles; Latin America and the Caribbean. The World Bank, Washington, DC: (mimeo).

Alam, A and Rajapatirana, S (1993). Trade policy reform in Latin America and the Caribbean. World Bank Policy Research Working paper No. 1104, Washington, DC.

Anderson, JE (1979). A theoretical foundation for the gravity equation. *American Economic Review*, 69, 106–116.

Anderson, JE and van Wincoop, E (2004). Trade costs. *Journal of Economic Literature*, 42, 691–751.

Arndt, SW (1969). Customs union and the theory of tariffs. *American Economic Review*, 59, 108–118.

Athukorola, PC and Jayasuriya, S (2000). Trade policy reforms and industrial adjustment in Sri Lanka. *The World Economy*, 33(3), 387–404.

Baier, SL and Bergstrand, JH (2001). The growth of world trade, tariffs, transport costs, and income similarity. *Journal of International Economies*, 53, 1–27.

Balassa, B and Bauwens, L (1988). *Changing Trade Patterns in Manufactured Goods*. Amsterdam: North-Holland Publishing Company.

Bergstrand, JH (1985). Gravity equation in international trade: Some microeconomic foundations and empirical evidence. *Review of Economics and Statistics*, 67, 474–481.

Bergstrand, JH (1990). The Heckscher–Ohlin–Samuelson model, the Lynder hypothesis and the determinants of bilateral intra-industry trade. *Economic Journal*, 100, 1216–1229.

Bhagwati, JN (1993). Regionalism and multilateralism: An overview. In *New Dimensions in Regional Integration*, de Melo, J and Panagariya, A (eds.), pp. 22–51. Cambridge: Cambridge University Press.

Bhagwati, J and Panagariya, A (1996a). Preferential trading areas and multilateralism — Strangers, friends or foes. In *The Economics of Preferential Trade Agreements*, Bhagwati, J and Panagariya, A (eds.), pp. 1–78. Washington, DC: American Enterprise Institute.

Bhagwati, J and Panagariya, A (1996b). The theory of preferential trade agreements: Historical evolution and current trends. *American Economic Review*, 86, 82–87.

Bruno, M (1972). Market distortions and gradual reforms. *Review of Economic Studies*, 39, 373–383.

Cavallo, D and Cottani, J (1991). *Argentina*. In *Liberalizing Foreign Trade*, Papageorgiou, D, Michaely, M and Choksi, AM (eds.), Vol. 1, pp. 1–67. Oxford: Basil Blackwell.

Chan, KS (1991). Bilateral trade negotiations and trade diversification. *Journal of Development Economics*, 36(2), 243–257.

Chenery, HB and Syrquin, M (1975). *Patterns of Development 1950–1970*. London: Oxford University Press.

Collie, DR and Su, Y-T (1998). Trade policy and product variety: When is a VER superior to tariff. *Journal of Development Economics*, 55(1), 249–255.

Corden, WM (1966). The effective protective rate, the uniform tariff equivalent and the average tariff. *Economic Record*, 42, 200–216.

Corden, WM (1974). *Trade Policy and Economic Welfare*. Oxford: Clarendon Press.

De la Cuadra, S and Hachette, D (1991). *Chile*. In *Liberalizing Foreign Trade*, Papageorgiou, D, Michaely, M and Choksi, AM (eds.), Vol. 1, pp. 169–319. Oxford: Basil Blackwell.

de Pineres, S, Gutierez, A and Ferrantino, M (1997). Export diversification and structural dynamics in the growth process: The case of Chile. *Journal of Development Economics*, 52(2), 375–391.

Disidier, A-C and Head, K (2008). The puzzling persistence of the distance effect on bilateral trade. *Review of Economics and Statistics*, 90, 37–48.

Dodzin, S and Vamvakidis, A (2004). Trade and industrialization in developing economies. *Journal of Development Economics*, 75(1), 319–328.

Drysdale, P and Garnant, R (1982). Trade intensities and the analysis of bilateral trade flows in a many-country world: A survey. *Hitotsubachi Journal of Economics*, 2, 62–84.

Edwards, S (1993). *Latin America and the Caribbean: A Decade after the Debt Crisis*. Washington, DC: The World Bank.

Eichengreen, B and Irwin, DA (1998). The role of history in bilateral trade flows. In *The Regionalization of the World Economy*, Frankel, JA (ed.), pp. 33–57. Chicago: University of Chicago Press.

Evenett, SJ and Heller, W (2004). On theories exploring the success of the gravity equation. *Journal of Political Economy*, 110, 281–316.

Galiani, S and Sanguinetti, P (2003). The impact of trade liberalization on wage inequality: Evidence from Argentina. *Journal of Development Economics*, 73(2), 497–513.

Grubel, HG and Lloyd, PJ (1975). *Intra-Industry Trade: The Theory and Measurement of International Trade in Differentiated Products*. London: Macmillan.

Haberler, G (1936). *The Theory of International Trade*. London: Hodge and Company.

Halevi, N and Kleiman, E (1995). Regional versus non-regional integration: The case of the Middle East. Hebrew University of Jerusalem (mimeo).

Harberger, AC (1991). *Trade Policy and the Real Exchange Rate.* Washington, DC: World Bank Economic Development Institute.

Harrison, A and Hanson, G (1999). Who gains from trade reform? Some remaining puzzles. *Journal of Development Economics*, 59(1), 125–156.

Helpman, E (1987). Imperfect competition and international trade: Evidence from fourteen industrial countries. *Journal of Japanese and International Economics*, 1, 62–81.

Helpman, E, Melitz, M and Rubinstein, Y (2008). Estimating trade flows, trading partners and trading volumes. *Quarterly Journal of Economics*, 123, 441–448.

Hoekman, B and Djankov, S (1997). Determinants of the export structure of countries in Central and Eastern Europe. *World Bank Economic Review*, 11(3), 471–487.

Hummels, D and Levinsohn, J (1995). Monopolistic competition and international trade: Reconsidering the evidence. *Quarterly Journal of Economics*, 110, 799–836.

Hummels, D (2001). Toward a geography of trade costs. Unpublished Manuscript, Purdue University.

Kemp, MC (1969). *A Contribution to the General Equilibrium Theory of Preferential Trading.* Amsterdam: North-Holland Publishing Company.

Kleiman, E (1976). Trade and the decline of colonialism. *Economic Journal*, 86, 450–480.

Krueger, AO (1993). Free-trade arrangements as a protectionist device: Rules of origin. *NBER Working Paper* No. 4342.

Krugman, P (1991). The move to free trade zones. In *Policy Implications of Trade and Currency Zones*, pp. 7–41. Federal Reserve Bank of Kansas City.

Kuznets, S (1958). Economic growth of small nations. *The Challenge of Development*, Chapter 1. Jerusalem: The Eliezer Kaplan School of Economics and Social Sciences, The Hebrew University. Reprinted in Robinson EAG (ed.), (1960). *Economic Consequences of the Size of Nations.* London: The Macmillan Press.

Limão, N and Venables, AJ (2001). Infrastructure, geographical disadvantage, transport costs and trade. *World Bank Economic Review*, 15, 451–479.

Linneman, H (1966). *An Econometric Study of International Trade Flows.* Amsterdam: North-Holland Publishing Company.

Lipsey, RG (1960). The theory of customs unions: A general survey. *Economic Journal*, 70, 496–513.

Markusen, JR (1983). Factor movements and commodity trade as complements. *Journal of International Economics*, 14, 341–356.

Meade, JE (1955). *Trade and Welfare*, The Theory of International Economic Policy, Vol. 2. Oxford: Oxford University Press.

Meade, JE (1955b). *The Theory of Customs Unions.* Amsterdam: North-Holland Publishing Company.

Melvin, JR (1969). Comments on the theory of customs unions. *Manchester School of Economics and Social Studies*, 36, 161–168.

Michaely, M (1962a). *Concentration in International Trade.* Amsterdam: North-Holland Publishing Company.

Michaely, M (1962b). Multilateral balancing in international trade. *American Economic Review,* 52, 685–702.

Michaely, M (1963). *Concentration in International Trade.* Amsterdam: North-Holland.

Michaely, M (1977). *Theory of Commercial Policy: Trade and Protection.* Oxford: Philip Allan, Chicago: University of Chicago Press.

Michaely, M (1980). The economic significance of peace with Egypt. *Economic Quarterly* (in Hebrew), 105, 116–122.

Michaely, M (1981). Income levels and the structure of trade. In *The World Economic Order: Past and Prospects,* Grassman, S and Lundberg, E (eds.), pp. 121–161. London: The Macmillan Press.

Michaely, M (1984). *Trade, Income Levels and Dependence.* Amsterdam, New York: North-Holland.

Michaely, M, Papageorgiou, D and Choksi, AM (1991). In *Liberalizing Foreign Trade: Lessons of Experience in the Developing World,* Papageorgiou, D, Michaely, M and Choksi, AM (eds.), Vol. 7. Oxford: Basil Backwell.

Michaely, M (1996). Trade preferential agreements in Latin America: An *ex-ante* assessment. World Bank Policy Research Paper No. 1583, Washington, DC.

Moneta, C (1959). The estimation of transportation costs in international trade. *Journal of Political Economy,* 67, 41–58.

Mundell, RA (1957). International trade and factor mobility. *American Economic Review,* 47, 321–335.

Ohlin, B (1935). *Inter-regional and International Trade.* Cambridge, Mass.: Harvard University Press (*Revised Edition,* 1967).

Panagariya, A (1995). Rethinking the new regionalism. World Bank Conference on Trade Expansion, Washington, DC: (mimeo).

Panagariya, A (1996). The free trade area of the Americas: Good for Latin America? *The World Economy,* 19, 495–515.

Papageorgiou, D and Michaely, M (1995). Trade liberalization: The recent experience. The World Bank, Washington, DC: (mimeo).

Pigato, M, Farah, C, Itakura, K, Jun, K, Martin, W, Murell, K and Srinivasan, TG (1997). *South Asia's Integration into the World Economy,* Washington DC: The World Bank.

Primo Braga, CA, Safadi, R and Yeats, AJ (1994). Regional integration in the Americas: "Déjà vu all over again"? The World Bank, Washington, DC: (mimeo).

Redding, S and Venables, AJ (2006). The economics of isolation and distance, Chapter 5. In *WTO at the Margins,* Grynberg, R (ed.), pp. 145–163. Cambridge: Cambridge University Press.

Robinson, EAG (ed.) (1960). *Economic Consequences of the Size of Nations.* London: The Macmillan Press.

Romer, P (1994). New goods, old theory, and the welfare costs of trade restriction. *Journal of Development Economics,* 42(1), 5–38.

Rybczynski, TM (1955). Factor endowment and relative commodity prices. *Economica*, 22, 336–341.

Sologa, I and Winters, LA (1999). Regionalism in the nineties: What effect on trade? The World Bank, Washington, DC: (mimeo).

Srinivasan, TN (1986). The costs and benefits of being a small, remote island, landlocked, or ministate economy. *The World Bank Research Observer*, 1, 205–218.

Stolper, WF and Samuelson, PA (1941). Protection and real wages. *Review of Economic Studies*, 9, 58–73.

Summers, L (1991). Regionalism and the world trading system. In *Policy Implications of Trade and Currency Zones*, pp. 295–301. Federal Reserve Bank of Kansas City.

Syrquin, M (1992). Industrialization, integration and trade in Latin America. The World Bank, Washington, DC: (mimeo).

Tinbergen, J (1962). *Shaping the World Economy: Suggestions for an International Economic Policy*. New York: The Twentieth Century Fund.

Vanek, J (1965). *General Equilibrium of International Discrimination*. Cambridge, Mass.: Harvard University Press.

Viner, J (1950). *The Customs Union Issue*. New York: Carnegie Endowment for International Peace.

Wonnacott, P (1998). The role of history in bilateral trade flows: Comment. In *The Regionalization of the World Economy*, Frenkel, JA (ed.). Chicago: The University of Chicago Press.

Wonnacott, P and Wonnacott, R (1981). Is unilateral tariff reduction preferable to a customs union? The curious case of the missing foreign tariffs. *American Economic Review*, 71, 704–714.

Yeats, AJ (1998). Does Mercosur's trade performance raise concerns about the effects of regional trade arrangements? *World Bank Economic Review*, 12, 1–28.

Author Index

Subject Index